༺ Historical Memory in Africa ༻

MAKING SENSE OF HISTORY

Studies in Historical Cultures
General Editor: Stefan Berger, Director, Institute for Social Movements, Ruhr Universität Bochum, Germany
Founding Editor: Jörn Rüsen, Emeritus Professor at the Institute for Cultural Studies, Essen, Germany

HISTORICAL MEMORY IN AFRICA

Dealing with the Past, Reaching for the Future in an Intercultural Context

---

Edited by
Mamadou Diawara, Bernard Lategan, and Jörn Rüsen

berghahn
NEW YORK · OXFORD
www.berghahnbooks.com

First published in 2010 by

Berghahn Books

www.berghahnbooks.com

© 2010, 2013 Mamadou Diawara, Bernard Lategan, and Jörn Rüsen
First paperback edition published in 2013

Library of Congress Cataloguing-in-Publication Data

Historical memory in Africa : dealing with the past, reaching for the future in an intercultural context / edited by Mamadou Diawara, Bernard Lategan, and Jörn Rüsen.

      p. cm. — (Making sense of history; v. 12)
  Includes bibliographical references and index.
  ISBN 978-1-84545-652-8 (hardback) ISBN 978-1-78238-083-2 (paperback)
ISBN 978-1-78238-084-9 (retail ebook)
    1. Africa—Historiography. 2. Historiography—Social aspects—Africa.
  3. Collective memory—Africa. 4. Memory—Social aspects—Africa.
  I. Diawara, Mamadou. II. Lategan, Bernard C. III. Rüsen, Jörn

DT19.H577 2010
960.072--dc22

                              2010007982

British Library Cataloguing in Publication Data

A catalogue record for this book is available from the British Library.

Printed in the United States on acid-free paper.

ISBN 978-1-78238-083-2 paperback   ISBN 978-1-78238-084-9 retail ebook

Contents

Introduction

Mamadou Diawara, Bernard Lategan, and Jörn Rüsen

This book is the outcome of an international research project jointly sponsored by the Stellenbosch Institute for Advanced Study (STIAS) and the Kulturwissenschaftliches Institut Nordrhein-Westfalen (KWI) under the title *Dealing with the Past, Reaching for the Future*. It examines the ambiguous nature of historical memory during times of social upheaval and transformation, focusing on a variety of cases from a number of African countries to illustrate the multifaceted and diverging roles of historical memory in dealing with the past, interpreting the present and anticipating the future. While the focus is decidedly on Africa, the contributions are placed in an international comparative context by including intercultural perspectives from the North and the East. These show striking similarities, but also marked differences characteristic of the ways historical memory functions in different cultural contexts. The book concludes with a selection of texts that deal with the praxis of memory, trauma, forgiveness and healing.

Given the vast amount of literature – both scholarly and popular – that already exists on the subject of historical memory, why another book? The main purpose of this publication is to address a structural lack in the memory discourse, namely the relationship between memory and the future – hence the subtitle: *Dealing with the Past, Reaching for the Future*. The issue of the future potential of memory therefore forms a recurrent theme throughout the volume. This interest also explains two further characteristics of the collection – the focus on Africa and the inclusion of contributions from other cultural contexts. Africa provides a wide spectrum of cases ranging from the most destructive use of historical memory to remarkable examples of constructive reassessment of the past. But in order to understand such contrasts more fully, these cases need to be considered in a wider, intercultural context.

Historical memory involves a complex set of mental processes that function on different levels of human activity in everyday life: on the level of official rituals and symbols, in historical instruction in schools and universities, in historiography as an academic discipline, in popular culture, in entertainment, films, monuments and memorials. It has personal, local, regional, national, supranational and universal dimensions, and it integrates nearly all realms of human existence, including religion, morality, political convictions, individual and collective identity, cognitive understanding and aesthetic perceptions. It is an important mental and social site of struggle for social differentiation and recognition, for political legitimacy, and for perceiving the self and the other.

In essence, memory fulfils a 'sense-making' function. The contributions to this book provide a kaleidoscope of examples of how this process works. Africa has experienced both the unspeakable and the unimaginable. The killings in Rwanda, Burundi and the Democratic Republic of the Congo – often in the name of a falsified historical memory – are a constant reminder of the reality of disaster and its unspeakable dimensions. On the same continent the unimaginable happened when the bulwarks of apartheid were breached by resistance, negotiation and reconciliation. Drawing on examples from the Congo and South Africa, Jewsiewicki illustrates the role of memory in the formation of individual and collective identities and how it can be used to resist, to escape the strategic intentions of others and to give a new content to the identity and self-understanding of the individual and the group. But memory can also be a 'multi-channeled' process, as Joubert shows in her analysis of oral and performative ways of remembering, making it a rich and powerful tool for orientation in the present and for opening future perspectives on human action. Even on the most abstract level, the way in which we remember has consequences. Macamo argues that the ahistorical way in which 'Africa' (itself a modern construct) is recollected by Africans and non-Africans alike has direct consequences for social theory and for the practice of sociology in an African context. The same happens (as Diawara shows) when memory is fragmented and elements of the past (in this case 'local knowledge') are treated in an ahistorical way. This leads to a mindset that is informed only by the present, which perpetuates unhelpful divisions such as the distinction between 'developed' and 'non-developed' societies.

The *mode* of the memory process therefore is as significant as its content in a specific situation. The need to establish a sense of continuity and of identity almost inevitably leads to strategies of selection, delineation and exclusion when dealing with the past. These in their turn result in fragmented, divisive and contested memories. The dominant mode in this case is that of *justification* in terms of the past. The result is that every event and every phrase becomes ambiguous, as Bisanswa shows with reference to Congo-Zaïre: the colonial period is remembered as paradise or as hell, independence is interpreted as liberation or the return to primitiveness. These conflicting memories provide the basis for group mobilization and the emergence of ideologies.

As long as justification is the default mode of memory, the chances of breaking out of this mindset and getting beyond one's own past remain slim. How then can the tide be turned, and how can the intensely desired 'memory of crossing' (Bisanswa) be achieved? It is here that the structural deficit in the memory discourse becomes most obvious. Without bringing the future potential of memory into play, any form of 'crossing' remains unattainable. This calls for a different kind of reading – a reading of history 'against the grain', approaching it from the perspective of the future, rather than from the past. As Bisanswa shows, the crossing is not a return to the past, but a detour through the past towards the future. This supposes a process that favours transient movements and the willingness to cross existing boundaries. It reopens fixed positions and focus on alternative possibilities. In short, this change of perspective is based on the priority of what is possible over what is real (Jüngel 1969).

With such a change of perspective, the mode of memory discourse also changes – from justification to inclusion, to mediation, to complementation. Shifting the focus from what is real to what is possible reveals alternative ways to configure the past and envision the future. However, there are different ways to conceptualize the future and not all of these are suitable to develop a 'future oriented' memory, as Lategan shows. Furthermore, the quest for one grand narrative is no longer attainable. Rather, we are witnessing the complementary coexistence of multiple memories. A prominent example is the concept of the 'rainbow nation' in the post-1994 rhetoric in South Africa, perhaps most eloquently articulated in Thabo Mbeki's famous speech 'I am an African'. There is, no doubt, an element of artificiality in any such reimagining. Ghosh reminds us that one of the aims of the politics of commemoration is to control its reception. In his analysis of the centenary celebrations of the South African War, Grundlingh shows what bizarre forms the process of appropriating and controlling memory can take. Nonetheless, it is at the same time an insistent, if awkward, expression of inclusiveness. Harries provides further examples of attempts to produce a new, more consensual history in South Africa. It remains an ongoing challenge – recent developments triggered by changes in the ANC leadership have demonstrated anew that this project is still in a fragile stage.

The search for a more inclusive form of memory is therefore no panacea. But it does enable us to explore other, often-neglected dimensions of the memory process. As Rüsen insists, there is an inevitable logic involved here: once memory moves beyond commemorating the past and contemplates its role in the present and its significance for the future, it has to find ways to integrate negative, even traumatic events of the past to form a new historical identity. It thus becomes clear that issues like trauma, mourning, confession, forgiveness and reconciliation have to be considered as part of such an extended understanding of the memory process. In fact, their inclusion raises new questions. Bisanswa asks: How do we achieve redress? Is forgiveness enough for reparation? Is the airing of the wrong a precondition for reconciliation? From the experience of Gobodo-Madikizela with Eugene de Kock it would seem – in line with normal expectations – that confession is indeed a prerequisite for forgiveness. But the story of Eva Mozes Kor provides us with an example of forgiveness without prior confession. Han Sang-Jin, meanwhile, is confronted with a dilemma: what happens when perpetrators refuse to admit and apologize? Here we catch a glimpse of the universal relevance of these issues.

This serves as a reminder that although Africa offers a rich source for the study of memory, its experiences are by no means unique. In fact, exploring the nature and use of historical memory in this context raises generic issues and universal concerns. One of these is the function of the different components of a 'future-oriented' memory. This requires more sustained attention to processes like mourning, forgiving, reconciliation and restoration, but also to strategies to overcome the burdens of the past. It is generally accepted that forgetting is not a solution, since it leads to strategies of suppression by which the past is not forgotten but remains enormously powerful in influencing the minds of people beyond their awareness and control. Moralizing is another strategy to distance oneself from these burdening experiences. It can be done by both victims and perpetrators. But a strict moralistic approach to historical memory contains the danger of continuing exclusive strategies based on a clear-cut distinction between good and evil. Moralizing attitudes and strategies are natural, but they have their limits as well. The complexity of historical experience does not allow an absolute distinction between right and wrong. In addition, those who moralize unintentionally follow a logic of exclusion that prohibits the 'crossing of memory', that could lead to a more inclusive and complementary understanding of the human condition.

For this reason this book ends with documents of forgiveness and reconciliation. When considering the vast variety of historical cultures all over the world today it becomes evident that more energy is needed to generate the kind of historical sense that will take us forward. This is true not only for Africa, of course, but for other continents as well. The crimes against humanity committed in East Asia, for example, still cry to be recognized by those who perpetrated them and their offspring. Only in a very few cases has this cry been heard, and steps towards reconciliation have been taken in fewer cases still. In this regard, examples from other cultural contexts can encourage similar processes elsewhere.

Three cases were chosen to represent this precious way of overcoming inhumanity by remembering. They come from three countries, each of which has to deal with a horrifying past: South Africa with apartheid, South Korea with its past of a brutal authoritarian regime, and the West (mainly the Jewish and the German people) with the Holocaust. All these cases present a traumatizing past in a perspective of memory that opens up a future perspective in contrast to the horrors of the past. This is achieved by employing different modes of making sense of the past. Despite their differences, each of the three cases documents the chances of healing the wounds that were inflicted in the past through the mental power of forgiving. The documents present the voices of victims who plead, not for a moral condemnation of the perpetrators (though they do not negate the necessity of morality), but for a recognition of the perpetrator's human nature as a potential chance for regaining their humanity. At the same time, it becomes possible for victims to overcome their victimhood. With this documentary presentation, the book ends by opening up a future perspective for all strategies engaged in making sense of the past by creating a historical culture in which the memory of an inhumane past can lead to the vision of a more humane future.

Summary of Chapters

Chapter 1

Elísio Macamo argues that social theory is a specific mode of making sense of the past, present and future. In order to do this, it relies on a particular form of historical memory. He illustrates his hypothesis by depicting the way in which African social reality is recollected by Africans themselves – in the face of the strong development of sociology in Europe. The intriguing question is why African intellectuals, under conditions comparable to those that gave rise to sociology as a discipline in Europe, have not produced a sociology of their own.

Macamo shows how the study of social change in the Europe of Emile Durkheim and Max Weber relies on a basic distinction between 'modern, industrial society' characterized by change and 'traditional society' resistant to change. Africa is an example of the latter, and the (unintended) consequence is an ahistorical concept of African society. 'Africa', in fact, is a modern construct resulting from the way Africa is 'remembered', and the absence of sociology in Africa reflects the negation of the modernity of that construct. The alternative is not a rejection of sociology, but the development of a sociology that gives full recognition to social change in African societies. Macamo uses his work in a Protestant mission in Mozambique to illustrate this alternative approach. His conclusion is a plea for the africanization of sociology as one of the most privileged ways of acknowledging the relevance of historical recollection for the constitution of social reality.

Chapter 2

Annekie Joubert highlights the important role of oral memory in African societies in making sense of present-day events. Her chapter draws on meticulous research of the oral culture of the Lobedu and Hananwa communities in South Africa's Limpopo Province. She illustrates the advantages of oral culture as a 'multi-channelled' form of history that consists of telling, seeing, hearing, smelling and experiencing history. This not only offers alternative forms to single-channelled historical documentation, but also points to powerful ways in which memory is used to uncover the past for the purpose of political reconciliation in the present, and for future perspectives on human action. Oral memory provides an arena within which the processes of re-reordering and reinterpretation can take place. It enables the reconciliation of different experiences and memories, and facilitates a process of reestablishing identity amongst peoples torn apart by memories of violence and war.

Memory should be more than factual accounts of events if it is to provide a connection between the present and the past. Memory should be understood as the bringing the *past* back into the arena of the *present,* where stories become performative utterances, that is, historicizing gestures, where people *live* the past, and where trauma becomes *living* memory. The presence of the past, as chanted in traditional praise poetry or performance poetry, witnessed during the TRC hearings or acted out in memorial practices, connects us with our present situation. Joubert concludes that it is important that 'modernity' commits itself to fostering oral memory as a living archive and creative extension of single-channel history. 'An orality that is healthy is infinitely bigger than its material expression. We are all storytellers. Our stories sustain us, carry us, carry our values, our beliefs, our identities.'

Chapter 3

Bogumil Jewsiewicki examines the role of historical memory in the formation of individual and collective identity in contemporary African societies. The rise of audio-visual media brought with it a transfer of authority from the historian as critical mediator of news to the witness as representative of the community who produces the 'truth', certified by the authenticity of experience. One consequence of this transfer is that identity is organized not so much in terms of time, that is, in terms of historical evolution and sequence, as in terms of space, that is, illuminating the present by making elements of the individual's experience contemporary. Memory thus acquires a certain 'indiscipline' that enables the subject to resist, to escape from the other's strategic actions and give a specific content to the subject's identity and self-understanding.

Jewsiewicki illustrates this form of identity formation with two examples. The first is from the Congo, where a historical memory of redemption was developed as the narrative of the nation. Using a Mobutist-era painting by a popular artist from the city of Lubumbashi, he illustrates how this is as much a unique work as it is a synthesis of Congolese memorial icons. The biblical figure of Moses is used to evoke memories of the precolonial slave trade and the colonial era as well as the failed rebellions preceding the Mobutu era, and to relate these to the contemporary situation of the artist. The second example is from South Africa, where the restitution of the memory and remains of Saartjie Baartman is driven by the desire to establish a historical continuity of the nation that goes beyond apartheid. Nelson Mandela and Tutu on the one hand, and Thabo Mbeki on the other, represent the use of two different memory strategies to ensure this continuity with a pre-apartheid past.

Chapter 4

Justin Bisanswa offers (in what is virtually a literary essay) unconventional insights into the way that memory functioned in strife-torn Congo-Zaire during the colonial era and also at the time of its independence. Mingling personal reminiscences with conflicting memories and understandings of history, he illustrates how selective and divisive memory can be if it remains caught up in a justificatory mode. Every event and every phase becomes ambiguous – the colonial period is remembered as paradise or as hell, independence interpreted as liberation or as the return to primitiveness. This is especially evident in the way journalism constructs alternative interpretations of the situation based on selective memories and informed by preconceptions, which then acquire the status of 'reality'. This applies to representations of personages and events and to the explanations of both the colonial era and the time of independence.

Bisanswa argues that the effect of memory will be divisive, as long as it remains a static memory of justification. What is needed is a dynamic 'memory of crossing', characterized not by fixed locations and certainties but by mobility and transient displacements. It is a discourse that is cautious, critical and open to change. Such a memory of crossing became evident in some of the events surrounding South Africa's Truth and Reconciliation Commission.

Chapter 5

Mamadou Diawara demonstrates the dire consequences that ensue when the link with the past is lost and the focus is on the present and, even more so, on the future. This is especially the case in development studies. The Office du Niger in Mali is a case in point, where the protagonists of development operate from a presentist mindset while the past comes into view only in the form of 'local knowledge', which is already discredited. Ironically, historians become victims of the development policy that they study. Not only do they repeat the divisions between the 'developed' and 'non-developed' sectors of society, they also unwittingly perpetuate them. Diawara argues that local knowledge (and its context of social and temporal production) is to development what historical knowledge is to the future: it cannot be artificially separated from what generates it. Thus, one must begin with a complex whole, not with its isolated elements, no matter how available and tempting they may be. The failure to consider the past in constructing a future has not concerned development specialists, so their approach is bound to fail. He ends with a plea for the recognition of the important contribution that local knowledge can make to the writing of history.

Chapter 6

Albert Grundlingh examines the way in which historical memory functions in the post-apartheid South Africa. Although the country's divisive past is in no small measure responsible for the multiplicity of ways in which memory works in this context, the advent of democracy brought with it new emancipatory choices that hamper the chances of constructing a unified public memory.

Grundlingh uses the centenary commemoration of the South Africa War of 1899–1902 as a case study to demonstrate the unavoidable "contamination" that occurs when different groups seek to appropriate historical memory, not only for the immediate present but also as a way to ensure its control in the future. By the same token it is equally germane to note the permutations and gyrations of those who have inherited a particular memory and had to defend it in a context of dramatically shifting power configurations. Democracy opens up new opportunities, and when it does, rival claims to control historical memory can emerge. The way in which the state took control of the official commemoration in Brandfort shows that debates over commemorations are not primarily focused on different versions of the past or intended to assert the authority of scholarship, but are geared to invite inquiry to try and explain the way in which commemorations as such are constructed to derive maximum benefit from the past in the present.

Chapter 7

Patrick Harries provides an overview of the politics of memory in the 'new' South Africa. He contends that the political changes in the early 1990s initiated a sea change in the way the country looked at its past. Scholars became less concerned with the causes of apartheid than with the consequences of the ideology that, since 1948, had dominated South Africa. He describes some of the ways in which the new South Africa is attempting to produce a new, more consensual history and discusses how these changes are registered and received by different communities. His focus is on the contribution of historical memory to the transfer of power from the white minority to the black majority in South Africa. He concentrates on three areas to illustrate this contribution: the role of the state in the celebration of memory, the impact of community museums, and the influence of the market and tourism in general on the public history of post-1994 South Africa.

Chapter 8

Bernard Lategan examines the possibility of speaking of the future potential of memory. This interest stems from the experience of the ambivalent nature of memory, which becomes especially visible during major social transformations. On the one hand, memory can strengthen individual and collective identity by emphasizing links with the past. On the other hand, it can provide a basis on which to deal with change and construct the future. In the first case, historical memory is often used to justify entrenched positions, to reinforce existing stereotypes and to resist change, rendering it impossible for individuals and groups to envisage themselves as part of a positive future. In the second case, historical memory serves as a point of orientation in a time of uncertainty, providing direction and a sense of continuity. In this role, it has the potential to mediate between conflicting positions and to transcend existing differences, thereby facilitating change. In doing so, it enables individuals and groups to anticipate a constructive future and to participate in the process of bringing this about.

An important precondition for memory to fulfil this role is an explicit future orientation. It has to offer more than just coherence in historical knowledge and historical presentation. Several types of future orientation are discussed, as is the need to deal with the unexpected and contingent. In conclusion, some recent examples are given of how a future-oriented memory works in practice.

Chapter 9

Jörn Rüsen provides a counterpoint to the preceding essays from a German perspective. He takes as his point of departure the Holocaust experience to trace how the process of historical sense-making proceeds when dealing with a borderline experience of this kind – an experience that negates and even destroys the principles of historical interpretation. In doing so he offers a comparative framework for the other contributions. He maintains that the interpretive work of historical consciousness is a procedure of identity building, and that dealing with the Holocaust is a radical example of this process. He first analyses the different ways in which historical consciousness of the event shaped German identity in the post-Holocaust era. He then describes how this process went through three different stages – concealment, moralization and finally historization.

Building on the basis of his specific case study, Rüsen takes up many of the themes already raised by his co-authors and shows that the three stages and their sequence could arguably also apply to other cases of coming to terms with burdensome pasts. The real challenge is how to do history today – how to integrate negative, even traumatic events of the past into a concept of historical identity. The final part of his essay is devoted to an in-depth discussion of the crucial role of mourning and forgiving in dealing with catastrophic experiences. Moving beyond concealment and moralization (which constitutes an abyss of mutual exclusion) is essential if victims and perpetrators are to regain a shared humaneness. Mourning and forgiving can lead to the recognition of the humaneness of those who have radically lost or violated it. This forms the constitutive level of human intersubjectivity, in which recognition of others is a primary condition of human life.

Chapter 10

Ranjan Ghosh writes from an Indian perspective. He takes as his point of departure the myth of Rama and his birthplace Ayodhya and the production and proliferation of memory of the injustice perpetrated by Emperor Babur, who ordered his nobleman Mir Baqi to destroy the temple at Ayodhya and build a mosque instead in 1528–1529. Ghosh shows how Ayodhya became a strategic campaign to create a common memory, a feeling of *participation mystique,* and thereby a 'heritage' that would seek a communal consolidation around issues: Hindus have been wronged by the construction of the Babri Masjid at the 'sacred spot' where Lord Rama was born; the temple that stood at this holy site was pulled down to construct the Babri Masjid; such desacralization should unite the Hindus to embark upon a temple rebuilding mission. Through the politics of commemoration a master narrative is created that can negate the contesting claims of re-visioning this particular issue of Hindu history. The project of representing the past is carried over to the act of controlling the reception, which in turn creates the uncontested zone of collective memory.

Chapter 11

Han Sing-Jin brings an East Asian perspective to the discussion of historical memory. He describes the context in which a dialogue took place in 1997 between Kim Dae Jung, former President of the Republic of South Korea, and a group of students of Seoul National University. He not only provides an extensive background to the event, but also comments on the motives of Dae Jung in forgiving two former military presidents and opponents. He then uses the event to examine his own dilemma: what happens when perpetrators refuse to admit to and apologize for their wrongdoings? Is forgiveness still possible in these circumstances? The example of Dae Jung provides for him the key to deal with this ethical dilemma.

Chapters 12 and 13

The volume is concluded by two personal accounts of historical memory in action, each of which in its own way concretizes the theoretical concepts discussed in the preceding chapters. Pumla Gobodo-Madikizela writes of her encounter and eventual reconciliation with Eugene de Kock, one of the prime perpetrators of violence and death in the apartheid era, and Eva Mozes Kor, a surviving twin of the Mengele laboratory in Auschwitz, reflects on her path to healing.

Bibliography

Jüngel, E. 1969. 'Die Welt als Möglichkeit und Wirklichkeit: Zum ontologische Ansatz der Rechtfertigungslehre', *Evangelische Theologie* 29: 417–42.
Mbeki, T. 1998. *Africa – The Time Has Come.* Cape Town: 31–36.

Part I

Part I

FROM AN AFRICAN PERSPECTIVE

CHAPTER 1

Social Theory and
Making Sense of Africa

Elísio Macamo

Introduction

The purpose of this chapter is to argue that social theory is a specific mode
of making sense of the past, present and future. In order to do this, it relies
on a special form of historical memory. The hypothesis is that African social
reality becomes visible in the manner in which its experience by Africans is
recollected. In this sense, this chapter will speak directly to the role of African
intellectuals in theorizing such experience. The bulk of the argument will bear
directly on a question that can be assumed to retrieve the empirical and the
epistemological dimensions of the central claim. This question is whether there
is an African sociology, here understood as the modern way of engaging reflex-
ively with the experience of social reality. In answering this question special
attention will be given to the constraints upon African intellectuals, which will
be further elaborated with reference to a specific instance of what will be called
the ambivalence of African modernity.

'Sociology, like so many other things, is a European invention', Birgitta
Nedelmann and Piotr Sztompka write in an introduction to a collection of essays on *Sociology in Europe: In Search of Identity* (1993: 1). How, then, could the
claim be justified concerning the relevance of sociology to the recollection of
African social experience? In fairness to Nedelmann and Sztompka, it must be
added that the claims they lay on sociology are, themselves, very sociological
in nature. They are not claiming that sociology is a European invention out of
any chauvinistic sense of ownership; rather, their point is that sociology was the
offspring of a particular time in European social development that Koselleck

(1979) described aptly as *Sattelzeit,* a time of rapid social change. Basically, the claim is that historical and political factors were at work behind the emergence of sociology. This is a useful point of departure to consider the possibility of sociology elsewhere. Unlike the great *négritude* poet Aimé Cesaire, who in 1952, to the enthusiastic applause of many, sang the praises of the people who 'invented nothing', I argue that Africans, in the course of their historical development, also produced, and were affected by, the same conditions that in Europe led to the development of sociology. Africans, however, did not produce sociology. The question, therefore, is why there has never been an African sociology.

The discussion of this question will proceed in three steps. First, it seems appropriate to start by attempting to clarify some important misunderstandings over the meaning of sociology and the effect these have on Africans as objects of study. The purpose of such an attempt is to take issue with the conceptual distinction between 'traditional society' on the one hand and 'modern, industrial society' on the other. This distinction is misleading, as it does not allow us to appreciate the import and impact of social change in colonial Africa. Secondly, and drawing from the discussion of the distinction between 'traditional' and 'modern' society, it will be necessary to reflect upon the conceptual status of Africa with reference to how African intellectuals have engaged with social change. I will draw on my own work on the subject (Macamo 1999) to make the point that Africa is a modern construct and that the absence of sociology in Africa reflects the negation of the modernity of that construct. Thirdly and finally, I will wind up with a look into research I have carried out on the impact of a Protestant mission in Mozambique (Macamo 2001; 2002) and how it has been informed by the reflection on sociology in Africa. My conclusion will be a plea for the africanization of sociology as one of the most privileged ways of acknowledging the relevance of historical recollection to the constitution of social reality.

Traditional Society vs. Modern Society

To some, the direction in which things are going may appear all too obvious: this might appear to be yet another exercise in West-bashing. While in a sense this is indeed the case, it will be shortly argued that since African intellectuals are deeply implicated in the project of modernity, it is also an exercise in self-flagellation. Sociology as a social science was conceived and given content by such figures as Auguste Comte, Saint-Simon, Emile Durkheim, Max Weber and Georg Simmel to name but a few, none of whom was African. Just for the sake of argument, however, what if Max Weber had been African? After all, he seemed to have a keen interest in matters of the spirit. Certainly his major concern would not have been the question of why capitalism developed only in the West, but perhaps why Western capitalism prevented the development of capitalism in Africa or something similar, assuming, of course, that capitalism is what we all want. 'African Spirits and the Ethics of Western Capitalism?' Weber, of course, was not African, but if he had been African, would he have existed? In other words, would his engagement with society – his experience of modernity – have been acknowledged?

These questions would not be necessary if the dominant perception of sociology in Europe as the study of modern, industrial society did not imply the existence of an opposite, traditional society, contemporaneous but distant geographically. No sociological account of the emergence of sociology as an intellectual pursuit is complete without reference to the conditions that called for it in nineteenth-century in the first place. Indeed, the major social, political and economic transformations associated with growing industrialization and the need to find adequate solutions to the ensuing problems led to the development of a way of looking at social relations, which basically constituted them as empirical realities. The science of society did not emerge because there was something out there called 'society' that was crying out for study. It emerged because there was a longing for the invention of such a thing. Sociology provided the tools for describing it and in the process made it visible not only for study but also for interventions of all sorts.

The sociology of Émile Durkheim is particularly enlightening in this respect. Those of us who are inclined to a more interpretive way of doing sociology have grown accustomed to calling Durkheim's sociology names. To be sure, this is a habit that his often unbearable positivism seems to invite. But one of the most interesting, if not the greatest achievement of his sociology, was his attempt at defining the object of a science of society. A careful reading of his methodological essays will show that the concepts he wanted sociologists to use in order to account for society are not only descriptive tools, but also building blocks through which he actually invents society. One of the most striking things one learns when one goes through his methodological writings is precisely this dialectic between knowledge of society and the possibility of society.

Durkheim's notion of 'social facts' (1988) is a case in point. For him the notion of a social fact refers to ways of behaving, doing things and relating to other people that are not individually determined but given, influenced from outside. Central to his definition of a social fact is the idea that the social is constituted via external constraints. From this understanding of the social flows the logical conclusion of a whole held together functionally. We act in certain ways because we are members of a family and have roles within it that are independent of our individual will and are determined from outside of us. In other words, social facts refer us to the constitution of society by allowing us to see what it is made of and where it starts and ends.

Durkheim's call for treating social facts as things drives the point home about the way in which the descriptive moment can also be the moment of constructing a reality. Arguing against those who would rather concentrate on ideas about society as the proper subject of sociology, Durkheim points out that it is not ideas that are central to sociology, but the facts of social life that can be observed, as things, in the functioning of society. Not the idea of morality, but the set of rules guiding behaviour; not the idea of economic value, but economic exchanges in a given setting; not the idea of evolution, but the specific development of a given, historical society.

The aim of this essay is not to endorse Durkheim's sociology, but to take it as an example of how the emergence of sociology was linked to the discovery of society in a particular way. Durkheim's methodological statements are not just claims for the scientific status of sociology, but also statements about social relations as a whole at a time when they were being threatened by rapid social change. Sociology helped to raise awareness to something larger than immediate and individual social relations. It contributed towards making visible something that was no longer taken for granted and, with its analytical tools, helped to actually constitute society as an empirical reality.

Herein lies the genius of classical sociologists who, in the turbulence of rapid social change, discerned something much larger with which individuals should engage. Sociology was in an important sense one response to the search for community in the face of rapid social change. It offered an idea of a radically different community, one no longer based on status and face-to-face interactions, but rather based on contract, anonymity and functional interdependence, to name but a few distinctions. If this way of understanding the origins of sociology is plausible and accurate, it seems clear that the idea that sociology studies industrial, modern society needs to be qualified in order to make sense at all.

Sociology studies modern industrial society to the extent that it represents it in contrast to an assumed opposite, namely 'traditional society'. Taken as ideal types in a Weberian sense, both traditional and modern society can be quite illuminating. However, in the development of sociology the perception that these are just ideal types gave way to a belief that both traditional society and modern society were accurate descriptions of actual reality. From representing and constructing society, sociology was turned into a science that described something that existed independently of the terms of analysis employed. The history of 'the problem of order' offers interesting insights into this development. Since it is too complex to go into right now, brief mention could be made of Talcott Parsons, who reduced the development of sociology to the study of the problem of order (1967). Having interpreted the classics in this way, he proclaimed American middle-class society as the solution to that problem, for which his particular brand of sociology had contributed important insights. With the development of sociology, especially functionalist sociology, social relations lost their dynamism, ceased to be processes and became essences.

This belief in the actual existence of modern society went hand in hand with a belief in the actual existence of its opposite, namely traditional society. In disciplinary terms there occurred a division of labour that made anthropology the study of 'traditional society'. Often, African scholars complain that this division of labour is fuelled by racism, since more often than not the perception that anthropology was the study of primitive society was consistent with colonial ideology, even if we should be wary of drawing too close a link between anthropology and colonialism.

It could be argued that this division of labour was the result of a basic misunderstanding of the origins of sociology. And this becomes readily apparent if we cast a look at what classical sociologists had to say about different types of society. Durkheim, again, provides the best example. Durkheim (1984), as is broadly known, distinguished between two types of society, namely a society based on mechanical solidarity versus a society based on organic solidarity.

Now, in drawing this distinction Durkheim was not describing actually existing societies, even if on a superficial level we may be inclined to think that these distinctions corresponded to reality. Again, a society based on organic solidarity was what Durkheim saw as the most likely outcome of the process of change that was sweeping across Europe, even if in his most pessimistic mood he feared that anomie would end up reigning supreme; in any case, the distinction between mechanical and organic solidarity reflected both his epistemological as well as practical interests. As far as his epistemological interests were concerned, the distinction helped him to place the changes in an explanatory framework that, in a teleological sense, allowed him to account for the breakdown of forms of social integration. Rapid social change did not necessarily mean the end of social cohesion, but perhaps the beginning of an era in which social integration would be achieved in a different manner. As for the practical interest, this was tied in with sociology itself, since the distinction also allowed him to lend legitimacy to sociology as the science that would provide the means through which social order could be made possible.

The Conceptual Distinction in Africa

This conceptual distinction between traditional and modern society has had quite devastating effects in Africa. Indeed, understanding sociology as the science of modern, industrial society has had the effect of removing history from the concerns of sociology and of confining societies branded 'traditional' to the past and perceiving them, as Shalini Randeria (1999) pointed out in a recent essay on these matters, as the past of Europe. In his *Time and the Other* (1983), Johannes Fabian argued along much the same lines with his point to the effect that in dealing with non-Europeans, anthropology had tended to regard them and their institutions as Europe's past. Early armchair anthropologists had provided the justification for this understanding of anthropology when they argued that non-European societies were not chronologically old, only old in structure, which rendered them interesting for the long march of European modernity.

We should take a closer look at the effects of this conceptual distinction by discussing the conceptual status of Africa. In doing this, the point should be made that the conceptual distinction between traditional vs. modern society may account for the absence of an African sociology. It may also be a useful indicator of the forms taken by the ambivalence of modernity in Africa.

Some of the conditions that led to the development of sociology in Europe were not absent in Africa. Indeed, over the past one hundred years or so there occurred a process that it is fair to regard as the birth of Africa. In other words, the rapid social changes brought about by increased contacts with the outside world and, particularly, colonialism made Africa as an empirical reality possible. Or better still, before colonialism there was no such thing as Africa, only small or large polities and societies that defined themselves in parochial terms. This argument, which is spelt out in more detail in a book with the title '*Was ist Afrika?*' (Macamo 1999), is that Africa is a modern construct made potentially possible by European colonialism, but ultimately invented by Africans themselves in their attempts to cope with modernity.

This, of course, is bound to sound like the chicken and egg riddle. Who came first, Africans or Africa? In fact, we can use the term 'Africans' as shorthand for those who thought up Africa and, in the process, reinvented themselves as such. In Africa there are basically two positions on the status of the continent. One position holds that there is an original African community that was thrown out of history by European colonialism. The challenge for this position is to recover this original community and use it to rehabilitate the continent. Movements like *négritude, African socialism* and *African personality* are examples of this position. The other position maintains that Africa is a European invention, serving no other purpose but the European will to power. Those who maintain this position also argue as a consequence that there is no point in seeking a return to an original Africa, for this has been lost for good – and in any case, Europeans would not allow it – and concentrate, instead, in describing the way in which Europe represents Africa (Mudimbe 1988).

These positions come especially into view in the long-drawn debate concerning the question whether there is an African philosophy (Wright 1979; Ruch and Anyanwu 1981; Neugebauer 1989). Those who argue that there is one, define it in terms of a unique African way of perceiving the world – *la philosophie bantoue* – whereas those who say there is no such thing as an African philosophy argue that this unique African *Weltanschauung* reflects the ideological hold Europe has over our imagination. A closer look at these debates takes us back to their origins in the middle of the nineteenth century, when former slaves in America were returned to Africa. The debate documents more than fundamental disagreements about philosophy. In fact, there is a sense in which the debate itself was constitutive of Africa in a way that seemed to be lost to those participating in it.

Returning slaves were the first to posit Africa as a category *sui generis*,[1] much in the same way that sociology became the means through which industrial society began to be represented. Men like Edward Blyden, Samuel Crummel and Africanus Horton, among others, interpreted the experience of slavery, colonialism and political disenfranchisement as moments in the construction of an African community of destiny and values. Where there had been no sense of belonging together, of Africa if you like, struggles for political rights, cultural recognition and economic emancipation gave reality and substance to it.

One of the main reasons why African intellectuals engaged in inventing Africa failed to see their intellectual activity as a crucial moment in that invention has to do with the conditions under which intellectual discourse in Africa emerged. These conditions were largely determined by European ideas about non-Europeans. The conceptual distinction between traditional and modern society was central to these European ideas. Assured by intellectual debates at home that seemed to confirm their daily experience of life in the 'heart of darkness' – to use Conrad's famous literary description of Africa (2002) – colonialists went about their work in Africa as if they were indeed dealing with traditional societies and were unable to countenance the possibility that the native might also be experiencing modernity.

The colonial understanding of Africa was based on two assumptions, namely either the need to preserve traditional society as appropriate for Africa, or the belief in the need for Africans to embrace European ways. The British policy of indirect rule is a good example of the former, while the French and Portuguese assimilationist policies are illustrations of the latter. Both assumptions were normatively loaded. It was not the experience of social change by the African that was at the centre of these policies, but Europeans' patronizing attitudes towards Africans.

The possibility of an African discourse on Africa was deeply constrained by this to such an extent that African intellectual discourse has been, in fact, one long bitter, frustrated and pedantic monologue on European perceptions of Africa. It has always been constrained by the need to choose between two alternatives, traditional or modern, and while often hostile to the former, African intellectual discourse has perceived itself as an argument against the latter. The irony of it all, however, is that this soul-searching was and continues to be constitutive of Africa. This is why, against the popular notion that there is something intrinsically African in the way of life of ordinary, often rural Africans, I, for one, deem it more appropriate to argue that intellectuals are the real Africans; the others are but Ashanti, Yoruba or Zulu, which, of course, should not rule out that 'Africans' in the constructivist sense employed here might carry along such specific identities.

In the book on the meaning of Africa (Macamo 1999), I discuss the paradoxical nature of this attitude. It is as if African intellectuals were caught up in

a trap, freedom from which would mean the end of our hold on reality. Africa
is a product of modernity, and yet the only way Africans can engage with it is
by adopting a discourse that on the surface is critical of modernity. Now, one
consequence of this dilemma has been the inability and failure of African intellectuals to develop conceptual and analytical tools to describe the experience
of modernity by Africans. We have been loud in our moral indignation against
the evils of colonialism, but deafeningly silent in engaging with modernity's
impact on us. Let us now try to illustrate the need for engaging with modernity
with reference to empirical work done on the relationship between work and
societal order in Africa.

The Relationship between Work and Society

I researched the influence of a Swiss Protestant mission on the work ethic in
Southern Mozambique for about four years. My initial interest in the issue
came from observing a disproportionately strong influence of members of this
church – the Presbyterian Church of Mozambique – on national politics and
the economy. Popular perceptions of this influence do not take notice of the
religious aspect; rather, there is the belief that the country is dominated by the
Southern ethnic groups. Since I also come from the South and never felt that
I had been privileged in any way, I tried to understand the sources of this perception. Looking at the number of Southerners in government and industrial
positions, I was struck by something they shared, namely their membership of
the Swiss mission church. I also noticed that these were not just individuals, but
whole families that extended their influence through strategic marriages.

Not only did they seem to wield a lot of influence, but they also stood
out in terms of their level of education, economic achievement and strong
sense of purpose. What struck me more about the whole story was that these
were members of a Protestant denomination that had been persecuted by the
colonial state, which perceived itself to be Catholic[2] and saw all other Christian
denominations as unpatriotic and heretical. How had these religious minori-
ties risen to such prominence? Was there anything in the missionary work of
the Swiss that could account for it? After all, this was a strong Calvinist church,
committed to the values of hard work, virtue and honesty as a celebration of
God's glory. In order to find out more about the links between the Swiss and
industrious Africans, I conducted research in a rural village in Southern Mozambique, where the Swiss mission has been since 1912. I wanted to find out
whether there was anything in the work attitudes and life conduct of the African members of the church that could point me in the direction of a possible
influence of the Swiss.

The results were quite sobering, as anything really is in Africa once one
descends to the empirical level. While I found that members of this commu-

nity did, indeed, stand out in terms of educational achievement, employment and sense of purpose, I was unable to establish a link with Swiss Calvinist theology. What is more, their success was relative and did not really say much about non-members' commitment to the value of hard work and good moral conduct. I interpreted the material I had collected as telling me that rather than the mission having had an influence on the people, it had actually been used by the people as a resource in their attempts to master the changes that have swept across Africa and through these people's lives for over 100 years. One particularly striking and graphic illustration of this was the Swiss's dismal failure, in spite of their best and fanatical efforts, to make Africans stop believing in witchcraft. While the church officially and in public pronouncements abhors magic and anything related to it, in private members cannot make sense of anything without recourse to it, as I myself experienced when on my arrival I was the object of a tug of war between rival church ministers who accused one another of witchcraft. The one in whose house I ended up living told me my good spirits, not guardian angels, had led me to his protecting arms. Then there is the story of a practising witch doctor, one of the most active and fervent members of the church, who told me of his wish that the church and witch doctors could come together to fight superstition.

I complemented my research with archival work that could help me find a plausible explanation for the hypothesis that the church was used by the people as a local resource for coming to terms with social change. The evidence, as I see it, is overwhelming. The second half of the nineteenth century, when the Swiss mission ventured into Southern Mozambique, was a time of deep and rapid change.[3] The region was under the military control of Zulu invaders, who themselves had been pushed out of South Africa by superior British and Afrikaner firepower. The despotic rule of the Zulu was challenged also by the Portuguese, who laid claims over the territory and sought to enforce them by military means. The coast had for a few decades been a centre of international trade (Smith 1970), not only in slaves, but mainly in elephant tusks, salt, agricultural produce and hides. This trade was controlled mostly by Africans, although the Portuguese claimed authority over the bay region. Also at this time, massive numbers of Africans were flocking into the diamond mines and sugar plantations of South Africa, where they were drilled into industrial discipline and from where they returned home with values, attitudes and outlooks at odds with those of their original communities.

'Traditional' society was breaking up. Wars, new economic opportunities and new outlooks placed old normative systems under enormous strain as wealth acquired through trade, migrant labour or military involvement became more important than traditional forms of defining the status of individuals. I think it is fair to say that the transition to new forms of management of individual lives, as in the case of those who became mine workers, plantation workers and so on, was not a difficult one. Indeed, an American historian, Keletso Atkins, has shown for South Africa that in most areas there was a direct correspondence between traditional occupations and new ones. In the early days of industrialization and urbanization in South Africa the laundry trade was dominated by a class of people who had specialized in curing hides. Later discriminatory policies in favour of Indians and lower-class European migrants ended this dominance (Atkins 1993).

Things began to change as Portugal became increasingly able to assert its authority over the territory. There were three main factors behind this, but I shall concentrate on one, as it became central to the management of social relationships. The first was the Berlin conference in which Africa was carved up among colonial powers. Portugal's claims over Mozambique were granted 'legal validity', if you like. The second was a successful military campaign by Portugal against the Zulu rulers of Mozambique. The third and most important factor was the regulation of labour, which became the centerpiece of Portuguese colonial policy and the stone upon which the colonial state was built.[4]

The Portuguese regulation of labour was a response to doubts in Portugal as to whether keeping Mozambique as a colony made any real sense. Many in Portugal argued that colonies should be given up, as they were only a strain on the country. Those who were for keeping the colonies – who not surprisingly were chiefly colonial officials – argued that the solution was not to give them up, but to make them profitable for Portugal. They pointed out that the key to making the colonies profitable was the intelligent use of native labour. Therefore, they criticized earlier Portuguese colonial policy, which by abolishing slavery and forced labour had, in their eyes, deprived Portugal not only of an important economic resource but also of the only means of civilizing the natives.

In 1899, they drafted a law on native labour whose main innovation was to allow colonial administrators to force natives to work if they failed to live up to legally established definitions of gainful employment. Those forced to comply with the regulations would do public works or work for Portuguese settlers, who always complained of a shortage of labour. If I may add a personal note, my own great-grandfather was beaten to death by a settler because he tried to escape into South Africa, where wages were better; even as late as the 1950s, my maternal grandmother was forced to work on road construction because her husband, who had gone to work in South Africa, had failed to return after the end of his labour contract.

The Portuguese regulation of labour was based on two assumptions. One assumption was that Africans were lazy and would only work if compelled to. Available evidence suggests, however, that this was not the case. The large migratory waves and the thriving international trade do not support this assumption. If anything, Africans were perhaps selective in the choice of employer and activity. Ironically, even the great colonial ideologue António Enes, the royal commissioner who chaired the commission that drew up the law on native labour, admitted that Africans were very industrious; the problem, in his view, was that earlier Portuguese legislation, which preached the equality of all Portuguese subjects, by removing the obligation to work in fear of hurting international susceptibilities concerning slavery, was encouraging the native to be indolent.

Tied to this patronizing assumption about the redemptive value of the obligation to work was the assumption held by colonial legislators that the passing of traditional society was devastating social relations and that something should be done about it. Given their lower position in the evolutionary scale, Africans, the argument went, were not yet ready to appreciate the advantages of civilization. The shock would be too great, so there was a need to introduce a series of measures that would ensure a smooth transition from traditional society to modern society. A few years after the passing of the native labour law, a new law was passed that created native political and legal institutions. These were modelled on Portuguese understandings of traditional African society and were for the most part based on South African codifications of African customary law, which were held to be valid across Africa.

The Portuguese response to social change in Africa was, therefore, to arrest it. The institution of two legal systems effectively removed history from African social relations by reinventing and stabilizing traditional institutions that had been under enormous strain and whose terms of demise Africans had been negotiating for some time.[5]

This is where I would like to bring the Swiss mission back into the story. Unlike Portuguese colonial authorities, the mission did not attempt to arrest social change. Instead, it rode the wave. And this was largely the work of Africans themselves. For a start, Swiss missionaries did not go to Mozambique; their church was taken to Mozambique by migrant labourers in South Africa who had been converted to Christianity. In the early days, returning migrant labourers would lead huge awakening meetings in urban and rural areas, funded by economically successful Africans, and would seek to establish new communities based on faith.[6] The leaders were often literate Africans who drew from many sources – as early as the end of the nineteenth century, there were translations into Shangaan (the local vernacular) of the works of leading black American thinkers. As Portugal gained more control of the country it cracked down on these, forcing several leaders into exile in the islands of São Tomé e Príncipe and Cape Verde.

As these awakening groups became more assertive they caught the eye of Swiss missionaries, who fought hard to wrest control of the church from Africans. A leading historian of this church, the Dutch theologian Jan van Butselaar, has written that some Swiss missionaries had their hand in the exile of leading African figures. Whatever actually happened in those turbulent days, the fact is that by the end of the century, and with Portuguese authority firmly entrenched, Swiss missionaries had gained control of the church and massive numbers of Africans were joining it in an open rejection of Portuguese rule.

What made the Swiss mission alluring for Africans was not so much the theology, which Africans heartily adopted, but the opportunities it opened for education, vocational training, access to medical care and, above all, the sense of community it offered Africans who had for some time been in search of one.[7] Unlike the Catholic church – the state church in colonial Mozambique, which in the early days had funded its activities through the sale of alcohol in urban centres and accepted anyone who professed belief – the Swiss missionaries, true to their Calvinist tradition, required from converts not only belief in the Christian god, but also a true Christian life. This spoke to many Africans and explains, I believe, why this church was successful in attracting African converts in spite of the fact that Portuguese rules on assimilation required christening, something people could easily obtain by joining a Catholic church, where the priests were more concerned with numbers.

In their struggle with their own social, political and economic environment, Africans came to see Christianity, particularly the kind preached by Swiss missionaries, as an important resource in the domestication of fate. It allowed them to give a new sense of purpose to their lives, to establish new normative frameworks for social relations and, above all, to imagine new communities that would emerge out of the turmoil in which they lived.

The outstanding position of African members of the Presbyterian church in Mozambique does not, in my view, rest so much on their earlier and better access to education, vocational training and health care – very important resources in themselves – but rather on the sense of community they have been able to create, foster and rely on in their daily lives. Against the background of social change the community has been the most stable element in people's lives and a space for negotiating the terms of their incorporation into modernity.

Conclusion: Sociology and Historical Recollection

The conceptual distinction between traditional and modern society has been instrumental in denying Africans' experience of modernity. The Portuguese colonial authorities, working on the assumption that there were fundamental differences between Europeans and Africans, denied the latter historicity. Indeed, they simply assumed that African societies do not change over time, and that they preserve institutions and roles that can be retrieved whenever they are needed. At the same time, Portuguese authorities pursued policies that in effect sought to arrest social change. They reacted to ordinary Africans' engagement with the challenges of modernity by seeking to confine them to traditional institutions modelled on what they thought they should look like.

The Swiss missionaries, on the contrary, wittingly or unwittingly, rode the wave of these social changes. The institutions, as well as the normative framework their missionary work put in place, proved extremely valuable to ordinary

Africans. Indeed, they were used by the latter as resources in their efforts to come to terms with social change. Africans responded to the denial of modernity by the Portuguese colonial authorities by seeking to fulfil the promise of modernity within the institutional and normative frameworks made available to them by the Swiss mission.

The ambivalent nature of modernity in Africa (Macamo 2005) produced African social reality and structured Africans' experience thereof. While ordinary Africans coped as best they could with this ambivalence, African intellectuals engaged with modernity in very specific ways. For reasons that had to do with the way in which Africa had become an object of scientific interest and also the objective historical conditions under which modernity became an issue in the continent, most intellectuals developed a critical attitude towards modernity in general. Indeed, intellectuals either sought to recover a sense of identity presumed lost in the wake of colonialism or they challenged the representation of Africa and its assumption as truth revelation. In doing this, however, they failed to develop an autonomous field of intellectual analysis and reflection that could have allowed them to engage in a more direct way with African social reality. In other words, they did not develop an African sociology.

Even though African intellectuals did not develop an African sociology, there exists a sociology of Africa. This sociology needs to be africanized. The africanization of sociology consists of two equally important processes. First, there should be a conscious attempt to place the recollection of the past at the centre of reflections on the present. In other words, African intellectuals must make their implicit recognition of the constitutive role of the past much more explicit by engaging in a more direct way with Africans' experience of modernity as it manifests itself in social reality. This requires (this is the second process) a recognition that the future of Africa is open and can be shaped by Africans' own intervention. I borrow the basic idea from Koselleck's notion of 'futures past' (1985) to draw attention to the role of historical awareness in making Africa possible. The africanization of sociology, therefore, refers to a process whereby Africa reveals itself as a modern construct and becomes available for sociological analysis through the experience of that modernity. A call for an African sociology, therefore, is a plea for us to engage with that experience.

Notes

1. This formulation is drawn from Irele (1975).

2. Although at times it was very anti-clerical. This was especially the case during the Republican years early in the twentieth century.

3. Harries (1994) offers a beautiful description of this period in his history of migrant labour. See also Rodney (1971).

4. For a full account see Macamo (2003); for the theoretical statement of the problem, see Conrad, Macamo and Zimmermann (2000).

5. These findings are compatible with the argument made by Mamdani (1996).

6. For a good account of the early history of the mission see van Butselaar (1984).

7. If I am right in this interpretation, then Bayart's notion of 'extraversion' (2000) must be taken with a pinch of salt.

Bibliography

Atkins, K.E. 1993. *The Moon is Dead! Give us our Money! The Cultural Origins of an African Work Ethic, Natal, South Africa, 1843–1900*. London.

Bayart, J.-F. 2000. 'Africa in the World: A History of Extraversion', *African Affairs* 99: 219–267.

Cesaire, A. 1952. *Cahier d'un retour au pays natal: Présence Africaine*. Paris.

Conrad, J. 2002. *The Heart of Darkness*. London.

Conrad, S., E. Macamo and B. Zimmermann. 2000. 'Die Kodifizierung der Arbeit: Individuum, Gesellschaft, Nation', in J. Kocka and C. Offe (eds), *Geschichte und Zukunft der Arbeit*. Frankfurt am Main: 449–475.

Durkheim, É. 1984. *The Division of Labor in Society*. New York.

Durkheim, É. 1988. *Les règles de la méthode sociologique*. Paris.

Fabian, J. 1983. *Time and the Other: How Anthropology makes its Object*. New York.

Harries, P. 1994. *Work, Culture and Identity: Migrant Laborers in Mozambique and South Africa, c. 1860–1910*. London.

Irele, A.F. 1975. 'Négritude et African Personality', in A.J. Smet (ed.), *Philosophie africaine: Textes choisies*. Kinshasa: 151–168.

Koselleck, R. 1979. *Vergangene Zukunft: Zur Semantik geschichtlicher Zeiten*. Frankfurt am Main.

Koselleck, R. 1985. *Futures Past: On the Semantics of Historical Time*. Cambridge.

Macamo, E. 1999. *Was ist Afrika? Zur Geschichte und Kultursoziologie eines modernen Konstrukts*. Berlin.

Macamo, E. 2001. 'Protestantische Ethik und die Geister Afrikas', in U. Bauer, H. Egbert and F. Jäger (eds), *Interkulturelle Beziehungen und Kulturwandel in Afrika: Beiträge zur Globalisierungsdebatte*. Frankfurt: 185–168.

Macamo, E. 2002. 'Biographical Knots', in Y. Elkana, I. Krastev, E. Macamo, and S. Randeria (eds), *Unraveling Ties: From Social Cohesion to New Practices of Connectedness*. Frankfurt.

Macamo, E. 2003. 'Work and Societal Order in Africa – Negotiating Social Change', in W. Lepenies (ed.), *Entangled Histories and Negotiated Universals*. Frankfurt am Main: 281–309.

Macamo, E. (ed.). 2005. *Negotiating Modernity: Africa's Ambivalent Experience*. London and Dakar.

Mamdani, M. 1996. *Citizen and Subject: Contemporary Africa and the Legacy of Late Colonialism*. Princeton.

Mudimbe, V.Y. 1988. *The Invention of Africa: Gnosis, Philosophy and the Order of Knowledge*. London.

Nedelmann, B. and P. Sztompka. 1993. 'Introduction', in B. Nadelmann and P. Sztompka (eds), *Sociology in Europe: In Search of Identity*. Berlin and New York: 254–276.

Neugebauer, C. 1989. *Einführung in die afrikanische Philosophie*. Munich, Kinshasa and Libreville.

Parsons, T. 1967. *Sociological Theory and Modern Society*. New York.

Randeria, S. 1999. 'Jenseits von Soziologie und soziokultureller Anthropologie: Zur Ortsbestimmung der nicht-westlichen Welt in einer zukünftigen Sozialtheorie', *Soziale Welt* 50(4): 373–82.

Rodney, W. 1971. 'The Year 1895 in Southern Mozambique: African Resistance to the Imposition of European Colonial Rule', *Journal of the Historical Society of Nigeria* 5(4): 509–536.

Ruch, E.A. and K.C. Anyanwu. 1981. *African Philosophy: An Introduction to the Main Philosophical Trends in Contemporary Africa*. Rome.

Smith, A. 1970. *The Struggle for Control of Southern Moçambique, 1720–1835*. Los Angeles.

Van Butselaar, J. 1984. *Africains, missionnaires et colonialistes: les origines de l'Église Presbytérienne du Mozambique (Mission Suisse) 1888–1896*. Leiden.

Wright, R.A. 1979. *African Philosophy: An Introduction*. Washington, D.C.

CHAPTER 2

History by Word of Mouth
Linking Past and Present through Oral Memory

ANNEKIE JOUBERT

Introduction

One of the most prevalent deficiencies of oral memory is its transient nature, that is, the forgetting that occurs continually with the passage of time and the increase in people's age. The past seems to inevitably recede with the elapse of time and the occurrence of new experiences (Schacter 2001: 12–13). Experimental evidence gathered by scholars as early as Ebbinghaus in 1878 to Thompson in the 1990s indicates that 'memory after a day was close to a verbatim record of specific events; memory after a week was closer to a generic description of what usually happens' (Schacter 2001: 15). The recollection of when and where an event occurred, or who said what, seems to be notably ephemeral. This is particularly important for our discussion, since the focus of this contribution will be on the authoring and translation of memory in oral traditions through modes such as praise poetry and various forms of oral narration and testimonies into 'history' (Minkley and Rasool 1998: 90). The 'pasts' of black communities in South Africa, until recently, mainly consisted of an oral culture with an 'oral historical memory' where stories, poems and songs were passed down from one generation to the other by word of mouth.[1] Working with an oral culture and an oral historical memory requires the tapping of people's minds, the watching of performance events, and the listening to their stories – their recollections of the past, based on hearsay, memoirs, eyewitness accounts, emotions and experiences.

Although these forms of oral history have always been in our midst (even before the beginning of history writing), they have never received the promi-

---

Notes for this section begin on page 48.

nence in South Africa that they should. Historians, ethnographers and anthropologists, working in a culture where the overwhelming emphasis is put on literacy and not on orality, paid little attention to the use of oral memories, especially those narrated by African people. Harris (2000: 112) argues that both custodians and scholars demonstrate a determination to view and to utilize oral history as 'source for history' rather than as 'history in its own right'. Wright (2000: 126) agrees with this notion when he states: 'Generally speaking, relatively few western historians, radical or otherwise, have been concerned to question the notion that "the past" has its own objective existence "out there", independently of any historian.'

It seems then that until recently, researchers of the past believed that the past can to some extent become known to us as it actually happened or as it truly was. The truth of the matter, however, is that the past 'can be known only through the narratives, or stories, which particular people under particular circumstances write or tell about it' (Wright 2000: 126). Especially in a country like South Africa, where black communities had little opportunity to produce their own history, and where the country is still rife with racial bigotry and ethnic animosity, we can only speak about 'pasts' and no longer of 'the past', since different people tell different stories about the past.

This chapter explores the power of oral performance as a mode of communication in the presentation of the past. The examples used point out the multi-channelled (auditory, visual, tactile, olfactory) communicative process that is transmitted in performance, in contrast to the severely limited channel capacity (visual) of the print medium as generally used in historiographic writing. The first part of this chapter shows how a deeply rooted form of oral art, namely praise poetry, is still, even in new forms and manifestations, operative in African communities. It further argues in favour of the inclusion and reappropriation of these forms of orality in the process of serious historiography. The second part illustrates the emergence of a universal trend whereby the past is remembered through multi-channelled communication processes (that is, in the form of *performance*) for the purpose of political reconciliation, the creation of 'new' identities and the sharing of future perspectives.

Memory through Oral Praise Chanting as an Articulation of History

What relevance, if any, do the elaborately dense and rich oral traditions of African societies have in the reinterpretation of the past? Do praise poems from the past still have the capacity to be used as voices in today's public space, and in the understanding of the past and production of a future? In answering these questions we have to remember that oral art never exists in isolation but coexists with the communal lives of people, as acted out in different ceremonies and occasions. In this way all oral discourses in African societies (including praise poetry) are to some or other extent intertwined and impact on each other. Oral cultures seem then to use more activity-based knowledge and memory, which they extract largely from their 'performed' lifestyles. Memory, through oral art, represents actively collective experiences: what is memorable to remember in a particular community, and how it will be remembered – indeed, serving as a vehicle in the preservation of the past.

The long tradition of praise poetry provides evidence of an engagement of this form of oral art in various issues, ranging from colonial encounters, leadership, bravery, suffering and wars to political action, public commentary and self-identity. The continual use and importance of praise poetry in South Africa became evident during the Truth and Reconciliation Commission (TRC) as one of the old witnesses chanted his lineage in order to introduce himself. Raditlhalo (2004: 37) explains the preamble of the witness, as recounted by Antjie Krog in her book *Country of My Skull* (1998):

> Punctuating each one of his nineteen generations of forebears by striking his knobkerrie on the floor, Chief Anderson Joyi would not countenance beginning his testimony without outlining his ancestral lineage; and in explaining why he began his testimony in this manner, he said that these names gave his story a 'shadow', placing in perspective what had happened to him. This granted him the ability to endure past and present.

The function of one's lineage has great importance since it not only identifies the individual, the family and the clan, but also anchors a person's belonging in a community and cultural group. This 'belonging to' played an important role during the TRC hearings, since communities, cultural and linguistic groups were deeply divided. The chanting of Chief Joyi's lineage not only introduced him to the audience present, but also distinguished him in terms of culture and language, by doing so marking him as one of the victims.

The intellectual strength, historic importance and symbolic competence of oral praise poetry have long been recognized. Scholars such as Opland (1983), Barber (1989), Gunner (1999, 2003) and Kaschula (1999, 2004) have indicated how the regenerative power of memory can make praise poetry at the same time part of the present and the past. Kaschula (2004: 47) explains it as follows:

> The reemergence of the oral poet or *imbongi* in southern Africa, and the griot in West Africa, as part of national literatures during and after the struggles for liberation has been borne out by the numerous performances in honour of, for example, Senghor in the 1960s and Mandela in the 1990s.

The use of old forms of praise poetry in contemporary performances confirms the fluidness and adaptability of tradition.[2] By invoking figures from the past such as the Zulu king Shaka, the Xhosa resistance figure Sandile, Mzilikazi the founder of the Ndebele people of Zimbabwe, the Basotho king Moshoeshoe, the Hananwa chief and war hero Ratšhatšha, or the Lobedu queen Modjadji, contemporary praise poets pull formerly distinct 'national' figures into the arena of present political debate, and the creation of identity. According to Gunner (1999: 54), this form of contemporary oral praise poetry produces 'the possibility of a more hybrid history far more suited to the many "nations" present in the new South Africa in terms of language and remembered histories and traditions'.

Recently the multi-channelled ways of presenting historical accounts have gained prominence and are now recognized next to the previously exclusive written documentation of 'high history'. A further development in this regard is the way in which modern technology and especially the Internet influence the global oral discourse.[3] The interaction between the oral word and tech-nology facilitates, according to Kaschula (2004: 47), 'a world-wide audience for contemporary poets'. The term technauriture[4] is used by Kaschula in his insightful essay to point out the emergence of technologized orality in the form of contemporary poetry such as performance poetry, which includes rap, dub-poetry, slam, izibongo, kwai-jazz, direto, dithoko and kiba. A powerful example of this kind of oral discourse is the rap song 'I Remember District Six' from the rap band Prophets of da City's most recent album *Ghetto Code*. Ac-cording to Brown (2003: 15) the band 'explicitly link their sound and perfor-mance with a sense of placement and displacement, combining oral testimony, melodic jazz, and the rapper's own voice of remembrance'.

The performance poet Kgafela Oa Magogodi, who is also a columnist for *Y-Magazine,* wrote in 'The Spoken Word' about the scene of contemporary spoken poetry as it unfolds in South Africa and abroad:

> The intervention that the young lions and lionesses of the word make in the ter-rain of popular culture and political memory must be recorded. True, there's a voice in the process of becoming. If you must catch it still warm, pay attention to THE WORD.[5]

From these quotations it becomes clear that memory and orality are in-creasingly used in exciting new ways of performance to create awareness around societal issues and to interpret contemporary reality. This simultaneously em-braces many different cultural phenomena and cultural fields, enabling us to relate art, politics, history and society in a new way with one another.[6]

When the poems from which I will be quoting are performed in modern times, it demonstrates that the activity of praising and chanting cannot be re-stricted to a static notion of tradition but is rather a form of art that is constantly relevant to both the past and the present. Gunner (1999: 50) supports this view by stating that 'it is part of the "labours of remembrance" used in the turbulent present to recall a perhaps equally turbulent past, but used nevertheless as part of an active remembering of a community's history, and used as part of the way in which it sees itself in the present.'

Before I quote from the first praise poem, I want to return to the scepti-cism raised earlier about the deficiencies of oral memory, namely its transience and its ephemeral nature. This scepticism underestimates both the neurological processes underlying oral memory and the array of mnemonic techniques supporting it. Both written and oral memory rely on selection and interpretation, but in the case of the latter, the process of remembering is enhanced in several ways. Recent research has shown that specific neurological processes occur when we experience events or acquire new facts and information. Unless the neural connection is strengthened by subsequent retrieval and accounting, it will dissipate as time passes and interference occurs. The principal technique in countering this transient state of memory is to enhance elaborate encoding through visual imagery mnemonics.[7] Oral cultures utilize mnemonic devices such as rhyme, rhythm, metaphor, and formulated patterns to assist their memory. Episodes and incidents that are discussed, often retold, rehearsed or performed are therefore 'more' protected from transience, whereas those that are never mentioned fade more quickly (Schacter 2001: 16–17). In the case of oral art, and especially the genre of praise poetry, the repeating of historic information through multi-channelled performance events improves the memory of what is repeated. The distributing of these repetitions over time, and in context, seems to result in better memory than massing all the information together (Schacter 2001: 48). Vansina (1980: 272) explains how oral devices are used to strengthen memory:

> Oral tradition is a memory of memories in the most literal way, since the message is learned from what another person recalled and told. Given its dependence on recitation, it is reassuring to know that all memorization has a verbal dimension to it. In fact many mnemotechnical devices, such as rhyme, verse, assonance, etc., make use of the phonemic characteristics of a language to ensure a more faithful rendering.

This seems to be especially important in oral cultures where all experiences are shared and performed within communities, and voiced in an oral, visual and communal way. Remembrance then, takes place much more easily through performance, where multiple faculties such as seeing, smelling, touching and gesture are employed, than the mere remembrance through imagination, which a written text evokes in the mind of the reader. Oral art then, tends 'to make the songs and poems from the past serve the goals of the present for the sake of the future. It is only when tradition is dying that it begins to lose contact with the present and becomes a preserver of its own past rather than a continuator' (Kgobe 1989: 11).

The 'performing' of experiences as part of daily life enforces in oral cultures the memory of people, and denounces the claim that oral historical memory is a less faithful source for historic research. Oral memory (performance) should in my view be reincorporated in the living memory of the modern world, and should not be just part of remote and long-ago peoples. Aristotle addressed the issue about truth and accuracy as early as the fourth century B.C.:

> The real difference (between history and poetry) is this, that one tells what hap-
> pened and the other what might happen. For this reason poetry is something more
> philosophical and serious than history, because poetry tends to give general truths
> while history gives particular facts.[8]

The first two poems from which I wish to quote had their origins in a war fought by the Hananwa, a Northern Sotho-speaking community living at Blouberg in the present-day Limpopo Province of South Africa, against the forces of the Zuid-Afrikaansche Republiek (ZAR) in 1894. What prompted me to look into the Hananwa's oral memory was the total dominance (in written documents) of a white perspective over the past hundred years on the Hananwa leader Ratšhatšha, and the events of 1894 (Kriel 2004: 790). Although there are different and shorter performance versions of the praise poems to be discussed, they all refer to two main issues, namely the bravery and integrity of Kgalushi Leboho (alias Ratšhatšha), the then chief of the Hananwa, and their betrayal by the chief's half-brother, Kibi. What is most interesting, however, is how the memory of this war has been kept alive by a rural community and is even evoked today to serve changing needs of successive generations in the present contexts of performance events.

The first poem is in honour of Chief Ratšhatšha, who reigned over the Hananwa during the time of the 1894 war. As a result of their leading role in the then Transvaal Republic, the Hananwa people were perceived to be a threat by the government of the newly established Zuid-Afrikaansche Republiek (ZAR). Mainly because of this perception, but also for various other reasons, such as the non-payment of taxes and the Hananwa's refusal to move to a new 'location', the ZAR government declared war on the Hananwa and their chief in 1894. After a two-month siege of his capital by the ZAR forces, the chief and his followers were forced by starvation and shortage of water to leave their mountain refuge and surrender to the ZAR troops.

For almost all colonized societies, the confrontation with colonial forces was an apocalypse. Many societies experienced 'deepened demographic disaster, as well as crises of leaderships' as a result (Hofmeyr 1989: 132–33). These were times of social change and adaptation, conditions that are often characterized by a yearning for the past. By continual performance of a historical incident, the poet is able to establish continuity with a heroic past. Recalling these traditions results in a feeling of security, in that images of continuity with the past are established. The following interpretation of excerpts of the war praise poem demonstrates the value of orality as a resource for reexamining experiences of resistance that lie at the core of South African historiography.[9] The living his-torical consciousness of the Hananwa presents us forcefully with a retrospective and inner account of a tragedy in the history of nineteenth-century Transvaal. The functionality of oral tradition and the practice of memory give us the op-portunity to 'hear' and 'see' the 'other side' of frontier history (Opland 1983: 51), an opportunity that could never have been possible had we relied only on the 'white side', as expressed through the limitations of written documentation and printed records.

Ratšhatšha's praise poem[10]

1. Leboho, you are hesitant
2. In the event of there being a battle, you would rather stay behind exposing others to the arrows
3. The spears that wipe out people
4. Tšhatšhaa the people with a rifle, Ranketane
5. Me, with a rifle, I wipe out people
6. Morwa Ngako saw the cannons firing at Moilatha
7. The cannon which wrecked the branches of trees
8. Only the bare branches of the water pear trees remained
9. Iiiuu! The water threatened to overwhelm Nketane
10. Then I, Masilo, took off my clothes

This war praise poem contains seventy-eight transcribed lines in total, of which I have selected certain sections for our discussion. The first quoted lines, from verse 3 of the poem, refer to the 1894 war and Ratšhatšha, the chief at the time. Leboho (alias Ratšhatšha) was neither bloodthirsty, nor war-hungry. In line 1 his people blame him for his reluctance to react to the approaching enemy, the ZAR forces. In lines 2 and 3 the people accuse Leboho, saying that in the event of war, he would rather not become actively involved and would thereby expose his people to the spears, the destructive weapons of the enemy, i.e. the auxiliary troops that fought on the side of the ZAR forces. *Tšhatšhaa* in line 4 is an idiophone imitating the sound of firing rifles, and adds to the descriptive quality of the line. It is also from this idiophone that Kgalushi's praise name, Ratšhatšha, derives.[11] He is also addressed as Ranketane (4), since one of his daughters was named Nketane.[12] From line 4, the poet rapidly takes the listener into the war, boasting of Ratšhatšha's excellence as a marksman (5), reporting on the firing cannons of the enemy (6, 7 and 8) and proclaiming his heroism when his daughter Nketane is endangered (9 and 10). Morwa' Ngako (6) was the wife of Jacob Mokgobu, one of the great Hananwa war heroes. She saw the cannons firing at Moilatha, the oldest tribal capital on the Blouberg mountain summit. Moilatha is situated east of Mount Serawe, towards Mothakeng, and is sacred to the Hananwa.[13] The onslaught of the ZAR artillery was so severe that the water pear trees (*Syzygium guineense*), which grow abundantly on the mountain, were stripped of their foliage (7 and 8).[14] Water, used metaphorically in line 9, symbolizes the attacking enemy. According to one interlocutor it seemed to the besieged people that 'millions' of Boer soldiers were ascending the mountain and gradually submerging it, like waves of water.[15] At this stage, Ratšhatšha (alias Masilo) decided to fight: he figuratively took off his clothes to come to the rescue of his beloved daughter, Nketane, who was being submerged by the water. Lines 4 to 10 illuminate the collective oral memory of the Hananwa: the suffering of their ancestors, and how Ratšhatšha, their leader, courageously defended them against Boer aggression.

The following selected lines from verse 6 comment further on the danger and casualties of the war and on Ratšhatšha's bravery:

11. Lord, have mercy on the people, the capital village is on fire
12. I Masilo, when I shoot I shoot selectively
13. I, Kgalushi, the one who escapes the bullets
14. Nobody dares to go over there at Senwe
15. The heads of people lie like stone walls
16. The heads of Blacks and of Whites

In line 11 the Hananwa people plead for mercy. They were betrayed by Kibi (half-brother of Kgalushi), who advised the ZAR soldiers and their allies to set fire to certain cattle kraals in the capital. Kibi knew that the Hananwa had dug grain pits in these kraals to hide the only food they had left. The dry cattle dung burned rapidly and caused such intense heat that the food supplies of the besieged were completely destroyed.[16] This is the fire in the capital that is referred to in line 11. The Hananwa maintain that Ratšhatšha (alias Masilo in line 12) was a very competent marksman, and that he selected only officers as his targets. In this line he boasts of his excellent marksmanship and the way in which he manages to escape the enemy bullets by sidestepping them.

The Senwe Valley referred to in line 14 is an important proxemic marker. This valley is situated on the southwestern slope of Mount Blouberg, east of the Leipzig mission station.[17] It was from this side that the Waterberg and Rustenburg Commandos ascended the mountain.[18] Lines 15 and 16 relate the severity of the battle that was fought there. Everybody was frightened to enter the valley because it was littered with the heads of the dead. These were so numerous that they gave the impression of stacked stone walls. The losses on both sides were huge and equally gruesome for the Hananwa and the ZAR forces. The unprejudiced manner in which the outcome of the battle in the Senwe Valley is reported suggests that no one was actually the winner in this senseless conflict. The harrowing experiences in the lives of the Hananwa people reveal *how, when,* and *why* people's memories are created.

The last quotation from this praise poem relates to verse 8, and comments directly on the perpetrators, the Boer forces and their leader president Paul Kruger:

17. They arrived without cripples, the Boers
18. Deformity was inflicted upon them by the Hananwa
19. We are from Manakatšhwe of Rasebudi of Kololo
20. What did you have in mind Paul, you instigator, when you sent children into the dangers of booming cannons

They came with no cripples in their midst (17), but then suffered wounds, in other words, physical deformity was inflicted upon them by the Hananwa (18).[19] The syntactic foregrounding of the noun Boers in line 17 to the end of the sentence emphasizes the identity of the enemy. During combat Ratšhatšha is constantly supported and strengthened by his proud heritage, being one who descends from Manakatšhwe of Rasebudi sa Kololo (19). In line 20, he addresses Paul Kruger, president of the ZAR, asking him what he had in mind when he sent young children into the danger of thundering cannons.

Ratšhatšha's war praise poem gives a comprehensive account of the 1894 siege of Blouberg. The recital of this praise poem during contemporary political and social gatherings links the present with the past through memory. The interaction with colonial powers is reflected in the praise poem and forms the backdrop and context, thereby confirming Harries's observation (1989: 82) that 'people choose, adopt and emphasize cultural symbols that they believe to be signs of a shared historical identity in order to benefit their class or regional interests.'

The poem also demonstrates the historic competence of the oral poet. The diachronic course of the events of the war as narrated in the poem is logical and tallies not only with other orally transmitted versions, but also with written documents. By assimilating all the cross-references among the proxemic markers, the listener is able to reconstruct a visual picture of the events of 1894 as experienced and remembered by the victims, the Hananwa. The mentioning of specific localities points, according to Gunner (2003: 136), 'to the importance of place names as part of the wider memory bank used by individuals to map themselves into place and time.' This is of course true for the Hananwa people as well, since the contemporary use of historical praise poems helps them (insiders) and us (outsiders) to gain a better understanding of the Hananwa's inner dynamics as a group, and their sense of identity in an ever changing South African context.

The next poem stands in direct contrast to the previous praise poem, which is chanted in honour of chief Ratšhatšha's bravery.[20] This poem can be regarded as 'negative praise' to brand Kibi (a half-brother of Chief Ratšhatšha) as a traitor, murderer and coward. Because of the content of the poem and the sensitivity surrounding the events of the 1894 war, the performer asked that his/her identity not be revealed, a request to which I acquiesce. I decided to include this poem, since it discloses a side of the 1894 war that has, until now, not been revealed in any historical documentation, but only lives in the memory of the Hananwa people themselves.

Praise poem for Kibi[21]
1. Kibi, scandalous person (despicable wizard)!
2. The disgrace of Mamoloko
3. The disgrace (guilt) for killing a beast is bearable but the death of a human turns on oneself
4. Kibi has four testicles
5. Two are pulling an ox wagon
6. Two are fanning the fire

The Hananwa's hatred for Kibi becomes abundantly clear as the poet addresses Kibi in the first line by calling him a despicable wizard or in Hananwa a *mamototwane* (a corpse that was brought to life by a wizard whose tongue has been removed and who assists the witches in carrying out evil and despicable deeds at night). Kibi is further referred to as 'the disgrace of Mamoloko' (2), because of the grave pain he inflicted on his father Matsiokwane, who was also known as Mamoloko. The idiomatic expression in line 3 becomes an important sign, since it is directed at Kibi, and points to his despicable deed of betraying his brother and thereby causing the deaths of his father and his own people. The expression literally means that the guilt one feels for killing an animal (beast) is bearable, but the punishment of having killed a human being cannot be escaped, and turns on oneself. His testicles are used metaphorically to expose his character in a derogatory way, as a traitor in line 5 and an instigator in line 6. Line 5 refers to Kibi's alliance (yoke) with the Boer forces, who used ox wagons in the battle against the Bahananwa, and line 6 refers to his role as instigator of the fire (conflict) between the Boer forces and the section of Bahananwa under his brother, chief Kgalushi (Ratšhatšha).

The war of 1894 against the Hananwa was only one of a number fought by the government of the ZAR against various communities in the former Transvaal. It can be argued that the ZAR used these confrontations to claim its authority over a newly conquered territory. In order to break the resistance of the people, men, women and children were indentured, in accordance with the ZAR Government Resolution, Article 1580 of 4 September 1894, as labourers on Boer farms all over the Transvaal. They had to work on these farms for a period of up to five years, earning only their keep (Van Schalkwyk 1995: 99–100). Marginalized people like the Hananwa, with a lack of commemorative acknowledgement, tend to shift their focus of memory to the private worlds of their own communities where private symbols, such as praise poems, ritual or 'sites of memory' take centre stage. The conscious memory of the Hananwa, as performed through their oral art, indeed tells the untold 'other' story, as Kriel (2004: 789) so convincingly explains:

> The memories of the Hananwa, the subordinates, were not presented on their own terms in written form until the last quarter of the twentieth century. It was thus via written accounts that the prevailing white hegemony was concealing the oppositional historical consciousness of the subjugated, a consciousness which indeed contradicted that seemingly hegemonic view.

The preceding discussion convincingly illustrates how oral memory can be reappropriated to shed light on remote pasts and how performance poetry can assist not only historians but all South Africans in developing a better understanding of the post-apartheid reality.

The third poem from which I have selected parts is a praise poem in honour of Modjadji, the queen of the Lobedu who form part of the northern branch of Bantu-speaking peoples of southern Africa. The Lobedu royal nucleus descends from one of the Rozwi states that gained prominence in the southern part of the former Karanga empire (Davison 1979: 211). They have been ruled for the last six generations by a female ruler, all bearing the dynastic title 'Modjadji', the legendary 'Rain Queen' (Balic 1990; Hilton-Barber 1996). Modjadji I, literally translated as 'the ruler of the day', ascended the throne in 1800. Her land was known as Bolobedu, the 'land of offering'. She became renowned as a rainmaker and was surrounded by an aura of mystery and awe because of her magical powers (see Kruger 1936: 101). She remained isolated, and it was this secrecy that brought her the greatest fame and reverence, fostering the idea that she was immortal.[22] Modjadji V (Mokope) (1980–2001) was inaugurated in October 1982. She died in June 2001, some days after the death of her daughter. Modjadji V (Mokope) was succeeded by her granddaughter Mmakobo (Modjadji VI). Mmakobo ruled for a short period until her untimely death in September 2005. She was the first Lobedu queen who had received formal education.

Royal praises are still recited in honour of the Lobedu queen. These poems are often compositions that contain the image of the queen, narrate her victories in battle, laud the Lobedu's ancestry and proclaim the queen's acquired fame. The mystery of immortality that surrounded Queen Modjadji I remained with all her successors and carries past memories into contemporary royal praises – linking past and present through the royal line of succession.

Praise poem for Queen Modjadji[23]
   1. You, Phaswa of Manaila

Line 1 represents the introduction or opening formula and consists of a royal praise, addressed directly to Queen Modjadji. By addressing her in this way the performer creates the necessary interaction between herself and the addressee, i.e. the queen. The presence of the queen is essential, since these poems are directed mainly at the queen and recited in her honour. The use of the archaic and lofty language in line 1 is difficult to translate or interpret. It does, however, indicate that oral art (praise poetry) is no static concept, but a dynamic and creative art in the 'mouth' of the poet. The oral poet can therefore make, in the words of Canonici (1996: 224),

> use of a wide collection of ideas (those stored in the shared memories of his culture which he **must know**), of expressions (often characterized by formulaic language to make remembering and reproducing easier: **knowledge of creative skills**), of themes and motifs that are commonly known and need no explanation (because they form part of this collective memory), in order to produce something that is both original and traditional, personal and common (**artistic ability of performer**).

An artist can therefore make use of carefully chosen words, imagery and gesture to create beauty and passion, to impress his/her audience, or to make a poem more easily remembered. Krige and Krige (1943: 28) are of the opinion that 'almost every Lovedu name has its praise, whoever might bear it.' The royal praises describe and praise the lives and deeds of important persons such as Mohale, who is regarded as the founder of the Lobedu during the cycle of kings, (the Lobedus are often referred to as the pigs of Mohale); Mogodu, also written as Mogudo (1750–1800), who is praised as 'Mogudo of Pheduli, Transformer of the Clouds, he kills as he lists and spares whom he likes'; and Queen Modjadji II (1845–1894), known as Masala-Navo, whose praise name means 'she who remains with them' (Kruger 1936: 103). Lines 2 to 6 deal with the military achievements of the Lobedu:

> 2. The time of your return after you had struck at Tzaneen
> 3. We slaughter a beast when we reach Modzinone
> 4. At Džadžalale the young men slaughter theirs
> 5. At the hillock where Nagana melted iron
> 6. Where the Euphorbia trees grow in abundance

Line 2 refers to the queen as initiator of the attack and serves as a reminder to potential enemies to fear her. As the military forces return from battle, the matured soldiers[24] celebrate their military achievement by slaughtering a beast at Modzinone (3). Modzinone, one of the Lobedu districts lying to the southwest of the tribal capital on the banks of the Mulodozi River, is referred to by Krige and Krige 1943: 176, 180) as Mudzinoni. At the same time, the young soldiers (4) celebrate victory by slaughtering their beast at a place called Džadžalale.[25] The poet gives an indication in lines 5 and 6 of the locality of Džadžalale: it is in close proximity to the hillock Šodone, where Nagana melted iron (5) and where the Euphorbia trees grow in abundance (6). According to the district map of Krige and Krige (1943: 176) Šodone also lies on the bank of the Mulodozi River, four districts to the north of Modzinone, which can, according to the scale indicated on Krige's map, be estimated at a distance of seven miles. The listener can reconstruct a geographical picture of the position of the returning soldiers by assimilating the cross-references between these two proxemic markers. Lines 7 to 9 deal with the physical location of the Lobedu ancestry:

> 7. You who go to Maolwe keep in mind that it is the place of the ancestors
> 8. Maolwe which is adjacent to Sekhuthini the walking stick of the sour plum, the blackish one of Dadža
> 9. Right there at Maolwe is the place where offerings are made at the shrines

These lines honour the Lobedu ancestry by celebrating the continuous chain of life, from the founding of the nation at Vokhalaga[26] to the present Maolwe (7),[27] where offerings are still taken today to the holy shrines of their ancestors (9). Line 8 reveals two other proxemic markers, which are of utmost importance in the Lobedu's line of ancestry. Sekhuthini (8) is a place adjacent to Maolwe that could, according to the map of Krige and Krige (1943: 176), be identified as a district southeast of the tribal capital. Sekhuthini was, according to Mathekga (1939), the place where Modjadji I lived after she moved from

Khethagone (Sehlakong). The other reference (Dadža) is metaphorically called the 'blackish walking stick of the sour plum', because the sour plum grows, according to my interlocutors, only in the Dadža Forest. A person using a black walking stick must therefore be of Lobedu origin, since the place is regarded as holy, cannot be entered by anyone, and should not be pointed at.[28] Dadža is mentioned in various sources as the place where the Lobedu found sanctuary after they fled across the Limpopo River. It lies, according to the district map of Krige and Krige (1943: 176), to the northwest of the tribal capital.[29] The poet expresses the most delicate nuances of meaning in this unit to metaphorically equate Vokhalaga, Dadža, Maolwe and Sekhuthini as being the same place, the place of the Lobedu royal ancestors. The poet returns in line 9 to Maolwe, the burial place of the Lobedu royals, the place where offerings are still made at the holy shrines. Krige and Krige (1943: 236) witnessed a *thogola* ceremony in August 1938 and give the following description:

> they sat round the shrine, the queen and sons and daughters near by, wives further away, while the small children were made to kneel on the lower side of the shrine, hands together and palms up. Pouring out beer on the mound, the queen said a prayer similar to the previous one, adding that the gods must tell one another and not leave any one out. Then, drinking a little herself, she placed the calabash on the ground for the next person to take up and drink. Each one in turn placed the gourd on the ground for the next to take up, till all the relatives had drunk, when it was returned to the queen. She drank once more, saying, 'He who gives to the gods must not remain hungry,' and laid the calabash upside down on the mound. The small children lapped up the beer from the ground, and trilling and hulosha marked the end of the ceremony.

These events, coupled with praises, clearly denote a religious intention in the lives of the Lobedu as they are used as a medium of communication between the living and the dead – the present and the past – to obtain the blessings of the ancestors who still hold a position of status in the lineage.

In the last quoted lines from this praise poem, the performer concludes the poem with an extensive royal praise in honour of Queen Modjadji:

10. Royal praise: Keeper of all districts of the people
11. Royal praise
12. Gole, the time of your return after you had struck at Tzaneen
13. We slaughter a beast when we reach Modzinone
14. At Džadžalale the young men slaughter theirs
15. Gole! Gole! The carnivorous beast of Mohale
16. If we want to execute (kill) we execute (kill)
17. If we want to leave alone, we leave alone

In line 10 the chief/queen is praised as the 'Keeper of all districts of the people', which can metaphorically be interpreted as the 'keeper of unity' within the Lobedu community.[30] Line 11 is an archaic royal praise in honour of Queen Modjadji, the meaning of which could not be explained by the interlocutors.[31] The use of this form of archaic language during a contemporary performance underlines the continuation that the Lobedu people wish to keep with their past. Lines 12 to 14 are a repetition of lines 2 to 4, praising the queen's military achievement. The last three lines (15–17) are fixed royal praises dating from the time of Chief Mohale (1633–1678), who is acknowledged as the founder of the Lobedu during the cycle of kings (Krige 1975: 57, 1985: 1–45). His reign will be remembered for the subjugation of the Khioga people (an aboriginal group), whom the Lobedu met in the Dadža Forest (Kruger 1936: 321–356; Krige 1937: 321–356; Mathekga 1939: 179). The queen is personified and equated with the carnivorous beast of Mohale (15): the fearsome one who executes if she wants (16) and spares as she likes (17). From this example it is clear that the praises of important people remain a testimony to commemorate them, or as Canonici (1996: 236) remarks: 'a praise, or an apostrophe, is often formulated in relationship to someone else, especially important members of the family. In an oral society a person is as good as he is perceived by others, and as important as his family, including his ancestors.'

Queen Modjadji is praised in this poem as a descendant of Mohale, member of the royal family, and founder of the Lobedu people. She has therefore the responsibility of representing the whole line of succession in person and deeds. This poem forms (according to interlocutors) part of the collective memory of the Lobedu people. It is the glorious property of the Lobedu people, and appeals to the group's past and present traditions. It captures generations of Lobedu history in dating back to the origin of the Lobedu people and their wanderings over a long period of time, reflecting on their genealogy, identity, religious beliefs and glorious chiefs and queens. The poem is therefore still recited at any important public occasion, not only in honour of the queen but also as a tribal salutation, adulation or laudatory praise in honour of the Lobedu people as a group (see Joubert 2004: 440–449).

Hananwa and Lobedu cultural geography and identity have to be interpreted in terms of past struggles for place, space and meaning, as well as current issues such as language, religion, education and all the cultural transformation processes that still continue in a postcolonial and post-apartheid era. The quoted examples clearly show that praise poetry can certainly provide 'a means of visioning both the past and the present, and of making memory part of present, contingent reality' (Gunner 1999: 53).

Relevance of Praise Poetry in Contemporary 'History Making'

The examples of praise poems discussed here represent an old art form with its roots deep in the social and political awareness of the people. The important role oral tradition plays in the reconstruction of the historical and cultural existence of nonliterate societies cannot be ignored. Praise poetry has the ability to capture the present through the past, 'and its appetite for events, is very well suited to commenting upon and memorializing the individual and the historical moment' (Gunner 2003: 140).

Largely marginalized, the Lobedu and especially the Hananwa had very little opportunity to take part in the making of their own history. Until recently, texts produced by the people of these two communities have been ignored (see Hofmeyr 1989 and Hamilton 1993). As discussed by Vail and White (1983), it has seldom been possible to establish the contribution of African perceptions in the unfolding of events that shaped their history. What is therefore needed is an 'insider' account of history where people experience and interpret it from a culturally reflexive point of view (Coplan 1987). The poems fulfill precisely the needs mentioned by Coplan, as they act as historical commentators with constant reference to important historical events. For example, Ratšhatšha's war praise poem gives a comprehensive account, from the Hananwa's perspective, of the 1894 siege of Blouberg. Also, the 'negative praise' of Kibi explains the long-standing rift between two sections of the Hananwa, while the praise poem in honour of Queen Modjadji sheds some light on the Lobedu's early migration from Zimbabwe, the genealogy of chiefs and queens, and the history of the group. The poems narrate the same historical information documented previously, but from the point of view of 'insiders', the people themselves. By superimposing these archaic forms of communication on current situations, members of the community are given an opportunity to actively take part in the creative process of 'history making' and the formation of an own identity.

However, it did become clear during our discussion of these poems that successful communication and understanding depends on a common memory shared by the performer and audience (the people). In other words, there must be some shared information that connects the present with the past. To achieve this, one needs to pursue an interdisciplinary and interactional transcription of all elements operative in the communicative process of oral art. It is a process that provides symbolic statements about common experiences and reflects popular consciousness, or as Vail and White (1983: 887) put it, provides us with history 'from below'. The historical use of these praise poems helps us to gain a better understanding of the Hananwa and Lobedu people's memories and visions and, as explained by Levine,[32] 'to better understand the inner dynamics of a group and the attitudes of its members, and to comprehend their sense of worth.'

Praise poetry is therefore a creative act of memory that comprises a complex and comprehensive communicative process of rhythm, music, gesture and drama, and goes beyond the mere words of the verbal utterance. Praise poems do not die with an individual, but remain, in the words of Dlomo as quoted by Canonici (1996: 226), 'an ornament to your life, a reminder and treasure, an inspiration and a glory to your family, friends and clan.' That is why the interlocutors told me that praise poetry expresses 'the soul and dignity of our people', not only then, but also now.

History through Oral Memory: A New Point of Convergence

Since the transition to an inclusive democracy in South Africa, numerous attempts have been made to improve our knowledge of the past by empowering
nonliterate and semiliterate communities. A 'voice' has been given to 'ordinary
people' in contrast to previous attempts to write history 'from above.' The purpose of oral history is now to answer questions, gain insights, uncover or, as
formulated by Denis (2003: 208), 'to bring to light as reliably as possible a frag-
ment of the past transmitted by word of mouth.'

Now, in the first phase of a post-apartheid South Africa, the focus of oral
memory as history has changed from resistance and oppression to reconciliation, reconstruction and transformation. In recent years, significant initiatives
have been launched nationally and internationally, aimed at the reworking of
memory in service of remembrance, reconciliation and history production.[33]
Some of the prominent discourses in oral memory have been the Truth and
Reconciliation Commission (TRC), set up in South Africa in 1996 to deal with
the memories of victims and perpetrators of the apartheid era; the 100-year
anniversary of the Maji Maji war against colonial rule in German East Africa,
1905–1907; and the sixtieth commemoration of the end of World War II. Of
special interest for this discussion is the commemoration of the liberation of the
Nazi death camp Auschwitz in Poland on 27 January 2005.

The act of historical remembrance has a special dimension in Africa, since
it forms part of Africa's natural oral storytelling (performance) tradition, which
involves three basic human actions: the act of remembering, the act of speaking and the act of listening (Denis 2003: 211). All three actions are imbedded
in a specific social and cultural context within which the articulated messages
(memories) are to be understood. In terms of this long-standing African tradition, the individual testimonies gathered by the TRC process function as much
more than a 'method of documenting a people's past, or as a product' (Denis
2003: 209). They should rather be understood as a form of oral narration – a
performance event – or as Hutchison (2004: 53) explains: 'theatre as counter-
memory has moved beyond traditional theatrical spaces to include the Truth
and Reconciliation Commission (TRC), a national forum where individual
stories intersected with South African history to offer new histories and communal memories.'

The 'arenas for discourse'[34] that were set up for the TRC in different towns
and locations created spaces in which some specialized forms of communication were uniquely licensed to take place. More than a mere exchange of
information, they became instead a human encounter. In these spaces deeply
divided individuals and groups were given a 'stage' to share memories that
had been repressed in the past. People used their own particular ways to narrate their remembered pasts, and most importantly to have their stories officially acknowledged. According to Du Toit (2004: 71) the mode of the TRC

was 'characterized by its focus on victim disclosure and acknowledgement of truths relating to human rights violation in a non-adversarial context of public reconciliation.'

The relatively non-violent transition from a totalitarian state to a multi-party democracy can be ascribed to the peaceful commitment amongst South Africans to coexist in spite of their differences. Teffo (1994: 5) agrees:

> there is no lust for vengeance, no apocalyptic retribution. … A yearning for jus-tice, yes, and for release from poverty and oppression, but no dream of themselves becoming the persecutors, of turning the tables of apartheid on white South Af-ricans. … The ethos of ubuntu … is one single gift that African philosophy can bequeath on the other philosophies of the world.

The open and participative performance mode of memory so typical of the TRC process drew heavily from the African concept of *Ubuntu,* which defines individuality in terms of its relationship with and to others. Western cultural norms and values are primarily based on the recognition of the uniqueness of the individual. African cultures, on the other hand, discourage the view that the individual should take precedence over the community and emphasize col-lectivity, communalism and consensus. The Northern Sotho proverb '*motho ke motho ka batho*' (a person is a person through other persons) articulates a phi-losophy and way of life that is embedded in humane compassion received from others. This unifying worldview of personhood is expressed almost identically in all nine South African Bantu languages. The cardinal belief underlying this figure of speech is that a person can only be a person through the goodwill or assistance of others. This goodwill is based on fundamental principles of com-passion, respect, human dignity, group solidarity, collective unity and reconcili-ation. For Desmond Tutu the term *Ubuntu* means

> the essence of being human. You know when it is there, and you know when it is absent. It speaks about humanness, gentleness, hospitality, putting yourself out on behalf of others. It means not nursing grudges, but willing to accept others as they are and being thankful for them. It excludes grasping competitiveness, harsh ag-gressiveness, being concerned for oneself, abrasiveness. (as quoted by Saule 1998: 11).

The essence of *Ubuntu* therefore lies in the 'wisdom' that our humanity is bound up inextricably with our fellow countrymen and women. When you dehumanize another human being you inexorably dehumanize yourself. This realization prepared the ground for forgiveness in many of the TRC cases and in this way contributed to the process of changing negative memories into more bearable and positive ones for the future.

The year 2005 marked the centenary commemoration of the start of the Maji Maji rebellion (1905–1907), a pivotal event in the history of early colonial Tanzania. Hundreds of thousands of people died or were displaced, changing the historical landscape of southern Tanzania beyond recognition.[35] Maji Maji (named after a water medicine [*maji*] that supposedly made resistance fighters invulnerable to the bullets of German colonizers) was the first manifestation of a united interethnic opposition to colonial rule in Africa, and more specifically to a policy of forced labour by the German administration in what was then German East Africa. The Maji ideology as articulated by Kinjikitile Ngwale drew on shared beliefs and resulted in an impressive unity across diverse cultural and linguistic groupings in southern Tanzania. Kinjikitile's traditional medicine (*maji*) became a 'national' medicine that promised 'national' victory over the German oppressors (see Gwassa 1972). Maji ideology, which played a central role in the revolutionary resistance against German colonial rule, clearly had a deeply rooted 'insider' or cultural basis. Written records (especially from a German perspective) are particularly deficient with regard to these aspects. It is therefore not surprising that many historians and other researchers interested in the Maji Maji war rely heavily on oral narration, eyewitness accounts or other oral genres such as poetry[36] or theatre. In the preface of their study on the Maji Maji uprising, Gwassa and Iliffe (1967: 1) write:

> We have deliberately chosen the documents from as wide a range of sources as possible, in order to show the variety of evidence available. About half the documents are **oral accounts** recorded by Mr. Gwassa during 1966–67, mostly in Matumbi. The remainder are official documents, letters, mission chronicles, **oral information** collected by other students, and various personal observations [author's emphasis].

Another important publication, *Kala Shairi German East Africa in Swahili Poems,* which appeared in 2002, covers the work of a joint German-Tanzanian effort. The editors tried to collect all the scattered historiographic poems from the period of German colonial rule in Eastern Africa between 1884 and the beginning of World War I in one volume. The collection includes praise songs as well as narrative poems that outline the struggle for power in former German East Africa. Many of these poems were only available in German publications. The importance of 'oral human encounter' becomes evident, since the researchers had to collect and digitize the material during field research in order to prepare the English translations (see Miehe et al. 2002).

A group of German students recently started the Maji Maji Bibliography Project[37] with the basic aim of encouraging historical research on the Maji Maji rebellion by providing ready access to a particular type of historical resource. Interestingly, the main criterion for the inclusion of a source on the web page was whether the author was a direct observer of the events of 1905–1907. The underlying notion of 'being an eyewitness' reconfirms the important role of memory and of choice, namely *what* will be remembered by *whom,* as discussed earlier in this contribution.

The 2005 symposium *Lieux de Memoire and the Maji Maji War,* held at the Wissenschaftskolleg in Berlin, was a commemorative event in itself. Professor James Giblin's opening lecture, 'The Maji Maji War 1905–1907: Colonial Conflict, National History and Local Memory', underlined the importance of local memory in this long and often forgotten war. Giblin's collaborative research on the oral history of the Maji Maji war has revealed the ways in which local Tanzanians remember the past through their own memorial practices, which are connected to landscapes and 'sites of memory'. These local sites encourage ordinary people to recover and collate their memories in an active way. The performance of memory provides discursive arenas not only for 'new history' outside of the formalized historic narratives, but also for the creation of identity and nation building in Tanzania.[38]

The reappropriation of oral narration, eyewitness accounts and oral genres such as poetry, theatre and memorial practices confirms the power of orality in the creation of history and the remembrance of the past. In contrast, the deficiencies of traditional historical accounts of the Maji-Maji war, reliant exclusively on written sources, are clear. The importance of orality and its multi-channelled modes of communication for historiography can therefore hardly be underestimated.

A final example: on 27 January 2005, world leaders gathered in Poland to remember the arrival of Soviet troops in 1945 and the liberation of the Nazi death camp in Auschwitz. I interrupted my writing to watch a special broadcast by the BBC from Auschwitz and returned to my desk touched by images and sounds, but most of all by narrated memories of survivors who were, and still are, shattered by the evil of inhumanity.[39] The commemoration of Auschwitz transcended the ordinary course of discourse and events in many ways. The interacting variables (physical setting, psychological ambience, participants, special genres of storytelling, chanting and singing, and interactional patterns of participants) provided the ground rules that governed this very significant and touching commemoration. Auschwitz itself was chosen to form the physical setting (performance arena) for the commemorations. The site is unique in more than one sense: it was the largest camp established by the Germans during World War II, and it had a double role, functioning as both extermination camp and labour camp. The way in which genocide was scientifically designed and engineered there adds to its prominence. Moreover, it was the only camp that had substantial numbers of survivors from different countries at the end of the war, who could tell the stories of what really happened there. The camp also remained physically intact, bearing witness to the brutality that characterized the detention of millions of people.

By using the real physical location, the commemoration became frightfully real and charged with associative values, not only to the commemorative event that was taking place at that moment, but also, and in particular, to the events that took place sixty years before. History was re-performed in contextualized words, scenes, noises, smells and action, relating it directly to today's examples of intolerance and crimes against humanity. A special psychological mood was created: the opening of the ceremony was signalled by a train whistle at the Auschwitz-Birkenau site, where a railway track brought hundreds of thousands to their deaths. Against the backdrop of towering watchtowers, flames lit up the darkening sky, sending a cloud of smoke over the camp. These visual and olfactory signs added to a chilling atmosphere, designed to be redolent of the smoke that hung in the camp at the height of the genocide as the bodies of victims burned in the crematoriums.

The central players (performers) of the event were the former inmates who narrated their memories of Auschwitz. These oral renditions were charged with deep emotions, creating a revised history 'for modernity', emerging from the actual lived experiences of survivors. The Polish survivor started his recollection of events by calling out his Jewish prison number, 4427. He ended his account with the following words: 'Our reflection must transform itself into responsibility, into lasting memory of what happened.' The French survivor's opening words – 'With my heart full of emotion …' – sum up her inner feelings. She urged mankind to join in a new undertaking, to unite and to fight against hatred and intolerance. The Roma survivor explained what a large mark the genocide has left on the collective memory of the Roma minority. He personified Auschwitz as being not only a place of remembrance, but also a place of warning – the conscience of the community of democratic states.

Six inmates and three Soviet ex-soldiers followed these testimonies by lighting the first candles at the main memorial. They were followed by world figures like Israeli President Moshe Katsav, Russian President Vladimir Putin, Polish President Alexander Kwasniewski, French President Jacques Chirac, and US Vice President Dick Cheney. The attendance of these leaders enforced the importance of the event. Different ecumenical prayers were said. The unique way in which the Jewish rabbi chanted the Jewish prayer for the dead – the *Kaddish* – made it not only a moving experience, but also a culturally specific one. Within this global gathering of mourning and remembrance, one group remains central: the Jews, the primary victims. The ceremony was brought to an end by the playing of a Jewish horn – the *shofar* – linking them to their ancient biblical past. Fire and sound were again used as unique closing signs as the rail tracks were lined with flames and the train's last whistle signalled the evil that men are capable of.

The act of historical remembering, as expressed during the TRC hearings, by Tanzanians through their own memorial practices or in the Auschwitz commemoration, mandate worlds of signification that are much larger and more complex than the isolated events. It is rather the degree of the different stories' dependency on a world outside of the conduct itself, and the ensuing interaction between stories and communities present and past, that define the stories and allow 'incomplete' stories to be 'completed' by the meaning found in the forces surrounding them (see Foley 1995: 5).

The point I wish to make is that the victims and perpetrators, as well as the listeners and viewers, had to draw on extra-memorizing contexts in the interpretation and understanding of the vast web of oral intercommunication that took place within those oral performance events. My plea is that tradition, memory and orality should not cease to continue to be arenas negotiating society's relationship between past and present. Modernity has the responsibility not only to stage current history, but also to revive the spirit of oral memory in making silent, ageless voices speak again.

Like praise poetry, oral testimony can become a vehicle for 'voicing' the histories of nations and the stories of ordinary people. The overlooked and forgotten 'oral pasts', performed and watched, can be interpreted as counter-memory to the vast number of 'official written records' from a segregated past under apartheid, and can create an alternative form of historical documentation (see Minkley and Rassool 1998: 90). The momentous public process (performance event) between interviewer(s) and interviewee(s) before an audience became, in the case of the TRC, even more important than the five-volume *Interim Report* published in 1998 and the *Final Report* that was submitted in March 2003, owing to the humanness brought about by face-to-face encounters between victims and perpetrators, and the fact that the hearings legitimized the voices of victims and, by doing so, 'irreversibly transformed the country's understanding of its own history' (Denis 2003: 209). Most importantly, the TRC contributed in defining South Africa as a democratic nation by opening up its archive to 'add new content, to reinterpret the old, and to making it globally accessible in a post-nation global environment through the worldwide web, and publication of its multi-volume report' (Muller 2002: 426).

Memory, remembering and forgetting (willful amnesia) in social contexts, have become crucial themes in history since World War II (see Tatum 1995: 152). The oral testimonies of Auschwitz survivors, surrounded by an atmosphere of death and horror in the physical location of the concentration camp, forcefully translated a tragic past into the presence of humankind. The commemoration did not necessarily contribute to 'hard core historical facts' – rather, it drove home the point of 'remember-not-to-forget'. It became not only a remembrance of the past, but also the collective memory of consciousness for modernity.

These postmodern ways of multi-channelled history – of telling, seeing, hearing, smelling and experiencing history – have become not only alternative forms to single-channelled historical documentation, but also powerful ways in which memory is used to uncover the past for the purpose of political reconciliation, and for future perspectives of human action. Oral memory provides an arena for the processes of reordering and reinterpretation to take place. It enables the reconciliation of different experiences and memories, and it facilitates a process of reestablishing identity amongst peoples torn apart by memories of violence and war (see Reynolds 1990). The remembrance of inhumanity, however, has no significance if it cannot be related to the present. Memory carries a 'lesson': that 'modernity' has a responsibility to live in respect for the dignity of humankind and actively counteract the phenomena of hatred, contempt, xenophobia, anti-Semitism and apartheid. Our remembrance must transform itself into responsibility – into lasting memory of what had happened (see Gobodo-Madikizela 2004: 102). This brings us to the essence of memory: the link between the past and the present that makes it existentially clear why slavery was banned, why colonialism collapsed, why apartheid could not be tolerated and why an Auschwitz should never happen again.

Conclusion

Factual accounts of memory seem not necessarily the ones that provide a connection between the present and the past. Memory is rather the idea of bringing the *past* back into the arena of the *present,* where stories become performative utterances – historicizing gestures – where people *live* the past and where trauma becomes *living* memory. The presence of the past, as chanted in traditional praise poetry or performance poetry, witnessed during the TRC hearings or acted out in memorial practices, connects us with our present situation. It tells us the stories of people's suffering, what they have experienced and how they will 'continue to experience in a society in which the promised changes are not yet a reality for them' (Gobodo-Madikizela 2004: 102). Thus, it is imperative that 'modernity' commits itself to fostering oral memory as a living archive – part of history and a creative extension of it. Harris (2000: 122) expresses this conclusively:

> An orality which is healthy is infinitely bigger than its material expression. We are all storytellers. Our stories sustain us, carry us, carry our values, our beliefs, our identities.

Memory draws on the past to inform the present, preserving elements of our present experience for future reference and forming a bridge across time to allow us to link our minds with the world (Schacter 2001: 206).

Notes

1. Vansina (1980: 262) refers to these stories as 'oral traditions'.
2. South African performance poets include Zolani Mkiva, Lesego Rampolokeng, Kgafela Oa Magogodi and the late Bongani Sitole.
3. Apart from Lesego Rampolokeng and Zolani Mkiva releasing compact discs of their poetry, they also have their own web sites, for example: http://www.music.org.za/artists/lesego.htm and http://www.music.org.za/artists/mkiva.htm. One can also find a variety of South African poetry produced in various languages on the site www.LitNet.mweb.co.za.
4. According to Kaschula (2004: 46), the term 'technauriture' encapsulates the emerging link between technology, literature and performance poetry.
5. http://www.kgafela.com.
6. See Tatum (1995: 152).
7. See Vansina (1980: 278 n. 34); Schacter (2001: 34).

8. Quoted by Small (1995: 164).

9. For the full version of this praise poem, see Joubert and Van Schalkwyk (1999: 29–47).

10. The war praise poem was recited at a political rally at Blouberg in 1989 by Agnes Leboho, on which occasion it was audio recorded by J. Van Schalkwyk, with the assistance of S. M. Moifatswane. I made a visual recording of the war praise poem as chanted by Raisibe Leboho on 11 February 1996 at Blouberg. Discussions with her, family members and local inhabitants contributed to more insight into their history and produced fascinating narration from the past.

11. Oral narration by Raisibe Lehobo, Blouberg Sesalong, 5 February 1996.

12. Oral narration by Raisibe Lehobo, Blouberg Sesalong, 5 February 1996.

13. The geographical site of the oldest Hananwa capital, Moilatha, on the mountain summit was identified by Thomas Leboho during field research.

14. Botanical identification of samples of these trees (pointed out to me by Simon, Hector and Jomo Leboho on the mountain summit, 4 October 1994), was done by botanist Fanie Venter, Pietersburg, 8 October 1994.

15. Oral narration by Hector Leboho (whose ancestors were participants in the 1894 war), Blouberg, 1 October 1994.

16. By June 1894 it was reported in the newspapers that as many as 600 houses had been burnt down (*De Volkstem,* 19 June 1894.) The grain was excavated from the granaries and used by the ZAR troops to feed their horses. Apart from this, numerous objects were also confiscated and no doubt looted. See Van Schalkwyk 1991: 27–30 and oral narration by Jomo and Matanzima Leboho, Blouberg summit, 5 October 1994.

17. Oral narration by Thomas and Jomo Leboho, Blouberg Mission Station, 12 February 1996.

18. Interview with Professor J. Bergh, Historical and Heritage Studies, Faculty of Humanities, University of Pretoria, February 1995. See Van Schalkwyk and Moifatswane 1991: 175–183.

19. The large number of casualties is attested to in an eyewitness account of the war. See C. Rae (1898).

20. See the same version of this poem in Joubert (2004: 423–425).

21. The praise poem was audio recorded on 30 September 1998 on the summit of the Blouberg mountain. The performer requested that no visual recording be made, and that his/her identity not be revealed.

22. See Joubert (2004: 232–245) for the royal genealogy of the Lobedu.

23. The poem was recited by Maphethola Ntšhaupa during a festive occasion held at the tribal capital of Queen Modjadji on 26 January 1996. For the full version of this poem and its Lobedu transcription, see Joubert (2004: 426–433).

24. Personal communication by Hans Booka and Makhoša Mathekga, Modjadji tribal capital, Bolobedu, 9 November 2001.

25. During my research in 1996 the name Džadžalale was explained as a river that lies between the tribal capital and Tzaneen.

26. The Lobedu royal group can be linked to the once mighty and powerful dynasties of the Rozwi states in Zimbabwe, also known as Vokhalaga (see Joubert: 2004: 224–231).

27. Maolwe refers to the sacred place where the Lobedu chiefs and queens are buried. It is situated southeast of the tribal capital. Interlocutors pointed this place out to me during a visit in November 2001. The elder brother of Modjadji I, Malegudu, had a daughter Magov who became a wife of Modjadji II. Modjadji III in her turn made Magovo the district head of Maolwe (see Krige and Krige 1943: 178).

28. I was warned by the elders (keepers of tradition) not to point at Dadža: 'You who point with your finger towards Dadža are breaking the law. Dadža is never pointed at, that is the place of the ancestors. It is the place of the ancestors of Modjadji of Mohale.' (January 1996).

29. I obtained permission to visit Dadža, and was taken by Mathekga to visit the Dadža Forest in January 1996. The Lobedu people moved, according to oral narration, first to Lebyene, then to Dadža, from where they moved to Sekhuthini, followed by Maolwe, and lastly to their current settlement, Khethakone.

50   *Annekie Joubert*

30. The Lobedu area consisted of 69 districts, according to the map in Krige and Krige (1943: 176), with districts 70 to 80 being subdistricts of the capital.

31. One of the interlocutors, Hans Booka, confirmed this archaic praise by commenting: 'Our ancestors brought it with them from Vokhalaga.' Personal communication, Modjadji tribal capital, Bolobedu, 8 November 2001.

32. As quoted by Georges and Jones (1995: 86).

33. To name a few of the many oral history initiatives in South Africa: Robben Island, the District Six Museum, the Centre for Popular Memory at the University of Cape Town, the Mandela Museum in Umtata, Constitution Hill Precinct, the Apartheid Museum, the Hector Pieterson Museum, the African Window Museum, Cato Manor Interpretive Centre, the Killie Cambell Collection, the Oral History Project that forms part of the ANC Archives at the University of Durban, and Isandlwana Battlefield.

34. See Foley (1995: 47) for a similar definition of the term 'performance arena'.

35. See <http://www.mhudi.de/maji>.

36. See the epic poem on the Maji-Maji war *Utenzi wa Vita vya Maji-Maji* by Abdul Karim bin Jamaliddini, collected by A. Lorenz in Lindi in 1912.

37. See <http://www.mhudi.de/maji/Bibliography-Source.html>.

38. See <http://www.wiko-berlin.de>.

39. My description of the commemoration event at Auschwitz is based on the special broadcast by the BBC on 27 January 2005.

Bibliography

Abraham, D.P. 1961. 'Maramuca: An Exercise in the Combined Use of Portuguese Records and Oral Tradition', *Journal of African History* 2: 211–225.

Alpers, E.A. 1970. 'Dynasties of the Mutapa-Roswi Complex', *Journal of African History* 11(2): 203–220.

Auschwitz commemoration, 27 January 2005. URL= http://news.bbc/co.uk/2/hi/europe/ 4214079.stm (consulted 26.11.2009).

Barber, K. 1989. 'Interpreting *Oríkì* as History and as Literature', in K. Barber and Farias P.F. de Moraes, *Discourse and its Disguises: The Interpretation of African Oral Texts.* Birmingham: 13–23.

Balic, S. 1990. 'Reign of the Rain Queen.' *Sunday Times,* 11 February 1990.

BBC: Special broadcast on Auschwitz commemoration, 27 January 2005.

Brown, D. 2003. '"Where shall I wonder under the thunder who's that black boys making that black noise step a little closer to the mike": Prophets of da City and Urban South African Identity', in J. Draper (ed.), *Oral Literacy and Colonialism in Southern Africa.* Pietermaritzburg: 145–169.

Canonici, N.N. 1996. *Zulu Oral Traditions.* Durban.

Coplan, D. 1987. 'Eloquent Knowledge: Lesotho Migrants' Songs and the Anthropological Experience', *American Ethnologist* 14(3): 413–433.

Davison, P. 1979. *The Material Culture of the Lobedu: A Museum and Field Study.* Unpublished master's dissertation, Stellenbosch.

Denis, P. 2003. 'Oral History in a Wounded Country', in J. Draper (ed.), *Oral Literacy and Colonialism in Southern Africa.* Pietermaritzburg: 205–216.

Draper, J. (ed.). 2003. *Oral Literacy and Colonialism in Southern Africa.* Pietermaritzburg.

De Volkstem (The Volkstem), 19 June 1894.

Du Toit, A. 2004. 'The Truth and Reconciliation Commission as Contemporary History', in S. Jeppie (ed.), *Toward New Histories for South Africa.* Landsdowne: 61–79.

Foley, J.M. 1995. *The Singer of Tales in Performance.* Bloomington.

Georges, R.A. and Jones, M.C. 1995. *Folkloristics: An Introduction.* Bloomington.

Geschichte-Gedächtnis (Maji-Maji). URL = http://www.mhudi.de/geschichte-gedaechtnis.html (consulted on 26.11.200).

Gobodo-Madikizela, P. 2004. *A Human Being Died That Night*. Claremont.

Gunner, L. 1999. 'Remaking the Warrior? The Role of Orality in the Liberation Struggle and in Post-apartheid South Africa', in D. Brown, *Oral Literature and Performance in South Africa*. Oxford: 50–60.

Gunner, L. 2003. 'Frozen Assets? Orality and the Public Space in KZN: Izibongo and Isicathamiya', in J. Draper (ed.) *Oral Literacy and Colonialism in Southern Africa*. Pietermaritzburg: 135–144.

Gwassa, G.C.K. 1972. 'Kinjikitile and the Ideology of Maji Maji', in T.O. Ranger and I.N. Kimambo (eds), *The Historical Study of African Religion*. Berkeley.

Gwassa, G.C.K. and J. Iliffe. 1967. 'Records of the Maji Maji Rising (Part One)', in G.C.K. Gwassa and J. Iliffe, *The Historical Association of Tanzania Paper No. 4*. Nairobi.

Hamilton, C.A. 1993. *Authoring Shaka: Models, Metaphors and Historiography*. Unpublished doctoral thesis, Baltimore.

Harries, P. 1989. 'Exclusion, Classification and Internal Colonialism: The Emergence of Ethnicity among the Tsonga-Speakers of South Africa', in L. Vail (ed.), *The Creation of Tribalism in Southern Africa*. London: 82–117.

Harris, V. 2000. 'Blindness and the Archive: An Exergue', in P. Denis, *Orality, Memory and the Past*. Pietermaritzburg: 112–123.

Hilton-Barber, S. 1996. 'The Skies May Have Opened, but for the Rain Queen the Magic is Gone.' *The Sunday Independent*, 14 January 1996.

Hofmeyr, I. 1989. 'No Chief, No Exchange, No Story', *African Studies* 48(2): 131–148.

Hutchison, Y. 2004. 'Memory and Desire in South Africa', in M.J. Banham, M.J. Gibbs and F. Osofisan (eds), *African Theatre: Southern Africa*. Oxford: 51–67.

bin Jamaliddini, Abdul Karim. 1933. 'Utenzi wa Vita vya Maji-Maji.' Trans. A. Lorenz in *Mitteilungen des Seminars für orientalische Sprachen an der Friederich-Wilhelm-Universität zu Berlin* XXXVI, no. 3: 227–259.

Joubert, A. 2004. *The Power of Performance: Linking Past and Present in Hananwa and Lobedu Oral Literature*. Berlin.

Joubert, A.P. and J.A. Van Schalkwyk. 1999. 'War and Remembrance: The Power of Oral Poetry and the Politics of Hananwa Identity', *Journal of Southern African Studies* 25(1): 29–47.

Kaschula, R.H. 1999. *The Transitional Role of the Xhosa Oral Poet in Contemporary South African Society*. Unpublished doctoral thesis. Grahamstown.

Kaschula, R.H. 2004. 'Imbongi to Slam: The Emergence of a Technologised Auriture', *Southern African Journal for Folklore Studies* 14(2): 46–58.

Kgobe, D.M. 1989. *The Oral Nature of Northern Sotho 'direto'*. Unpublished master's dissertation. Pretoria.

Kriel, L. 2004. 'Same War, Different Story: A Century's Writing on the Boer-Hananwa War of 1894', *Journal of Southern African Studies* 30(4): 789–810.

Krige, E.J. 1985. 'Descend and Descent Groups in Lovedu Social Structure', *African Studies* 44(1): 1–45.

Krige, E.J. 1975. 'Divine Kingship, Change and Development,' in M. Fortres and S. Patterson (eds.), *Studies in African Social Anthropology*. London: 55–74.

Krige, E.J. and J.D. Krige. 1943. *The Realm of a Rain-Queen*. London.

Krige, J.D. 1937. 'Traditional Origins and Tribal Relationships of the Sotho of the Northern Transvaal', *Bantu Studies* 11(4): 321–356.

Krog, A. 1998. *Country of My Skull*. Parklands.

Kruger, F. 1936. 'The Lovedu', *Bantu Studies* 10(1): 89–105.

LitNet: PoetryNet. URL = http://www.oulitnet.co.za/relax/vonanai_bila.asp (consulted on 26.11.2009).

Magogodi, K. URL = http://www.kgafela.com/profile.html. URL = http://www.vooruit.be/en/page/883 (consulted on 26.11.2009)

Maji-Maji Aufstand in DOA 1905-1907. URL = http://www.mhudi.de/maji/Bibliography-Source.html (consulted on 26.11.2009).

Mathekga, A. 1939. *Setŝhaba sa Balobedu le semelo sa bona*. (The tribe of the Lobedu and their customs). S179, K34/6. National State Archive. Pretoria.

Miehe, G., K. Bromber, S. Khamis and R. Großerhode. 2002. *Kala Shairi German East Africa in Swahili Poems*. Cologne.

Minkley, G. and C. Rassool. 1998. 'Orality, Memory, and Social History in South Africa', in S. Nuttal and C. Coetzee (eds), *Negotiating the Past: The Making of Memory in South Africa*. Cape Town: 89–99.

Muller, C.A. 2002. 'Archiving Africanness in Sacred Song', *Ethnomusicology* 46(3): 409–431.

Opland, J. 1983. *Xhosa Oral Poetry: Aspects of a Black South African Tradition*. Johannesburg.

Raditlhalo, S.I. 2004. 'Praise and Performance Poetry Past and Present: Possibilities for Regeneration', *Southern African Journal for Folklore Studies* 14(2): 34–45.

Rae, C. 1898. *Malaboch, Notes from my Diary on the Boer Campaign of 1894 against Chief Malaboch*. London.

Rampolokeng, L. URL = http://www.music.org.za/artists/lesego.htm (consulted on 26.11.2009).

Reynolds, P. 1990. 'Children of Tribulation: The Need to Heal and the Means to Heal War Trauma', *Africa* 60(1): 1–38.

Saule, N. 1998. 'Images of Ubuntu in the Essays of S.E.K. Mqhayi in Umteteli Wabantu (1912–1939)', *South African Journal of African Languages* 18(1): 10–18.

Schacter, D. 2001. *The Seven Sins of Memory*. New York.

Small, J.P. 1995. 'Artificial Memory and the Writing Habits of the Literate', *Helios* 22(2): 159–166.

Symposium: Lieux de Memoire and the Maji Maji War. URL = http://www.Tanzania-network.de/.../Maji/2005_April_Wissenschaftskolleg.pdf (consulted on 26.11.2009).

Tatum, J. 1995. 'Memory in Recent Humanistic Research,' *Helios* 22(2): 151–155.

Teffo, J. 1994. *The Concept of Ubuntu as a Cohesive Moral Value*. Pretoria.

Vail, L. and L. White. 1983. 'Forms of Resistance: Songs and Perceptions of Power in Colonial Mozambique', *American Historical Review* 88(4): 883–919.

Van Schalkwyk, J.A. 1991. 'Crocodiles, History and the Presentation of "Facts"', *South African Journal of Art and Architectural History* 2(1): 27–30.

Van Schalkwyk, J.A. 1995. *Ideologie en die konstruksie van 'n landelike samelewing: 'n Antropologiese studie van die Hananwa van Blouberg*. (Ideology and the construction of a rural community: An anthropological study of the Hananwa of Blouberg). Unpublished doctoral thesis. Pretoria.

Van Schalkwyk, J.A. and S.M. Moifatswane. 1991. 'The Siege of Leboho: South African Republic Fortifications in the Blouberg, Northern Transvaal', *Military History Journal* 8(5): 175–183.

Vansina, J. 1980. 'Memory and Oral Tradition', in J.C. Miller (ed.), *The African Past Speaks: Essays on Oral Tradition*. Folkestone: 262–279.

Wright, J. 2000. 'Thinking beyond 'Modernist' History', in P. Denis (ed.), *Orality, Memory and the Past*. Pietermaritzburg: 124–131.

Zolani, M. URL = http://www.music.org.za/artists/mkiva.htm (consulted on 26.11.2009).

CHAPTER 3

Historical Memory and Representation of New Nations in Africa

BOGUMIL JEWSIEWICKI

To live without a past is worse than to live without a future.
—Elie Wiesel

If you've waited 300 years for a vote, what's another five hours in the rain!
—A black voter (Cape Times, 28 April 1994)

I will begin the following considerations on the relationship between memory and history in the public space of contemporary Africa by briefly reflecting on the relationship between discourse on the past and the international political context of reconfiguring the state and the nation.[1] Taking the role of consensual political construction (the work of citizens) into account – a role that the French nation has played since the French Revolution – Nora's texts must be considered in the same manner as Renan's, each being the realm of memory of the national sentiment of its time.[2] The political discourse on self-determination that avails itself of modernism, particularly the anti-colonial discourse, avails itself of the French example. Such is also the case for the opposition – canonical in literature on the subject – between the German state model and the French state model, both held as ideal types rather than historical realities. Let us emphasize the distinction between national construction, which features historical continuity, and construction that overcomes (all the while recognizing) its discontinuities. More than canonical opposition between land and blood rights, this distinction allows us to use the ideal French and German types to reflect on recent uses of historical memory in the reconfiguration of the nation. In the new international context, the mediatization of public space calls for 'new' performances of the nation.

Since the middle of the nineteenth century and throughout the twentieth, transformations in the international system itself have conditioned the legitimization of sovereignty and influenced the delicate political balance between citizen membership and authoritarian control.[3] For historic reasons attributable to the role of Christianity, historical narration long served as a manner of performing the citizen's relationship to the past and the nation. At the end of the twentieth century, a narrative crisis denoted the exhaustion of a type of public performance without really putting the nation as affirmation of sovereignty into question. Postmodern prophets took the change in form and scale as a crisis of content. The Grand Narrative has been exhausted as a public form of legitimizing sovereignty. Nonetheless, narration is healthier than ever in the local space: it has become a natural vehicle for staging political, nonstate subjects such as community. The narrative has been 'democratized' into a multitude of stories wandering in search of an audience. Between historian and memorial relationships to the past, the historian's authority fails without affecting the narratives' and the narrators' legitimacy, particularly when the subject is in attendance as a witness of his or her experience.

In Western tradition, the historian distances him or herself from the witness, François Hartog says. This separation authorizes the historical operation and gives foundation to historical criticism. Historians extract 'historical' information from traces, such as the narratives of witnesses. They give order to this information, examine it and submit it to critique. Then, conducting a change of scale, they construct a narrative whose true subject is history (speaking in the name of the nation) rather than the historical actors themselves. The witness performs the miracle of memory and makes present an experience that no longer exists but appears to be real as opposed to the virtual reality of the media.

At the end of the twentieth century, the postmodern moment was marked not by the crisis of narrative authority itself, but rather by the mutation of this crisis. The transfer of authority – from the narrator to the arbitrator of narrative circulation – transformed public space. The narrative of the witness came essentially before the witness could master the reach of his 'voice' and the access to an audience. The transformation of how the media circulates information is largely responsible for this. The authority pronouncing the legitimate relationship to time is no longer the clerk professing from the elevated Chair of History, but rather an audiovisual authority that controls the scope of what is said, heard and seen in the public space. Witnesses seem more credible than historians; new audiovisual authority leaves their narratives apparently unharmed by mediation. Like the historian, but for other reasons, the witness tells what 'actually' happened. While the historian represents the state-nation, the witness stands for the human being 'without particular qualities' and brings the nation as a community into the present. The human witness (not the specialist on human beings) pronounces a truth certified by the authenticity of experience. Even when they lie, the witnesses' words remain authentic: they account for an experience. Not listening to the witness is equivalent to placing oneself above humanity and making oneself guilty of discriminating against the group that the witness represents. Modern art constructs the notion of authenticity in order to shelter itself from the arbitration of aesthetic judgment. Currently, this notion substantiates the reception of the witness and his narrative.

The communalization of audiences and constituents as political nonstate subjects was carried out on the grounds of recognizing the universality of human rights and the non-applicability of statutory limitations to crimes in respect thereof. As a human being without particular qualities, the witness represents a community. The case of Rigoberta Menchu is probably the first in which a witness was internationally recognized as a representative who brought her community into the world (despite its marginalization in space or time) and who held her own, mandated by a shared experience. The chapter dedicated to generation as community of experience and memory in Pierre Nora's *Realms of Memory* (1993) offers an analysis that can be transposed to other communities of experience such as destiny, spirituality, past suffering, current discrimination, etc. Collectives are endowed with spokespersons who are mandated by the communal experience, shared memory and disrespected rights, sometimes of former generations. These spokespersons reclaim the political rights that will sustainably reestablish recognition, reparation and restitution (Jewsiewicki 2004).

I believe that we must read political negotiations (including those that resort to violence) taking place on the African continent against the backdrop of these transformations. In the global arena, the subject's legitimacy rests on the forms that validate the legitimacy of continuity or discontinuity as a means for its own emergence. In our era, which is more postrevolutionary than postmodern, the first seems preferable. Strategies and arguments of legitimacy in regards to the representation of the subject are elaborated and strengthened in relation to this politico-media scene. Whereas in other eras only political representation counted, current mediatization, which values the effect of authenticity, values the presence of an absent who is distanced in space or time.

I present the issue of the subject in Africa with a résumé of my exchange (Jewsiewicki 2002a) with Achille Mbembe (2002) concerning the African discourse on self. The Cartesian tradition states that every human being is naturally able to express his identity. Without needing to follow a master, every man is able to reach the truth, wrote Descartes. However, along this path there is a trap: to arrive at truth, one must apply method. The method to express identity is narration, suggests Mbembe. Is it possible, then, to narrate self without mastering time? Deleuze, whom Mbembe quotes, regards time as the key to subjectivity, meaning that one cannot think and act as subject without mastering time as a dimension of his/her existence. At least in the tradition of Near Eastern monotheistic religions, mastery of the subject's identity refers to the time of narration, and narration refers to the book that presumes conversion. Explicitly recognized by the subject, subjectivity is likely to be implicitly taken away from the subject, unless he/she steps out of the time of narration, the time of history. To recognize the absolute sovereignty of grace transforms time into moments of its discrete manifestations. The privilege of authority disappears, and the past as time (duration) becomes open, suspended and waiting for an external intervention. Grace is immediate and comes down instantaneously to weld together the two sides of the present: the waiting for grace before its manifestation and then the waiting for the Second Advent. The presentist concept of time has become widespread today through the practice of Christianity in African Pentecostal-inspired churches. This practice upholds the subject's individualism face to face with God, devalues cumulative time, and abolishes the privilege of anteriority, exchanging conversions for elections.

Formulated in terms of co-presence rather than in terms of evolution, identity as relationship to the other defines the 'postmodern' moment. Organized by the category of space rather than that of time, is its enunciation performative-transactional (as Foucault would have said) rather than narrative? From a place where his memory is engaged (a '*propre*'), the subject makes the elements of his experience contemporary, thus illuminating the present and giving the concept of realms of memory its pertinence.

To deconstruct the theories of the African subject, Mbembe begins by identifying three forms of reflexivity in the Western tradition: (1) memory that recognizes, (2) meditation that opens into ascetism, the test of oneself as subject of the ethics of truth, and (3) (Cartesian) method that examines certitude. Then, he uncovers the African subject theories that are elaborated from the successive hardships of slavery, colonization and apartheid. He doubts that the collective crossing of these trials would unify African's aspirations of sovereignty, dignity and recognition. For Mbembe, being a subject in Africa does not presuppose having been a victim of these injustices and does not bestow upon the subject a special mission or an identity defined by a history that imposes the obligation to unite. The African's subjectivity is not a collective destiny forged by history or, even less so, by 'race'. The African subject's space is the now-present (Benjamin) that he masters through indiscipline. Indiscipline is not a strategy, while the space of tactics is not a *propre*. The subject's identity is developed in the experience and representation of the present: memory, as a way of taking stock of experience, illuminates the present by way of *praemeditatio malorum* (Foucault 2001).

Here, it is unlikely that the miracle of memory will be able to abolish time in order to resuscitate a lost truth. Anachronism offers memory a space, thus confronting the experience of before with that of now: both are current. The truth – lost and found again – of Mobutu's authenticity, of the glorification of black antiques, etc., knows not that it must give up the master's meditation and the subject's sovereignty. Whereas the experience of the last century has showed that the master – whoever he may be – finishes by confessing that he is a missionary, we see that indiscipline is all that remains for the subject.

For Mbembe, indiscipline is part of the African subject's *propre*. However, this particular space does not allow for any strategy. Indiscipline helps the subject resist, escape from the other's strategic actions and pretend, even to himself, that he has been converted. Is this the reason for the failure of postcolonial independence as new social order? After defeating colonial discipline, indiscipline as the subject's way of being could not found the new order, it could only bring about its failure.

The desire to meet – even surpass – the West in terms of 'modernity' lends a special urgency to the African subject's search for a 'fair' relationship to the past that will act as a foundation for the self-authentic subject. I propose that we examine from this angle two experiences of collective negotiation of international recognition of the self as a legitimate political subject. The predominance of human rights and the a-temporality that non-applicability of statutory limitations confers on these rights provide a vast audience for the experience of victims of the international system of slavery, colonization, neo-colonialism, etc. However, the authenticity of experience that the witness brings to the present calls for demonstrated continuity in order that compensation can be demanded for the wrongdoings inflicted upon several generations. In both cases, I will briefly examine the urban societies in Africa that consider themselves to be modern and are profoundly Christian, refusing to be passive recipients of the Christian message while they believe they hold the truth and are charged with its dissemination. Historic memory – the narration of suffering a community was subjected to – becomes a *propre* (in M. de Certeau's 1980 meaning) of the new nation.

The Congo: A Historical Memory of Redemption as Narrative of the Nation

My first example, from the urban culture of industrial Katanga, represents the ways of constructing a relationship with the past in urban Central Africa and, more generally, in urban Africa of the Christian tradition. The work of a popular painter from the city of Lubumbashi (Illustration 1), on which I base my demonstration, is as much a unique work as it is the synthesis of Congolese memorial icons. The structure of this historical memory dives down into the order of time of historical narration. The latter enhances the value of anteriority and takes origins for the emergence of evolution. The slave figure breaking his chains is as vital as the actualization of past experience (slavery, colonization, postcolonial oppression, etc.) and as the promise of a future. With a biblical ref-

Illustration 1. I am not a free man, Dessin Lascas, Lubumbashi (Congo), around 1972, col. B. Jewsiewicki.
Reprinted with the permission of the artist.

erence in mind, the slave is a figure of liberation who sees that the trials he was subjected to offer guaranteed redemption. The witness is elevated as prophet (Jewsiewicki et al. 1999).

In this way, the painting's caption is significant, especially the arrangement of sections of text. Let us remember that in this predominantly Roman Catholic country the bible was rarely accessible to believers without the mediation of a priest. Reading and writing, especially in French, opened up modernity as opposed to the traditional space of the village. Expressing oneself in French meant not only being liberated from 'tradition', but also taking up the role of redeemer and leader-missionary. The French caption that identifies the author's image as Moses refers as much to the Holy Book as to the principles of the Universal Declaration of Human Rights. The writing of 'Je ne suis pas un homme libre' (I am not a free man) puts the accent first on quality, ('homme libre', free man), and second on the subject's statement 'Je suis' (I am). The negation seems to be an afterthought, as if it did not belong to the initial formulation and was imposed upon it. Placing himself before his people is an act of bravery and a challenge that exposes him to others' envy and attacks by forces of the 'tradition'. Only solid protection from equal forces (supernatural ones) would be able to protect this solitary man. The reference to the exodus from Egypt and the mastery of French suggest that the subject, a man alone and disconnected from his village, benefits from such protection. Historically, from Léopold II (king of the Belgians and sovereign of the Congo Free State) to Mobutu and Laurent-Désiré Kabila, the leader of the Congo is a solitary figure.

Without a doubt, the chain-breaking figure witnesses (makes present) the collective experience of late nineteenth-century raids by slave hunters, well alive in social memory. Still in use in the 1960s, colonial schoolbooks remind us insistently that slavery was the Congolese people's condition before colonial intervention freed them. Yet the labor inflicted by the colonizer was long experienced as a new kind of slavery. The citizen's conditions under Mobutu's rule were experienced as a return to slavery. A man in underwear, called a *singlet* in Belgian French, represents the ordinary Congolese. Like Lumumba (a political Christ who died for the redemption of his people), who is also portrayed wearing these same garments, this figure is a witness who represents his people. Because he is bringing the past to the present, he delivers memory from silence.

A group of villagers painted to the right puts the accent on memory shared as performance. It looks as if these people are listening to the narrative and interjecting their stories. The chain breaker's experience is present, even if for him the act of breaking the chains announces slavery as past events. The experience of the past is made present without nostalgic intentions. This makes current an experience that illuminates the present in such a way as to prevent the return of phantoms from the past. In the background is a depiction of romantic village life. Examining this painting with the memorial icon '*colonie belge*' (Belgian colony) in mind (Jewsiewicki 2003) (Illustration 2) puts this disposition into perspective. The chain breaker's position in the middle of the image and his pose suggest that the figure of Moses contains three figures central to the *colonie belge:* the Congolese man who is flogged, the soldier who whips and the uniformed white man who approves the scene. The group of villagers who seem to be gathered to listen to the leader-witness also reminds us of the women of the *colonie belge,* who show the suffering and sorrow of the society subjected to (post)colonial slavery.

The painting was done in the middle of the Mobutist era. During the decade that followed, the work of memory and forgetting[4] was particularly intense in the Congo. The social and political relevance of the past was put into question, and this questioning was amplified by the effects of a major break with colonial past that had given meaning to politics and legitimated authority. The ideology of constructing the future under the stewardship of the state was finished, taking with it the legitimacy of the postcolonial double rupture: access to independence and failure of the early 1960s rebellions. The rebels were accused of wanting to replace modernity with precolonial 'barbarism', as depicted in colonial schoolbooks. The smothered rebellions were the foundation for Mobutu's political capital. The three decades of his reign were dominated by promises, amply interiorized by the population, of a radiant future closer than the distant colonization and the memory of the rebellions. The end of

Illustration 2. Belgian Colony, anonymous, Bunia (Congo), 1990, col. B. Jewsiewicki. Reprinted with the permission of the artist.

this illusion, as well as the revalorization of thirty years of Mobutism, opened society's door to the former rebel chief Laurent-Désiré Kabila, announcing a return to 1960 to rebuild the independence betrayed by Mobutu. It is important to mention that Kabila never offered to renew relations with the rebellions' revolution. Nor did he call for help from his former rebel companions, and he rarely conjured up Lumumba, whom he had formerly claimed was his model. Instead, Kabila proposed to the Congo to take up its history where it had gone wrong: 30 June 1960, the date of an event few Congolese remembered.

Throughout the 1990s, the change of generation as community experience came to a close (Jewsiewicki 2002b). The vast majority of today's Congolese population therefore has no experience of colonization and knows only a little from family members. The realm of experience has cracked, and the horizon of expectation is crumbled and smashed by the present, which has not passed ('crise multiforme', as the Congolese say). The desire to pull oneself away from the present is represented individually by the dream of emigration and collectively by the Second Advent. In both cases, experience here and elsewhere has lost its pertinence, and memory is furnished with anachronisms from colonial times. With only three or four generations at the most, social memory has relatively little depth in urban Congo. Under Mobutu, the colonial era and the times of the rebellions represented a repellent period, whereas the sovereign mastery of modernity was on the horizon of expectation.

Slavery is one of the main historical spaces of memory that, according to plan, establishes continuity between the slave trade and colonial (then postcolonial) subjugation. The coming of modernity for all, freeing all from slavery, is a work by Sisyphus. Since Lumumba, one Moses succeeds another – Mobutu at the end of the 1960s, then Tshisekedi followed by Kabila senior, etc. – none of them able (or even perhaps willing) to take up Lumumba's task of political redemption.

South Africa: Memory of the Nation, Lost and Found Again in the Quest for the Founding Moment

I do not believe that recent South African realities are deformed by insisting on a rehabilitation of the relationship between the past and the representations of this past within the presence of the 'new' nation. The will to establish a historical continuity of the nation that goes beyond apartheid now looks more important than reestablishing victims as what they would have been had apartheid not derided their rights. Because the reparation would be mainly political and symbolic, it will be the nation itself, with its 'historic' rights finally reinstated, that will benefit.

Here, the anachronism characteristic of the global movement of reparations is quite overt. Whether we are talking about individual rights of victims or about those of the nation, these rights are defined starting from the here and now and therefore follow political and economic processes – the effects of which must be cancelled, if not rendered to have no force and effect. However, a return to the past has not been postulated, and evolution of a society devoid of the kind of prejudices that must be compensated for is not a scenario that has been considered. There is nothing but memory to help stage – to tell, as the need arises – such operations and to reestablish continuity against the current of history. Witnesses authenticate this more by the suffering inscribed in their bodies, or in the bodies of their loved ones for whom they stand, than by speech. Saartjie Baartman is a most striking example of this. An aboriginal and a woman, she uncontestedly represents as much the country's first inhabitants – and thus the first victims of colonialism – as the victims of all denials of justice and all discrimination. A great symbolic charge surrounds the place and date of burial of the 'naturalized' remnants repatriated from the Musée de l'Homme in Paris. In President Thabo Mbeki's presence, on the supposed land of her ancestors and on Women's Day in South Africa, Saartjie Baartman stopped being an artefact of natural science, fabricated by imperialism and its science[5] that deprived her of her humanity. She became a symbolic mother-figure for all South Africans like her, whose right to humanity (sovereign existence) had been stolen. The displacement of the moment when national history began is striking, as is the symbolic nature of repatriation. In the terminology inherited from apartheid (which has not yet lost its meaning), as a Khoikhoi rather than a Bantu, she is an all-encompassing symbolic mother-figure throughout the world as well as in her own country. Standard South African history places the initial formation of coloureds in the miscegenation between Khoikhoi and whites. The aboriginal inhabitants of the African headland could be the people most closely related to African Eve, our common ancestor.

The two democratically elected presidents of South Africa, Nelson Mandela and Thabo Mbeki, successively emphasized two distinct approaches to repairing crimes of the past. Each approach looks to define the nature of the nation in its relationships with citizens and with the state. If citizens were reinstated – as least symbolically – in historic continuity and legitimacy by the TRC, the state that issued from the 1994 elections faced nearly half a century of rupture with legitimacy from various points of view, including that of the African National Congress (ANC).[6] Mandela and Tutu's ambition, which the TRC struggled hard to realize, was to make sure that there would be only one nation, which henceforth would never experience rupture of either legitimacy or continuity, and that citizens would share not only the present and the future but also the past (Jewsiewicki 2002c). The process of hearing the suffering and crimes perpetrated under the regime of apartheid by individuals on other individuals whom we may come across the street, listening to these individuals (rather than to functionaries or political figures) and recognizing the crimes committed against 'neighbours' rather than against 'terrorists' sought not only to render improbable the denial of personal responsibility for the past, but also to assume responsibility for the present.

National conscience forged in the challenge of being fully aware of the past – face to face with the wounded 'bleeding' body and soul of the victim – remains historic, but it cannot be shared, except in a memorial manner. Holding in one space (symbolically outlined as one of the nation's *propre* by the peregrinations of the TRC's hearings) the mourning of suffering and crime – the mourning for the nation broken in half – should forever prevent the negation of apartheid crimes and exorcise its phantom. Accepting apartheid as part of the nation's heritage was as important as granting criminal and civil amnesty to the perpetrators, who now were 'neighbours' exposed to the political and ethical judgement of their fellow citizens. Radio and television mediatization of audiences[7] was fundamental in creating a virtual space-time of the nation – a true cradle of the nation. In the spirit of repentance and forgiveness, all South Africans were expected to join in this mourning. The challenge was to teach individuals – all citizens since 1994 – not only how to live with the memory of apartheid, but how to become better for having acknowledged it. Making forgetting impossible, forbidding apartheid to be reduced to a parenthesis or accident of history, and rendering it impossible to hide behind the responsibility of individual perpetrators meant making this challenge into the reason for the South African 'miracle'. In the spirit of confession and penitence, and taking a psalm for national hymn, the community of the Christian tradition accepted its past and each individual accepted his or her own, grateful for moral and political redemption.

The end of apartheid became a political liberation for blacks and a moral liberation for whites; everyone benefited. Equals before the past and, in April 1994, equals before the present and the future, South Africans shared, for the first time in their history, their experience … of the past! A virtual nation of forgiveness and compassion, of repentance and abnegation, covers up the nation forged by violence. Were it not for daily life marked by AIDS, unemployment and economic disparities, this penitent memory, having already overcome the barrier of race, could have enjoyed a prolonged expansion, transforming apartheid into a trauma that founded the new nation.

Thabo Mbeki's first mandate was dominated by the inscription into the nation's historical continuation, of which apartheid made up an immediate past. It was essential for him to find South Africa's place in the concert of nations of the globalized world and in the universe of Africa and its diaspora. Change of temporary perspective was not favoured over bringing the memory of apartheid up to date. The discourse on the African Renaissance turned South Africa into a nation that, since its establishment as a colonial society, had not stopped resisting oppression (particularly racial and colonial oppression), and as such, it became the leader of black nations and peoples. Leslie Witz (2003) demonstrates how the commemoration of the founding moment (held to be the arrival of the first European colonizers in April 1652) changed in fifty years. Marking the inscription of racial domination at the heart of the Afrikaners' 'sacred' relationship to the promised land under apartheid, 1652 became the launch date of a 300-year battle for a democratized South Africa that would combat all discrimination. Apartheid, then, is no more than an episode and a parenthesis.

Since 1994, although the democratic form makes it 'new', the nation is nonetheless 'old' in its commitment (over more than 300 years) against all oppression. This representation of the past can be shared with those who claim the quality of Africanity, namely black Africans and Afrikaners or white Africans. The acquisition of this quality was the object of a controversy that broke out in 1999 in the South African press concerning Afrikaners' Africanity. Before, this quality was found at the heart of Afrikaner intellectuals' political negotiations with the political direction of the exiled African National Congress. The ANC leaders' acceptance that the African quality can be recognized in Afrikaners opened the way for political negotiation.[8]

Opponents of Africanity as a national quality that is conferred more by land than by blood evoke – in Renan's rather in than in Nora's spirit – shared experience and memories. Whether voluntary or not, apartheid's beneficiaries do not share the same experience or the same memory of apartheid as the victims. They have neither the same historical conscience nor the same responsibilities for the future. Putting collective experience and memory at the centre of the definition of belonging to the nation would restore the unity of blacks, which had been fractured by the heavily politicized renaissance of cultural and ethnic identities of Indians, Coloureds, Zulu, Xhosa, etc. Unity among all the oppressed (to call oneself Black was a political statement of resistance to oppression), strong from the apartheid era, took a blow from the multiculturalism of the 'rainbow nation'. Paradoxically, as an effect of the past political miracle, the memorial theatre of the TRC contributed to the idea that two distinct experiences and two distinct memories were inherited from apartheid. The last volume of the TRC's report on amnesty and definitive measures of reparation reinforced the feeling of conflict rather than that of a community of historic memories of the recent struggles against oppression.

The distanced past (especially the historic moments allowing all the candidates of 'African' quality, and not just the oppressed, to protest) is more fertile ground for the emergence of a new historical shared conscience. Long forgotten,[9] the participation of black Africans in the Anglo-Boer war (now called the South African War) was accorded a place of honour in the recent celebrations of the war's centennial (see Grundlingh's chapter in this volume). The site that was chosen for the ceremonial occasion was said to shelter the tombs of both Afrikaners and blacks. The presence of these 'witnesses' allowed history to pass into memory (as is shown by the impressive number of publications). By way of a member of the royal family brought to the site, Great Britain expressed its regrets for its imperialist intervention.

On the world political scene, Thabo Mbeki's support of Haiti's President Aristide during the controversial bicentennial celebrations of the independence of this first modern black republic prolonged the commemoration of the Anglo-Boer war as the first war against imperialism. In the context of the international community's abstention, the presence of the South African president at the side of the agonizing Haitian regime takes on meaning in the light of efforts to build the sense of belonging to the South African nation on the foundation of memory of the struggle against oppression. A century after 1804, South Africa's cause was the same as Haiti's had been then, but here the revolutionary victories were ephemeral. It was the peaceful victory of 1994 that transformed the world, putting South Africa in charge of leading black nations and black peoples. In May 1994, 'just like a referee proclaiming the winner, Mandela raised the hands of Vice-President Mbeki up to the heavens' (*Time Magazine,* 23 May 1994: 42), and racial oppression was thrown into the trash basket of history.

Notes

1. I give the term 'Representation' used in the title two meanings: (1) standing in the stead of someone we represent; and (2) bringing the absent to the present (Ricoeur 2000).

2. Nora (1993: 30) wrote: '[la] grande sortie du nationalisme traditionnel … , bien loin d'amener une exténuation du sentiment national, en a au contraire … libéré la dynamique.'

3. The emergence at the end of the twentieth century of the 'third force', primarily made up of populous organizations grouped into international associations, then nongovernmental organizations, is an excellent demonstration of the globalization (as imperial as it gets) of the circulation of information and (popular?) leisure culture.

4. Memory is distinct from written or oral history, whether it is question of space or work. Memory is built from witnessing, which brings to the fore an experience from the past. History, on the other hand, looks to establish a durable truth about the past. Anachronism – the historian's capital sin – is at the core of memory, which unfurls between the field of experience and the horizon of expectations. Memory makes present that which is absent. Yesterday, the past moment that memory brings to the fore could have evaded all efforts of memorial and could be again forgotten tomorrow. History is narrative, whereas memory is performative: it lends itself to bringing past moments back to the present, especially when the social or political forces are thrown out of tradition and when a regime of historicity decomposes.

5. To my knowledge no direct link was suggested during the burial, but celebrating this victim of Western science must not have displeased Thabo Mbeki, who challenged the connection established by this same science between the AIDS pandemic and HIV virus.

6. ANC President Oliver Tambo considered South Africa to have never really left the Commonwealth because the state under apartheid was not legitimate and did not represent its citizens (Hyam and Henshaw 2003: 349).

7. From the inside of her work as journalist, Antjie Krog (1998) provides an excellent summary of this. For further development, see Annie Coombes 2003.

8. Hermann Giliomee (2003: 192) quotes R.E.A. Hoernlé, a liberal from the 1930s, who in *Race and Reason,* released in 1945 in Johannesburg, qualified Afrikaners' domestic help as 'black Europeans', applying the same principle but in the opposite direction.

9. Marxist-inspired historiography dealt with this question by presenting black Africans as victims of an imperialist conflict, whether that of the British or that of the Boers.

Bibliography

Certeau, de, M. 1980. *L'invention du quotidien. I. Les arts de faire.* Paris. American translation 1984: *The Practice of Everyday Life.* Berkeley.
Coombes, A. 2003. *A Visual Culture and Public Memory in a Democratic South Africa.* Durham.
Foucault, M. 2001. *L'herméneutique du sujet: cours au Collège de France 1981–82.* Paris.
Giliomee, H. 2003. *The Afrikaners: Biography of a People.* London.
Hyam R. and P. Henshaw. 2003. *The Lion and the Springbok: Britain and South Africa since the Boer War.* Cambridge.
Jewsiewicki, B. et al. 1999. *A Congo Chronicle.* New York.
Jewsiewicki, B. 2002a. 'The Subject in Africa: In Foucault's Footsteps', *Public Culture* 14: 593–598.
Jewsiewicki, B. 2002b. 'Vers une impossible représentation de soi', *Les temps modernes* 57: 101–114.
Jewsiewicki, B. 2002c. 'De la vérité de la mémoire à la réconciliation. Comment travaille le souvenir? *Le Débat* 122: 63–77.
Jewsiewicki, B. 2003. *Mami wata: La peinture urbaine au Congo.* Paris.
Jewsiewicki, B. ed. 2004. *Réparations, restitutions, réconciliations entre Afriques, Europe et Amérique.* Cahiers d'études africaines. Paris: 173–174.
Krog, A 1998. *Country of My Skull.* Johannesburg.

Mbembe, A. 2002. 'African Modes of Self-Writing', *Public Culture* 14: 239–273.

Nora, P. 1993. *Les lieux de mémoire, t.3*. Paris. American translation 1996–1998: *Realms of Memory: Rethinking the French Past*. New York.

Ricoeur, P. 2000. *La mémoire, l'histoire, l'oubli*. Paris.

Witz, L. 2003. *Apartheid's Festival: Contesting South Africa's National Past*. Bloomington.

CHAPTER 4

Memory, History and Historiography of Congo-Zaïre

JUSTIN BISANSWA

> *Three torn, emerging countries (Rwanda, Burundi, Zaire), where the old order is collapsing in all directions . . . . But who on earth pigeon-holed, stigmatized these people as if they were flowers or butterflies; who else relegated them to this narrow category and locked them in the roles of slaves, masters, dignitaries, dissidents, but the colonizer and their administration, assisted by the church and later by all these foreigners who, thinking they were doing good, eager to understand, did the same labelling? How, over the years, could people of this region not accept as true this labelling foisted on them and use, in turn, the weapon of ethnicity?*
>
> —Colette Braeckman, *Terreur africaine*

There might be different ways of rereading the history of Congo-Zaire, Rwanda and Burundi. When Belgian journalists raised the question of the misery of the Congolese people with Mobutu, the marshal replied, alluding to the five years of 'chaos' shortly after independence: 'My people sing and dance. They enjoy peace.' One can recall today how the Lendu and Hema in Upper Congo killed one another. Also consider a statement that became common among my former students in Bukavu: 'I've learned that two days ago my father, my mother and all my brothers and sisters were killed by Rwandese soldiers.' This was reported in an emotionless voice and with an absolutely impassive face—calmly.

I cannot resist the temptation to reminisce about my arrival in Bukavu from Lubumbashi, via Goma, in November 1977. In Gisenyi, three kilometers away from Goma on the shores of Lake Kivu with its hotels, gardens and beach, I waited impatiently for dusk to see the sky from Mt. Nyiragongo turn red. I was fascinated. With its three thousand five hundred meters, the volcano seemed very close. The glowing incandescence turned yellow, red and purple. From time to time the crater spewed ash and small flaming rocks: fireworks. After my appointment as lecturer I visited the Parc Albert Reserve, and the sources of Mayi ya moto at Rwindi, between Lake Edouard and Lake Kivu, taught me that huge and fabulous forces were at work under my feet. Water, almost boiling, spurted out two meters above the ground. I went to see the Sake Plains: the lava, ten years old, was hard, black. Chaotic, dangerous tides of high black waves alternating with crevices, sometimes so deep.

I remained passionately interested in the volcanoes. Having learned their names and forms, I chased after them round corners and clouds: Nyamlagira, Mikeno, Karisimbi, Visoke, Sabinio, Gahinga, Muhavura. Karisimbi and Mikeno had white tops, for snow falls in Africa at 4,500 meters. Between Bujumbura and Uvira I remember the heat, the metallic whiteness of the surface of Lake Tanganyika, its immensity, and a young crocodile in the sand on the beach a few feet away from us. Then you get to Bukavu through the Kamanyola Valley. At certain places, the ravine is imposing. In Bukavu, I found fruit and flowers that I had never seen in Kasongo, where I was born. Many Belgian colonists used to spend their holidays in this region, when they did not go to South Africa, for it has Eden's climate, numerous colonists and large plantations, vast missions where young African priests were trained and great schools in Bukavu, Kigali and Ruhengeri. Observing villages in Kivu and Rwanda, I noticed cultivated terraces on the hills.

More than anything else, I have retained from my adolescence the hue of this province of Bukavu and its surroundings. When much later I read in Leonardo da Vinci's *Carnets* that in summer the mountains are 'sky-blue', and that 'from a distance, the shadowy flanks of the mountains are tainted more bluish and more beautiful than the sun-lit ones', it became evidence. I had known beforehand that these mountains are blue and unknowingly kept this blue in my retina – a memory that has remained with me all these years. After wars and my exile, I thought I had forgotten. The wound of this forgetting is another story.

Today, one hears only silence! Silence about the tragedy of the Congolese in the eastern region, about the tragedy of Tutsis and Hutus. Despite the silence, I have started searching. In 1972 Hutus were massacred in Burundi, and a million Hutus left their homes and fled abroad. The genocide was systematic. The same conflagration flared up in 1973, but then it was Tutsis who died; like those before them they were victims of Hutu militias, just as today's Hutus are the victims of a Tutsi army. Tomorrow's Hutus and Tutsis risk dying as long as mutilated children continue to ache in the missing hand or foot, suffering the loss of their missing mother or father. Tomorrow I will speak, I hope, of colours of life. I do not know if I will get to the heart of the issues that are still troubling me.

Another angle on this memory: at international gatherings a Belgian colleague repeats at every opportunity that on 30 June 1960, the Congo had 24,000 kilometers of paved roads, an enviable rail network, good health equipment, an impressive hospital infrastructure, the highest school attendance rate in Africa and the same level of development as South Africa, fifteen years ahead of Nigeria. All this is true and ought to be said. This colleague formulates the problem in terms of urgency and the immediate: the political power in the Congo cannot manage 'public affairs'. The certainty of being the bearer of truth is awesome. It is in itself violence. But one can also remember (and this represents an alternative memory) that after almost eighty years of Belgian colonization, when the 'model colony' gained its sovereignty on 30 June 1960, the Congo had only six university graduates, two of whose degrees were in psychology! Is it fair to compare the excellent achievements of the colonial system to the failures of the postcolonial period without evoking the circumstances or the context of the two periods? Inversely, the unspeakable cannot serve as a pretext to keep silent about the facts. What remains unsaid is due not to muteness, but to the fact that it raises the question how to share in a common encounter of something impossible to express, which affects the ability to make sense of what has happened. It is at this point that the believer and the nonbeliever can meet, by making this impossibility not a wall into which one runs, but a foothold to move forward in the night of significations. It is from here that the possibility of sharing and a way forward open for both.

Today, by this double denial – i.e. to keep quiet and to talk – the new generation is confronted with a debt of memory. We are all concerned with this task of restoring the truth because our wounds of memory have become a fundamental experience of our time in its distress and expectation. It is a fundamental experience because in us, acts impossible to punish or forgive have become possible. Our history can no longer be lived, nor thought of as before. Therefore, if this generation does not give in to the temptation to return to identity particularisms, it will be the one that will, for the first time, establish from catastrophes (slavery, colonization, apartheid, genocide, racism, etc.) a language worthy of our modernity, if we define the latter as Anette Wieviorka recently wrote in *Déportation et génocide*: 'Modernity is characterized by the fact that identity breaks away from the group, is no longer the initial given based on some simple elements, but a personal construct, aleatory, evolving and complex' (1992: 332). More than ever, the initial is exposed to the aleatory of the meeting with the neighbour and to the surprise of its otherness.

Be that as it may, Benoît Verhaegen (1966) retains the notion of 'crisis' to analyze the reality of contemporary Congolese society. Indeed, the history of the country is unique: political independence on 30 June 1960, followed by army mutinies, the parachuting of Belgian troops, Katanga's secession and then Kasaï's, and intervention of United Nations troops; the mysterious death of the UN Secretary General Dag Hammarskjöld, the arrest and assassination of

Lumumba, Mulele's rebellions, two coups d'état by Mobutu, two wars in Shaba, and temporary seizure of Moba by pro-Kabila troops; the democratization process, a long and incomplete transition, and a student massacre in Lubumbashi; embargo by the international community, Mobutu's expulsion of all Belgian cooperation experts, closure of all Belgian consulates in Eastern Zaire, and lootings in Kinshasa and in major towns in the country; assassination of Burundi's democratically elected (Hutu) President Melchior Ndadaye, massacre and massive exodus of Hutus to Eastern Zaire, assassination of Presidents Habyarimana of Rwanda and Ntiamirira of Burundi, flight to Eastern Zaire of Hutu populations from Rwanda, and the death of ten Belgian blue helmets; Opération Turquoise, the 1996 war waged in the Congo by Burundian, Ugandan and Rwandan troops, and the dismantlement of Rwandan refugee camps in Eastern Zaire; the advent of the former guerilla Laurent-Désiré Kabila and the exile and death of disease-stricken Marshal Mobutu in total solitude in Morocco; a new devastating war started in August of 1998 by Burundian, Ugandan and Rwandan troops, bringing panic and desolation to the civilian population (4 million dead) in Eastern Congo; the mysterious assassination of Kabila and, against all expectations, his succession by his son Joseph Kabila, who, it is said, has no political culture and no better intellectual preparation than three months of military training in China, yet curiously is supported by all Western powers; inter-Congolese dialogue followed by a new transitional government, despite growing insecurity and attempts at destabilization by Rwanda and Uganda – and so on.

In opening his chronicle *L'Odyssée Kabila: Trajectoire pour un nouveau Congo,* the Belgian Jean-Claude Willame, a former lecturer at the University of Lubumbashi in Katanga, offers a remarkable hypothesis on the Congo, provocative, but at the same time amusing: he sees some sort of 'return to the heart of darkness', to 'primitiveness', a curse (1999: 97). Obviously, many Africanists compare the postcolonial and colonial periods and find reasons to deplore the former and prefer the latter. The 1960s thus mark the end of 'civilization' and the return to/of darkness. The task may seem relatively easy. For a view that is not blurred by an ideology (regardless of its hue), this 'dialectic' evolution seems evident. The 'thesis': colonization or paradise is followed by the 'antithesis': independence or return to primitiveness.

Yet it is neither a predilection for darkness nor the fatalism of misfortune that Congolese reality brings, but an invading clairvoyance. This reality takes us beyond simplistic distinctions. Congolese history has not completed a circle since independence. There has been no return to the starting point, even if Congolese have somehow reclaimed the years of forgotten colonization and its rhetoric. In all likelihood, some Congolese reckon that they lived better under colonization. However, this does not mean that they were living a happier life but rather that under colonization (in comparison with the present), they enjoyed greater economic and social security and understood reality better. The world was so simple then. At the same time, though, most thought that it was worth changing the regime. This proves that the symbolic and spiritual values of change, after all, are still appreciated. The majority do not let themselves be fascinated by ideological simplifications offered by politicians and the media. They use multiple criteria to judge yesterday and today, and they do not confuse the present reality with yesterday's colonization. In the final analysis it is not a choice between victim and culprit, between damage incurred or wrong done: the stakes lie elsewhere. How does one speak in such a way that transmission is not traumatizing for the next generation? Indeed, there usually is, in every one of us, an imaginary identification with the other and his/her capacity to support transmission. Therefore, in the name of happiness supposedly to be safeguarded, one will rather choose compromise solutions. Is it not worth knowing how to get rid of certain memories in order to retain only good ones?

From this point of view, Congolese history of the past forty years has moved not in a circle but rather in a spiral. The opinion that is favourable to colonization cannot be ascribed to a 'bad information policy' of the education system, nor to the failing memory of the people who might have forgotten everything. They have forgotten nothing. They have rather, apart from a certain idealization typical of all memories, even those about a tragedy, moved the focus to new problems that have become topical: the drop in real incomes, wars, the uncertainty of the country itself, life, and the future. They can understand neither colonization nor the vicissitudes of the African postcolonial situation if they wish to forget that colonization derived its strength from the fact that it not only was imposed by the 'clamour' of bombs, which implies terror, but also was a response to certain popular aspirations, as the African novel of the 1960s suggests (Kane 1961; Mbembe 1988).

In a peroration of his own odyssey, Willame (1999), trying to understand 'the meaning of the trajectory',[1] uncovers the demise (and even the disappearance) of the Zairean state, which he traces to the collapse of the Kamoto mine in April 1990. He links this event to the rout of Mobutu's, then Kabila's armies, as well as to the protests against the currency. He observes the 'disinterest, the retreat of Western powers in this Central African region' (Willame 1999: 231). Yet the United Nations commission that investigated the looting of natural resources in the Congo observed that the loot went mainly to Germany, Belgium, the United States and Great Britain (see Bond 2002; Lutundula 2006; Nations Unies 2001). What should one think of this? The Congo apparently reaps misfortune from its own fortune. But facts are stubborn, and history does not obey the trajectory of our pen. Can one really believe that the Belgian colonial intervention in the Congo was merely a simple parenthesis, or as Bogumil Jewsiewicki aptly remarks (1995: 61), 'an interlude between the precolonial past and the postcolonial present'? It is through such stories, often widely publicized by the media, that the Belgian collective imaginary and a narrative identity are constructed, that most Westerners are informed about events in Central Africa.

Almost all historians recognize the presence of populations of Rwandan origin in mountainous Kivu well before independence. In *Banyarwanda et Banyamulenge* (1997), Jean-Claude Willame, a good historian, brilliantly highlights the causes and stages of migratory movements of these populations from the colonial period. The aim of the migration into Northern Kivu was firstly to remedy overpopulation in Rwanda and secondly to provide cheap labour to the Congolese economy. From 1949 to 1953, famine in Rwanda caused the influx of new Rwandan immigrants towards Masisi. From 1959 to 1961, the Rwandan ethnic massacres provoked another massive wave towards Northern Kivu. There have also been many illegal immigrants. As can be noticed, the label 'Banyamulenge', as applied to all these Rwandan people who settled in the Congo, bends the truth and is far from reality: alongside the Banyamulenge (inhabitants of the high plateau of Mulenge)[2] of Southern Kivu, there are other Rwandan migrants in the Congo (including refugees and illegal immigrants). The Banyamulenge, according to Willame (1997), gave themselves this label to distinguish themselves from Tutsi political refugees. By 1955, an area of 350 square kilometers allocated in Masisi to people from Rwanda became saturated. In 1959, these immigrants disposed of a territory of 1,500 hectares. On the other hand, we should not think that there is homogeneity or harmony among these groups of Rwandan origin. Recent history has revealed that the Banyarwanda of Northern Kivu have always enjoyed more political and economic advantages than the Banyamulenge of Southern Kivu. Increasingly, the latter are the first to complain. Hence one of the problems that analysts have not highlighted: failing to determine who is Congolese, one could ask who is Munyamulenge?

In December 1997, at a meeting of Friends of the Congo (Amis du Congo) to discuss the costs of reconstruction, Colette Braeckman, while interviewing Bizima Karaha, former minister of foreign affairs in Laurent-Désiré Kabila's government, asked him about his origin. He replied: 'I am from the territory [*commune*] of Tanganyika.' This answer can only reinforce doubts and skepticism among other Congolese, since at the time this territory did not yet exist in the political-administrative configuration or nomenclature of the country. Willame (1997) observes, without much detail, that the present Rwandan ambassador to Belgium is a former Zairean representative in an international organization in Geneva. Braeckman (1996) points out that Bisengimana Rwema, a Rwandan immigrant, was Mobutu's chief of staff for twelve years.

According to both analysts, shortage of land resulted in ethnic tensions in Kivu. Following Willame, Tsongo Mafikiri (1996: 46) thinks that dualism – due to the coexistence between customary practices and modern laws – engenders insecurity (cf. Laurent et al. 1997). According to him, after independence, colonial land legislation was abolished and various special organizations, notably the Special Kivu Committee (*Comité spécial du Kivu*), dissolved. The author alleges that the insufficiency of land, compounded by the grabbing of pasture in Masisi and Kalehe by Tutsi immigrant families, caused discontent among the indigenous population (Mafikiri 1996: 42–78).

Hence the persistence of the culturalist thesis, or the identity prism, according to which conflicts in Kivu are explained by ethnic resurgences. There are numerous representatives of this thesis: Willame (1997, 1999), Mafikiri (1996), Mugangu (2003), Braeckman (1996), Reyntjens (1994), Marysse and Reyntjens (1996–1997), and many others. What appears here is a stereotyping of specific features of the Hamitic people to produce the handsome, tall, intelligent Tutsi shepherd, who landed in the Great Lakes region in search of good pasture and whom the indigenous population, i.e. the Bantu, envy. Unknowingly, analysts of the Great Lakes region divide different tribal groups in the Congo into two groups: on the one hand are the Bantu, labeled 'indigenous'; on the other are Tutsis of Rwandan origin who are given many labels – 'imported populations', 'newcomers', 'foreigners'. The allochthonous term thus loses its extended meaning and no longer includes other Rwandan Hutu groups. This hypothesis does not take into consideration tensions that exist among other tribal groups in Kivu, notably between the Bashi and the Barega in their struggle for political power. Before the 1996 war that ended with the advent of Laurent-Désiré Kabila as head of state, Bashi and Barega leaders were meeting regularly to calm the tensions. Is it not worth meditating over L. Monnier's[3] thesis that power outclasses ethnicity?

Colette Braeckman is the only (Western) journalist who has highlighted the tragedy of Kasaï people in Katanga since the colonial period, and then in 1992 – to the indifference of so-called 'civilized' states and their media. She goes to the source of the violence and rightly draws our attention to 'classifications' and 'labels' used by the colonizer to depict these colonized people. Courageously she remarks that 'Belgium for a long time projected on Rwanda and Burundi its own passions: all along the conflicts between Hutus and Tutsis, it obstinately reads fragments of its own history' (Braeckman 1996: 10). But the *Soir*'s journalist herself falls prey to the very categorization she rejects. Speaking of populations of Rwandan origin in opposition to Congolese indigenous populations which she calls 'local' or 'indigenous', she writes (1996: 244):

> On the ground, Banyarwanda, thanks to their dynamism, have outclassed the local people. Vast and flourishing pasturelands of Tutsi shepherds arouse the envy of all and their children who successfully enter school or business also arouse envy. The Hutus, on the other hand, happen to be excellent farmers and farm workers in tea, coffee, and pyrethrum plantations.

Is the manner in which she refers to Kasaï people not paramount to making of them the equivalent of the Tutsis in the Congo? Certain terms applied to 'imported' populations are reused here (Braeckman 1996: 223):

> The Baluba from Kasaï are fairly successful. They seize the opportunity offered by colonization, send their children to white schools and convert en masse. Foremen and team leaders, but also employees, catechists, teachers, they became the first

relays of the Western culture. In mineral-rich Katanga, they quickly outclassed the local populations and even won the 1958 elections! Their social ascendancy obviously arouses envy.

On reading these texts about the Great Lakes people, one cannot but be struck by the inflation of epithets. This frantic need for epithets is evidence of the untimely, embarrassing presence of a journalist who prevents any freedom of decoding and, thus, buries words under their meaning. The expression used is now decoded merely as convention, rhetoric, form. The adjective is always expressive for Blackman, never representative. The journalist substitutes adjectives of subjective appreciation for adjectives of objective description. She exerts everywhere a despotic power on representation, constraining her readership to perceiving it only through the filter of her judgment and appreciation. The text thus evolves according to a Hutu-Tutsi bipolarization, with the positive and favourable a priori for the Tutsi while the Hutu appear as the evil of the Old Testament. One is thus led to a very expressionistic rhetoric of emotion where it is important that the feelings come out in a spectacular fashion. But here the phenomenon of reversal occurs: the superlativism is so caricatural that it discredits itself and, having become a cliché, allows itself to be read as 'rhetoric'. The narrative process transforms itself into a voice whose statement, devoid of its origin, acquires the autonomy of a rumour. The distance between speaker and hearer having being not consolidated but leveled, the levels of statement and reception are the same. In a technical structure, which is at the same time an ideological structure, this levelling is the result of a simulating and dissimulating writing. Information becomes disinformation and propaganda in defiance of and beyond reality.

There is continuity in the perception of the Great Lakes people and in the disfiguring mirror through which they will see themselves. Marie Gevers (1953: 81–87) spontaneously discovered this Great Lakes region – Rwanda and Burundi and part of Kivu (Bukavu and its surroundings) – on a visit to her children (See Bisanswa 2001). She observed the customs and traditional lifestyle of these people and interpreted dances of the Hutu, Tutsi and Twa. She described the Twa's dance (1953: 82) as miming an elephant hunt, and wrote of the 'hoe dance, performed by the Bahutu farmers' dressed in banana leaves:

> They dance without music. Only the hammering of their feet in the dust rhythms their progress. It seems that hits in the ground coincide with hits of the bare heel. The interval between hits is unique, too. It provokes in the audience some sort of anxiety. Does the rhythm correspond too much or too little to that of the human heart?

From a so-called ethnological distinction of the dance or demeanour of the three Rwanda's ethnic groups, Gevers is interested in the type of social link among what she called the 'three races'. More than social relationships, it is the endorsement of social roles that retains her attention. She attempts to show a division of the Rwandan society. But the barriers that are assumed to divide the three groups into three races in reality define race itself and place the observer and the whole of the colonial world in the position of an outsider. The experience proposed by Gevers of differences in dance or demeanour, of the mythical origin of Tutsis, is inherent in a mental attitude that she wrongly ascribes to certain members of the group and that actually characterizes her own perception of things. At times Gevers is fascinated by the 'elegant Tutsis', as Braeckman will be, much later. Their depictions of these 'imported' people of Rwandan origin – I borrow the phrase from Braeckman – in the Congo, or Balubas of Kasaï, give the impression of flying above the real, in company of gods and heroes of African legends.

A guest of Mgr Léon-Paul Classe, Apostolic Delegate to Rwanda, in 1939, Canon Louis de Lacger regards the Tutsis as the 'newcomers' of 'Caucasian type' characterized by an innate sense of commandment, like 'the Roman of Virgil'—the imagery speaks for itself—that they impose on 'simple' and 'semi-civilized' people, the Hutus and Batwas (De Lacger 1939: 56). Josias Semu-janga, of the University of Montreal, has shown that Alexis Kagame, repeating the Hamite myth, locates the origins of the Tutsis in Ethiopia (1996: 165). Conversely, for Filip Reyntjens, the Hutu is the eternal oppressed who ought to free him/herself (1994: 21, 131–132). (Even in the subsequent trading of insults between Reyntjens and Goyvaerts, the ethnic undertone remains, the former calling the latter a 'Flemish Tutsi').

One finds variations of the same ethnicist vision from one country to an-other. In the Congo, by recognizing the economic power of these 'newcomers', they make of the Munyamulenge the eternal oppressed to whom Congolese citizenship is denied and who must free themselves through armed struggle. Thus do analysts explain the so-called 'liberation wars' that started in Kivu in 1996 and 1998. Willame (1999), Braeckman (1996, 1999) and others call them rebellions[4] but add that these were supported by Rwanda, Uganda and Burundi to 'secure the borders' of these countries. In the meantime, all recog-nize that Rwandan, Ugandan and Burundian troops intervened in the Congo to dismantle Hutu refugee camps that were threatening the internal security of Rwanda. Willame (1999) writes that General Kagame acknowledged, on his trip to New York in August 1996, that war was inevitable in Kivu. The fact is that the war was made possible with the approval of Western powers. No one mentions that it ought to have been endorsed by the United Nations, which had been spending a million dollars per day since 1994 on behalf of Rwandan Hutu refugees. There were telltale signs: for instance, the closure of the Peace Corps Centre in Bukavu where American volunteers, officially, learned French before being deployed in African francophone countries. The official reason given was the breakdown of relations with Marshal Mobutu's regime, which the US government continued to support behind the scenes. At the same time, in June of 1996 the latter urged its citizens, including missionaries, to leave Kivu before 15 August, for security reasons!

In any case, when the war started in Uvira, no Western country condemned it. Western media, as the war raged in Lemera, spoke of a liberation war led by 'redoutable Banyamulenge warriors' (of whom Laurent-Désiré Kabila was the spokesman) in order to claim Zairean citizenship. That the trajectory of the war followed the geographic situation of Rwandan Hutu refugees raised no one's curiosity. Willame (1999: 41) notes judiciously that 'the Rwandan propaganda, relayed by Western press, credits the thesis of a rebellion undertaken by Banyamulenge, therefore Zaireans'.

Our time is a time of the loudspeaker and propaganda, and the life of the spirit is constantly falsified. Muller Ruhimbika, leader of the Milima Group (*Groupe Milima*), a nongovernmental organization grouping Banyamulenge, was the star of the moment. He was interviewed by all Western radio stations broadcasting to Africa. Only when the war got closer to Bukavu did these newscasts start speaking of an alliance of democratic forces for the liberation of Congo-Zaire whose declared objective was to end the dictatorship of Mobutu – who was in hospital in Switzerland! Nothing was said about this alliance or about those who constituted it. Kabila, surrounded by APR (Rwandan Patriotic Army) bodyguards, in Rwandan army Land Cruisers, appeared and spoke for the first time after the fall of Bukavu. A big city had fallen, without much resistance, and the war had to be justified to the jubilant audience in Kivu, who nonetheless was still shocked by the thousands of deaths and reticent about the presence of the Rwandan and Ugandan armies as well as mercenaries from Somalia, Eritrea and Ethiopia. In reality, Laurent-Désiré Kabila, (presented by Mwalimu Julius Nyerere, a champion of African socialism whose negative role in the region has not been yet discussed and analyzed[5]), ignored the true motivations of the war and had his own idea: power at all costs.

Kabila's odyssey is the fable of 'the biter is sometimes bitten'. His backers wanted to use him like a broom to justify the war in Zaire, but it was he who used it as an instrument. Against all expectations of the initiators of the war, he proclaimed himself head of state of the Republic of Zaire, which on 17 May 1997 he renamed the 'Democratic Republic of Congo'. Against the wishes of Zaireans (democratization, economic development, sovereignty), he protected the interests of Rwandan and Ugandan regimes. Were these only economic interests, or was there a commitment about ceding land in Kivu to Rwandans? Laurent-Désiré Kabila is gone, with his secrets, since 16 January 2001 when he was assassinated. Can we believe this rumour, which spread in Kivu in January of 1997, according to which the Rwandan army held him prisoner in Goma for some time, forcing him to sign a document by which he ceded Kivu to Rwanda through the Banyamulenge? The fact is that a week after this rumour, Kabila moved his headquarters to Kisangani.

However, in this region of Africa, as is the case elsewhere, rumours become truths and the scholar often surmises the point of view of the street based on conjectures and calculations. Like the famous Lemera accord! In the 1996 war Rwandan troops occupied the whole of Kivu. Had they not disbanded the Interahamwes (groups of young Hutu males who carried out genocide acts against Tutsis) and ex-FARs (Armed Forces of Rwanda) who had taken refuge after having committed the odious genocide? On 2 August 1998, trying to get rid of Kabila, who had become 'unmanageable', Rwanda, as in 1996, performed its exploit anew with the complicity of Congolese. But the context had changed: Mobutu, the common enemy, was gone. The population had not yet finished counting and mourning all its 1996 war dead. It was hard to believe that the Banyamulenge had rebelled because their security had been threatened following the return of the Rwandan army. The big losers were Banyamulenge, many of whom were removed from offices they had occupied since their easy victory of 1996. Some, such as Muller Ruhimbika, the spokesman of the liberation wars, took refuge in the West.

It is worth observing at this stage that in 1990, with the first FPR (Rwandan Patriotic Front) offensive against the Habyarimana regime, the regional geopolitics changed the image and identity representations of mountainous Kivu (Bisanswa 1999: 621–627). The FPR guerilllas were at the gates of Habyarimana's presidential palace when Mobutu sent troops of his special presidential division, commanded by General Mahele, to rout them. Many Rwandan and rwandophone families who were living in Zaire contributed to the FPR war, either financially or by sending their children to fight for the FPR. Tensions grew between indigenous communities and immigrant populations, the former accusing the latter of housing arms and ammunition caches and facilitating the infiltration of the FPR army in Zairean territory to attack Rwanda. Many young Banyamulenge enrolled in the FPR. When the latter took power, Banyamulenge families returned to Rwanda massively. Could they have left as a result of the exodus of Hutu populations to Kivu? In 1990, when the FPR military offensive for power began, the Hutu populations were still in Rwanda. Many Banyamulenge tore up their Zairean identity cards at the border, after having sold all their property.

What were the stakes of their alliance with the Tutsis of Rwanda? Back in Rwanda after the FPR victory, the Banyamulenge returned to Zaire in 1996 at the start of the APR war against Hutu refugee camps. All belonged to the victors, who proceeded with the looting of real estate and movables, seizure of posts across all the sectors, assassination attempts on traditional chiefs to replace them with Rwandans (Banyamulenge?), harassment of Kivu businessmen suspected of having collaborated with Hutu businessmen, legal proceedings including the recovery of properties sold to Zaireans when their owners were returning to Rwanda, victimization and violence (caning, spitting) against the indigenous inhabitants for minor misdemeanours, destruction of infrastructure, and loss of human lives. The 1998 war further isolated the Banyamulenge from other Kivu social groups, and then from the Congo, in accordance with the saying 'If you are not with me you are against me'.

Willame rightly notes (1999: 191) Colette Braeckman's bias in present-ing 'Laurent-Désiré Kabila's epic' in a favourable light in *Le Soir*. The gang of Bugera, Karaha and Masasu is presented as a new generation of Congolese politicians, patriotic and with integrity, who have broken away from politi-cians of the Mobutu regime. The fact is that, as long as Kabila was the ally of the Rwandans and the Ugandans, they could understand his acts, even with-out approving of them. The same applies to Western propaganda about Joseph Kabila, presented as the Messiah (his mother was from Wamaza in Maniema, it is said) that the Congo was expecting. But this *a priori* characterization in no way translates the Congolese social reality. It does not even reflect it. On the contrary, it muzzles it and rubs off its paradoxes and its contradictions. It merely invents a new order, reflecting the space of its own phantasms, which denies the real or transforms it in a rhetorical victory. The agony of today's Congolese is the agony of Tantalus: they are hungry in their own country, despite over-flowing granaries. They are condemned to roaming to feed themselves, while foreigners are drunk on milk and honey in the Congo.

The conclusion is clear: although better equipped than anyone else to understand and explain the realities of the Congo, Rwanda and Burundi in view of the traditional ideologies to which they relate, Gauthier de Villers (1996, 1999), Jean-Claude Willame (1997, 1999), Colette Braeckman (1996), Filip Reyntjens (1994), Marysse and Reyntjens (1996–1997) and their disciples fail to do so. For them, the profound meaning of the realities is beyond dialectic illusions, in the categorical willingness to help create a reality that has never existed. The apparent paradox of their essays is that they have brought a non-existent reality to fame by describing a middle ground between conscience and things, heavy like things and fascinating for our conscience. Their think-ing appears to rebel against this milieu, but understands it as an invitation to start the disheartening world all over again *ex nihilo*. For them, hope is reduced to mathematical formulas and the human condition to statistics. The illusory trajectory of the destiny of men and countries has paled to electronic plot-ting. The historian, the poet, the journalist are men of the word and of real-life experiences; we should not ask them to think about the historical totality *objectively*.

The way in which analysts like Willame and Braeckman construct the his-tory of the region is problematic because they do not distinguish clearly be-tween fact and interpretation. 'Facts' in themselves are not conclusive. They are ambiguous and in need of interpretation. It is when this interpretation is pre-sented as the 'truth' of history that it becomes misleading. Reality in this sense is a constructed reality. An inability to recognize this results in explanations that are just not credible, like the idea that the occupation of a large part of a country by armies from neighbouring countries, resulting in panic and terror, can be justified for reasons of so-called security.

The way in which memories of the past are treated is therefore not a matter of indifference. Remembering means the creation of a certain kind of reality in the present, a certain kind of self-understanding that can either hinder or facilitate the transition to the future. This is precisely why the analyses of Willame and Breackmann can harm peaceful coexistence between Banyamulenge and other groups in Congo instead of serving it.

Indeed, on this trajectory that should have led themselves from the imaginary to the symbolic, the Munyamulenge keep finding themselves and, thus, keep getting lost. Despite their aspiration to be part of the building of their fatherland (the Congo), they continually run into a fallacious image of themselves. They want to be Congolese, like others, but think that they are Tutsi first. Here begins a tragic misunderstanding between themselves and other Congolese. The Munyamulenge, perceiving him/herself as a dual being, wants in the final analysis to meet his/her own double, which we know can only be a mild or caricatural form of his/her own personality. The metaphor of the subject thus breaks into a series of fragments, of metonymic attributes. This makes him/her appear strange, even a stranger in and against his/her own country, praying in a church that is attended by no Congolese of any other tribe! Hence there persists this elusive character, wavering and ambiguous, that their countrymen assign to the Munyamulenge.

Here we are at the beginning of a myth and well into a magical and fairy-tale universe of African tales. From the logic of metonymy, we move to the logic of metaphor. This passage from metonymy to metaphor is completed in an oxymoron through the designation 'Congolese Tutsi', by which a person states his/her own spatiality as an expression of a growing tension in an attempt to solve contradictory extremes, and by which the making of a proper name into an adjective dissolves a national identity into an ethnic identity. The proper name, according to Michel de Certeau (1975), gives meaning to space. The name 'Congolese Tutsi' states a *before* and *after* – in sum, two memories – and the Munyamulenge is defined in relation to a referent (the Tutsi). In this way, s/he entertains an ambiguous relation, at the whim of circumstances and interests, with Tutsis and with the Congo. S/he is thus caught in a trap of two alternatives of which s/he is not the producer. S/he is rather an expiatory victim, consenting or resistant. S/he has even, since 1996, tightened the gaps of the trap.

As can be seen, various debates on African memory have aimed to anchor African history in a location that restates its specificity and its interactions: the origin (*unde?*), the proper location (*ubi?*) and the destination (*quo?*). But a reading of memory as crossing (*qua?*) initiates a new perspective. The quest therefore becomes one of the *crossing* of memory: where, by what, with what essential facts and what transfer and paradoxical effects does it articulate its plans (textual, sexual, ontophanic, ethical, political, historical, esthetic)? Reading in terms of *crossing* is based on the conviction that the much discussed question of origin (*unde?*) of memory is an impasse: the origin is often a projected anterior that is no longer the subject of questioning, but of an arbitrary response.

The Belgian colonial administration, Mobutu, Kabila Sr and Kabila Jr often explained the present situation in the Congo by reference to its past. Colonization meant in fact the beginning of the history of the Congo, because all that preceded it had to be wiped out. 'All was to be done again', it was always said. The colonizers explained their actions on humanistic grounds, with reference to the barbaric past of these 'tribes' who were killing one another. On independence day, Lumumba declared in his speech, which was not scheduled by protocol, that 'all was to be done again' after almost eighty years of Belgian colonization. Mobutu preached recourse to authenticity in order to distance Congolese from an assumed culture inherited from colonization. He renamed the country, the river and the currency. He justified his totalitarian power by reference to post-independence 'chaos'. Kabila followed the same line. He explained his dictatorship by saying that Mobutism had liquefied the state. He too changed the name of the country, the river and the currency. The national anthem 'Arise, Congolese' (Debout Congolais) was returned to its past glory. Dignitaries of the former regime were imprisoned. But on the day Kabila was sworn in as president of the Democratic Republic of Congo in Kinshasa, the students who had gathered at the Stadium of Martyrs sang the old national anthem of the Mobutu era, 'The Zaïroise'. They were alluding to the conviction that Kabila had sold out his country, which had become an object of exploitation by neighbouring countries (Rwanda, Burundi, Uganda, Angola) – in contrast to the Mobutu era, which in spite of its economic failure had maintained national integrity.

One has the impression, every so often, of a *new beginning,* with all the difficulties and uncertainties that birth implies. This sentiment is echoed by ordinary Congolese citizens: 'Everything is rotten, we must start afresh.' The beginning thus understood is often chronological instead of being an intensive beginning. The German language distinguishes between these two meanings of 'beginning' by using two verbs: *beginnen* would be an extended chronological beginning; *anfangen* an intensive beginning. Contained in *anfangen* is the verb *fangen,* which means to catch, to seize in a movement. *Anfangen* could thus mean a beginning that seizes an opportunity, catching something that occurs in a given history in a swift span of time where the *not yet* and the *never again* cancel each other out. When, for example, the renewal of the Congolese civil society and the beginning of a new political era were being mentioned, what was caught on the rebound? What was not caught?

Since 2002, at the end of the inter-Congolese dialogue, Congolese civil society has taken part in political decision-making. The country's economic situation is far from improving, and corruption and selfishness among the leaders is on the increase. Civil society leaders, who fought against what has been called the criminalization of the postcolonial state, were fighting, in fact, solely against their own marginalization from the affairs of the state. In a thousand ways, they have inherited the imaginary that they once fought in one of its manifestations. Often what they aimed at was only a swapping of roles in the same scenario. They used to speak on behalf of a civil society, but they were expressing only the thinking and not the movement itself. Any opposition accepts the risk of destroying the movement that it wants to redress. If it did not, no organization would ever redress its policy. How, then, can the fugitive temporality be caught and seized? How can the birth of events be seized and caught, not any more at the poles – white and black, colonizer and colonized, Belgium and the Congo, Africa and the West, Kabila and Mobutu, state and civil society – but in the crossing of these and other instances, such as subjectivity and transcendence? This is, I thought, reversing the critical perspective and militating in favour of auto-reflexivity, thanks to which critique becomes an arrow aimed at a subject with the idea of backfiring, which is pure chiasm in terms of the model of Adorno's negative dialectic. With the crossing, mediation, the rift, the in-between and hesitation enlighten the origin, because if the crossing is missed, the origin and finality have no meaning any longer.

Congolese live today with the split of belongings and the multiplicity of locations. The memory of the crossing is persuaded that they will never 'find again' the supposed 'Congolese authentic purity', the semblance of paradise of the colonial period, nor the apparent peace of which Mobutu used to boast. It favours not locations than can be assigned, but non-locations, interstitial spaces, transient displacements, the mobility of crossings and the fugacity of the event. The discourse of the crossing is cautious: it does not know where the sense is, but can indicate the impossible non-location where it sways. It is conscious that it does not dispose of firm ground, but of a territory that slips away. It is a stuttering that wonders how to outline what is not yet legible and, especially what, in the present history of Congo, are zones of bifurcation, retention, test and tension. It is a tale that no longer says 'In Congo, once upon a time', but rather 'In Congo, today'. The crossing does not work with the '*quid*' (what a thing is, what if means), but with the event, for 'that it occurs' (*quod*) comes before knowing 'what' (*quid*) occurs. The question of occurrence precedes here that of identity and essence.

The memory of the crossing is articulated in critiques and interrogations. In this perspective, we can reflect on the fatal dilly-dallying of the national sovereign convention. On this occasion, the (Congolese) Zairean society discovered what it was recovering, exposing openly its contradictions, uncovering its actors and testing its founding images. This memorable national sovereign convention was a vast forum of debates broadcast on television. The task consisted in writing up new rules of the advent of a new democratic order in Africa. The first act was to suspend the existing state constitution. Mobutu's regime was loathed. Corruption, economic criminality, assassinations and political patronage were castigated. From the 'national sovereign convention', a new democratic era in Zaire was ushered in with a comprehensive political agreement, which was to rule the transition period. Tshisekedi was elected prime minister. It was a mirage. This convention was supposed to represent an 'inaugural moment' (as if the word had not existed in Zaire before this gathering), but its participants forgot to dissociate politics from sense. The people's delegates rushed, like flies on carrion, to share managerial posts in the post-Mobutu era, and Mobutu blew the whistle for the end of the game.

The liberation of the word produced 'palaver' instead. Discussions on sense, on *living-together* and on the notion of community were suffocated by procedural quarrel about voting, the sharing of power, the future constitution, the status of new leaders and the fate reserved for their predecessors. In this cacophony, public opinion became an anonymous 'someone'. As soon as politics and sense are dissociated, and especially when the political debate turns on elections (of chambers, chanceries), there is a slip towards a subtle depolitization. The sidestepping of this question of sense gave a very consensual orientation to this debate, which aimed to be pluralistic and democratic. A 'pathos of the politic' was missing, whose role would have been to analyze mechanisms of mobilization and the main political passions. National conventions dealt with the effectiveness of power, not its affectivity. Political analysts of 'national conferences' did not feel concerned by passions during these conferences.

How could political passions, emotions and collective sentiments be put in place? What affective dispositions were motivated in the implosion of such or such regime in Africa? And why were dictatorial regimes (of Presidents Kérékou in Benin and Ratsiraka in Madagascar) that had been swept aside years earlier brought back into office by the same people who had ousted them? A Manichaean analysis of the politic in Africa cannot answer this question. The Cameroonian philosopher Jean-Godefroy Bidima (1997) invites us to turn to African palaver. For him, palaver, this politics of the word, a vigorous discussion that through discourse suspends the violence in a conflict, is an example of African politics, which today expresses the not-yet and by the same token remains very present. How is this traditional practice of conflict resolution useful today?

Africa knows a contradictory movement linked to the notion of conflict. On this continent, killings in Rwanda, Burundi and the Democratic Republic of Congo show every day the existence of the disaster and the unspeakable in it. Yet on the same continent, reconciliation tends the wounds of apartheid in South Africa. Through conflict and reconciliation, a normative problem emerges: in the wrong done or suffered, how do we give redress? Is forgiveness enough for reparation? Is the airing of the wrong a condition for reconciliation? In choosing to set not a tribunal, but a platform (the Truth and Reconciliation Commission), South Africa raised a moral problem with obvious legal stakes. Should we, in reparation in penal matters, discard the aspect of punishment to favour only public airing? Kagame's Rwanda, after the genocide, preferred, under the pretext of justice, the cycle of vengeance without end: Tutsis against Hutus, even in foreign territory where the Hutus had found refuge.

How is reparation without punishment possible? Can we forgive without conditions? Is the request for forgiveness the only precondition to forgiveness, or must we forgive exactly where it is impossible to forgive? The impossibility of forgiving seems to be the very condition of forgiveness: such is the lesson that South Africa seems to have given to the whole world through this platform. Of course, not all was solved, and the commission met with resistance and experienced failures that are still nascent. In contrast, by dealing with the genocide as an indelible event, as a decisive test of one's intentions and a spontaneous choice of the whole future of Rwanda and all its peoples, the Rwandan regime would like to presuppose that political questions can and must be posed and resolved in an instant. It must happen without flashback or recall that will require a face-to-face meeting with the unique, thereby uniting forever what seemed separable, opposes what was only the other.

For this new regime, the three meanings of the word order overlap. It is an order that brings order and that gives orders. Thus the whole social fabric becomes fragile like glass. The whole history becomes a duel without pauses, without inadvertences, without hazards, without the accusing stare of the moral imperative. If we think of the dynamics in which the Kagame regime is involved, we would think that the action of a government is a series of strikes by which it defends itself against death. But it would thus only be convulsions. If there is action, one must invoke inquiry, facts, a discussion (even if only with oneself), arguments, a preference for this over that. Who will judge the true line, the true situation, the true history? No one, that is, with the ethnic group as a laboratory of history, elucidation of the present, by oneself, becomes truth. We are thus at the end of realism: as we reason under the category of pure facts, political time is atomized into a series of decisions in the presence of death.

The memory of the crossing rejects the nostalgia of identity issues because the past is the non-achieved whose possibilities are about to hatch. The crossing is not a return to the past but a detour through the past towards the future. This supposes a process that favours transient movements. The crossing wants to be a gap always open, thereby rejecting both a neurotic or demanding approach and dissolution in a smug universalism. It is the opening of the sides, dilatation of partitions, outflow of pores, connection of seams and crossing of frontiers. With the non-achieved, Congolese memory changes. The paramount chiefs, the triumphs and the appointments kept, are not important. What counts are all the absences and appointments missed by Congolese history. To articulate Congolese history implies describing its silent contour in the past/present. It is to restore missing links that express themselves (without being heard) not in what is said, but in the half-said and the not-yet said. In the memory of the crossing, the important thing is not what Congolese space has been, nor what colonization, the state and the market have made of it, but how it enables the opening of the subject to the possible. What are 'favourable spaces' by which the possible can occur in the Congo?

After the Rwandan and Burundian genocides and the massacres in Congo-Kinshasa, black African thinking is being put to the test for wrongdoing and it is this that will lead African memory to submit this wrong to the test of thought in order not to understand it (from what categories?) nor to explain it (with what reasoning?), but to question it without expecting any answer. Should we state, like Adorno (1978: 287) on Auschwitz, that genocides prove the failure of culture? In African discourses, nothing will ever be as it was in the past, and it is the whole of African education that should realize the presence of the monstrosity in itself. Education, Adorno (1984: 207) believed, would have a meaning (after the catastrophe) only if it led to a critical reflexion on oneself. Black African memory has questioned slavery, colonization, and apartheid. This dolorous and accusing tendency showed to Western humanism its ambiguities and the ruses of its discourse. Negro-African memory relied on (and had faith in) African culture and its virtues (solidarity, communutarism, honesty) to criticize this 'invented' Africa by colonial historiography and rebuild an authentic future (cf. Mudimbe 1994). We were obviously criticizing the unwieldiness of African culture. However, on the whole, this should 'found' African history and praxis. For once, inflection will be on African culture itself and not on its link with the West.

The catastrophe inaugurates self-reflection that will be this stop, this distance, this rift and this threshold where the truth of 'thought' will be to think against 'thought' itself – which itself will dress the wound. After all the complacencies on African solidarity, spiritualism and communitarianism, the thought must, after these genocides, massacres and apartheid, strangle itself by thinking against itself. With this genocide in its innards, from now on stating will be contradicting. African memory, from now on, stands at the threshold and will enter into itself only through this strangulation, this narrowing from which it exited. And if present African rhetoric, with its vanities and arrogances (development, democratization, globalization), wishes to prolong the painful silence of the cry of the suffering of the dead, the genocides of Rwanda-Burundi, massacres in Eastern Congo and apartheid are there to untie the tongue and uncover rationalizations. Any African diction during the crossing will thus run into this 'intercalary call' that will remind us of these events, and diction will always be inter-diction. Memory in Africa thus becomes the nucleus of a break. The break of an African language that articulated with assurance the event of genocide, like that of apartheid, indicates to African history a horizon devoid of the certainty of big words. How can one speak of ethics and morals of the crossing from catastrophes, separations and discontinuations?

The wish for a better life, with and for the other in institutions almost fair, at least in principle, favours the translation of *I* to (the) *other*. In an allotropic move—this crossing towards (and by) the other, this spinning around the other—any break, any irruption, any faux pas is accession to dialogue. This ethics begins with the impossible relation to the other and continues with the requirement of an understanding that does not understand. In the appreciation of wrong, there is 'wrong suffered' and 'wrong done'. Colonization and slavery were 'wrong suffered' by Africans, whereas Rwanda's and Burundi's genocides are 'wrong done'. It is the latter that must interrogate the archetypal regime that is the foundation of African cultures in an interrogation whose phrasing opens another history and whose writing and reading are no longer done at the same rhythm, nor at the rhythm of the same, but with the cadence of the different. Through the catastrophes of Rwanda, Burundi and the Congo, 'it is not a country nor a continent but the world that the cry implicates; it is not a person but all' (Jabes 1963: 51). In this movement, the words will reappear, worrying and inquiring words, devoid of their great pretense to state the meaning not understood by an African culture that no longer understands –. The true identity of the present African memory is thus to refuse any identity, to outwit any easy identification, to mistrust assignations in order to cross like a melody. The texture of this melody will be made of fulls and empties, affirmations and denials, questions and answers, answers to unasked questions, of conjectures made and quickly denied. Discourse will be caught in its impossibilities, where one will be able to read the stated, delirium and the variations of an affirmation in a move that, like life, does not expresses fixedness but espouses an ironic and fertile change.

The division is not external to political society; so long as there is desire there is division, plurality. The important thing is thus not to hide division and conflict by postulating *reconciliation around the One* (who can take the figure of national unity, of the enlightened guide, of the ruling party, of the parliamentary opposition, of the ethnic minority or majority etc.), but to acknowledge plurality, division and conflict by multiplying *procedures* of provisional suspension of conflict. This notion of procedure implies discussion, which in turn supposes that citizens act and think in public space. Such a programme can be anything but simple and unique!

African memory, examined through identity, alterity, utopian institutions and projections, reveals that finitude, non-accomplishment and crises are historical opportunities. A well-oiled tradition of a dualist understanding of African problems (traditions vs. modernity, patriarchy vs. matriarchy, whites vs. blacks, the universal vs. particularism, past vs. present, present vs. future) often forgets critical self-reflection. A critical look at a given history mistrusts dualities and the irreducibility of oppositions to favour *translations, chicanes,* these crossings and crises that establish themselves when the same meets the other. These meetings and these crossings (the same who becomes the other) often produce the *novum*. Thus, for example, from apartheid in South Africa there emerges a new legal experience where tolerance, pluralism and forgiveness prevail. 'We are from a location, we create from this location, links, but for the former and the latter to have their meaning, they must be … denied, outdated, transgressed' (Maffessoli 1997: 73). The irony that consists in transgressing and denying one's launching location transforms itself in hope, for in this move of surpassing oneself something nascent always happens.

To write memory is thus useful. Memory associates contemplation and action with a bias for things and the content of words' content. It yields objects, but it is also a means to rejoin things and return to the source of expression before it transforms in words or thoughts. Thus it makes better, in that it discharges us of the desire for revenge and false hopes, which, disappointed, turn to resentment. 'To repair the world' (in this sense, to think is also dressing the wound), to retain it for a time in the workroom of expression, is also to play with it, in a ludic way of taking it seriously. Like a mischievous and cheerful 'ludion', the historian of memory refuses to lecture: s/he tries and finds. S/he marvels once at his/her findings and redoes it, starts afresh, always at the beginning. To be happy, make happy, be caught in surprise endlessly, between words and things, at their secret meeting point, under agreed upon words, near their games. The writing of memory is a serious game and thus a matter of literature – that is, of *life;* in the way Marcel Proust understood it.

Notes

1. This is the title of the seventh and last chapter of the book.
2. Banyamulenge are neither the first nor the sole inhabitants of the Mulenge high plateau.
3. I am quoting from memory.
4. It suffices to read Verhaegen (1966) to understand the difference between the present reality in Eastern Congo and what constitutes a rebellion.
5. Having enjoyed international reputation for having given up power, on the surface, but remaining the master of the game, Mwalimu Julius Nyerere can be considered the kingmaker in the Great Lakes region. It is Nyerere who imposed Kabila on Museveni and Kagame. It is he who once more recommanded Wamba dia Wamba, Professor of History at the University of Dar-es-Salam, to coordinate the heterogeneous movement called RCD (Rally for Congolese Democracy).

Bibliography

Adorno, Th. W. 1978. *Dialectique negative.* Paris.
Adorno, Th. W. 1984. *Modèls critiques.* Paris.
Bidima, J.-G. 1997. La Palabre: Une juridiction de la parole. Paris.
Bisanswa, J.K. 1999. 'L'année 1998 en République démocratique du Congo', *Revue canadienne des études africaines* 33: 621–627.
Bisanswa, J.K. 2001. 'Le voyageur et son double', in P.S. Diop and H.J. Lüsebrink (eds), *Littératures et Sociétés africaines: Regards comparatistes et perspectives interculturelles.* Tübingen.
Bond, J. 2002. 'Les financements des projets miniers en RD', dans Emery Mukendi Wafwana et alii, *Rapport du séminaire sur la contribution du secteur minier à la reprise de l'activité économique*

congolaise, tenu au Grand Hôtel du 22 au 23 avril 2002, Kinshasa. http://www2.ifc.org/ ogmc/files/rapportsurleseminaire.pdf. Consulted on 12/12/2008.

Braeckman, C. 1996. *Terreur africaine.* Paris.

Braeckman, C. 1999. *L'enjeu congolais l'Afrique Cenrale après Mobutu.* Paris

Certeau, M. (de). 1975. *L'écriture de l'histoire.* Paris.

De Lacger, L. 1939. *Le Rwanda.* Kagbayi.

Gevers, M. 1953. *Des mille collines aux neuf volcans.* Paris.

Jabes, E. 1963. *Le livre des questions.* Paris.

Jewsiewicki, B. 1995. 'La Mémoire', in C. Coulon and D.-C. Martin (eds), *Les Afriques politiques.* Paris.

Kane, H. 1961. *L'aventure ambiguë.* Paris

Laurent, P.J., T. Mafikiri, P. Mathieu and S. Mugangu. 1997. *Conflits fonciers, relations ethniques et violences au Kivu.* Louvain-la-Neuve.

Lutundula, A. 2006. Exploitation des resources naturelles en RDC. Assemblée nationale, commission spéciale chargée de l'examen de la validité des conventions à caractères économique et financier concludes pendant les guerres de 1996–1997 et de 1998. http://www.congoline .com/documents/Rapport_Lutundula_pillage_2006.pdf. Consulted on 23.04.2003.

Maffesoli, M. 1997. *Du nomadisme: Vagabondages initiatiques.* Paris.

Mafikiri, T. 1996. 'Pratiques foncières, phénomènes informels et problèmes ethniques au Kivu (Zaïre)', in G. Villers (ed.), *Phénomènes informels et dynamiques culturelles en Afrique.* Brussels and Paris.

Marysse, S. and F. Reyntjens. 1996–1997. *L'Afrique des grands lacs.* Paris.

Mbembe, A. 1988. *Afriques indociles: christianisme, pouvoir et État en société postcoloniale.* Paris.

Mudimbe, V.Y. 1994. *The Idea of Africa.* Bloomington and London.

Mugangu, S. 2003. La gestion foncière rurale au Zaïre: réformes juridiques et pratiques foncières locales. Cas du Bushi. Brussels.

Nations Unies 2001. Conseil de sécurité, *Rapport de la mission du Conseil de sécurité dans la region des Grands Lacs,* mai. Additif, S/2001/521/add.1, 30 mai. http://www.un.org./french/docs/ sc/scmissionsfr.ttm. Consulted on 23.04.2003.

Reyntjens, F. 1994. L'Afrique des grands lacs en crise. Paris.

Semujanga, J. 1996. 'De Cham au mythe hamite dans le discours du savoir en Afrique: Le Rwanda dans le miroir de l'Europe', *Discours social/Social Discourse* 8(1–2): 157–178.

Verhaegen, B. 1966. *Rébellions au Congo.* Brussels.

Villers, G. (de). 1996. Phénomènes informels et dynamiques culturelles en Afrique. Paris.

Villers, G. (de). 1999. République Démocratique du Congo: Chronique politique d'un entre-deux-guerres Octobre 1996–Juillet 1998. Paris

Wieviorka, A. 2003. *Déportation et génocide.* Paris.

Willame, J.-C. 1997. 'Banyarwanda et banyamulenge: Violences ethniques et gestion de l'identitaire au Kivu', *Cahiers Africains,* 25. Brussels.

Willame, J.-C. 1999. *L'Odyssée Kabila: Trajectoire pour un nouveau Congo?* Paris..

CHAPTER 5

Remembering the Past, Reaching for the Future

Aspects of African Historical Memory in an International Context

MAMADOU DIAWARA

He who does not remember is chastised by the future.
(Motto on a postcard in the 'Fire and Flame'
exhibition, Essen 1994)

It has been almost a generation since Reinhart Koselleck provided us with the polemical book *Vergangene Zukunft* (1979)[1]. Eleven years later, it was published in French as *Le futur passé*. The title of this chapter echoes that of Koselleck's book, which, using anthropological terms, treats the past *as* an 'experience' and the future *as* a 'horizon of expectation'. Koselleck (1990: 11) analyzes 'a particular present' and 'its future becoming the past'. François Hartog (2003),[2] in his fine book devoted to *Régimes d'historicité,* challenges Koselleck's rather mechanical and Eurocentric reflection. Hartog takes a different approach to the distinctions between present, past and future (2003: 19). For Koselleck, historical time is the product of a tension between the field of experience and the horizon of expectations, a thesis that Hartog criticizes: 'The lesser the experience, the greater one's expectation.' Hartog accurately observes that the distance between these two domains has grown to such an extent that today it borders on a complete rupture. The future is replaced almost entirely by the present. We have entered 'a perpetual present, incomprehensible and nearly unchanging,' what the author calls 'presentism' (1996: 33, 2003: 28).[3]

One might well ask: Why consider Koselleck at all, in the context of this publication? First, because development specialists, the subject of the following pages, tend to express themselves in dichotomous terms. They differentiate

Notes for this section begin on page 101.

the present from the past and they focus on the future, their preferred goal. Like after the Second World War, during the time of the Japanese and German economic miracles, or the 'trente glorieuses', today they heed the clarion call celebrating technological progress. Second, development experts (whether they are expatriates or not), are directly or indirectly anchored in the Western presentist universe. Faithful to a socio-evolutionary model, they seek to ensure that 'developing nations' follow the path of Western-style development. They ineluctably push the 'developing nations' towards a future considered radiant, though illusory. Some African cadres and technicians act in a similar manner, often more uncritically enthusiastic about the benefits of progress than their Western colleagues.

My intention here is to document the break between development studies centred on the transformation and dynamics in the present, on the one hand, and the works of historians focused on the past, on the other. A paradox obscures the ultimate goal of development and its agents. Development aims for the future as a universal credo that all capitalists and socialists, conservatives and revolutionaries alike translate into the present (Chazan et al. 1992: 5–17; Scott 1998; Ellis 2002: 4–5).[4] A close examination of what is said and done in the swarming intellectual field of development reveals a fixation on questions of the present, and even the future, but not a word about the past, unless it is cloaked as local knowledge.

The negation of the past is obvious in the eloquent example of Lesotho, which James Ferguson has so passionately narrated (1990: 25 ff.).[5] In this admittedly extreme but real case, the World Bank experts' feasibility study of the Thabatseka project turned the country into a rural land living from subsistence production. Emigration to South Africa, one of the pillars of the local economy for generations, was intentionally obscured. The slate of the past was wiped clean.

Can one build a present with the future on the horizon but without a past? It goes without saying that present, future and past correspond to three temporalities. How can specialists of corresponding disciplinary fields, many of whom are unaware of one another, come together and contribute to a better implementation of development programmes? How can considering these issues promote an alternative configuration of questions and methods of history? There are many parties involved: development experts and anthropologists as well as historians. Let us review the liabilities dictated by their professional background and circumscribe what everyone (including the locals) should have gained.

Historians and Anthropologists in the African Disciplinary Trenches

Historians have inherited certain disciplinary divisions that they overcome only with difficulty, despite brilliant analyses that have resulted in criticism of these classifications. Our time has been reduced to the comfortable diptych of prehistory followed by history. The latter is divided into the Middle Ages, the Modern Era and the Contemporary Period, inter alia. From an African perspective, this first division has provoked stormy debates. Lacking a written tradition, Africa found itself relegated to the shelf of prehistory. The division between the colonial and the precolonial eras has also provoked substantial debate on the continent (Mudimbe and Jewsiewicki 1993). I will not revisit this issue. Instead, I will first analyze the incontestable advances of historians, then their insufficiency in view of today's challenges. I shall then turn the question over to the anthropologists.

Historians and Their Limits

It goes without saying that the notion of development is a direct result of European-African contact. This is especially evident in francophone Africa. The 'politique de mise en valeur' promoted by the French colonial government was the culmination of French metropolitan treatment of the colonies that would later be termed 'development'. Furthermore, seeking a new mission after the war, nongovernmental agencies from 1945 onwards refocused on the colonies and former colonies (Cooper 1994, 1999; Van Beusekom 2002: xix). If the concept of development has been clearly expressed in these African latitudes, one must not neglect the long history that was its result. Van Beusekom (2002: xxii; cf. note 6) insists that the concept is older than World War II. She situates it between the first and second World Wars and demonstrates convincingly that it rests on the idea of France's civilizing mission (Conklin 1997). I believe that the origin of both the concept and the will to develop characteristic of European milieus can be placed much earlier. The clear allusion of C. B. Wadström in 1794, reported by Lamine O. Sanneh, illustrates it well (1999: vii). I argue that contact with the Occident was the birthplace of the concept and practice of development. This contact with the West was sometimes celebrated, sometimes contested.

Certain historians have wanted to reduce the history of the continent of Africa to the arrival of the Europeans: before Europe, there was no history. Voices, notably those of Ade Ajayi (1969) and Cheick Anta Diop (1955, 1967), rose in a swell of debate against this myopic colonial version. But these authors threw the baby out with the bathwater in their vehement reaction, reducing the colonial period to a parenthetical comment that does not belong to authentic African history (Moniot 1995; Mudimbe et Jewsiewicki 1993; Cooper 2002: Introduction). Cooper's work (2002: 4, 14–15) sets the record straight, in the sense that he rejects the traditional pre/postcolonial division. For him, this dichotomous formula forces a choice of breaking with either colonialism or continuity. He underlines the complexity of the situation by showing that the colonial regime was certainly dominant, but not to the extent it wished, and certainly not with the efficiency it desired. The Africans upset the imperial logic (see also van Beusekom 2002).

The studies devoted to the colonial period are numerous, once one takes into consideration the relative abundance of oral and especially written documentation as well as the increased professionalization of Africanist historians. Urban history, youth history, work history, the history of development and economic history, to name only a few, are henceforth part of the curriculum (Goerg 1991). Despite the quality of these works, they are not free from gross errors. I will cite three of them.

On the subject of research on the concept and praxis of work, Gerd Spittler (2003) rightly notes that historians and anthropologists have contented themselves with the colonial period. Colonial situations were certainly analyzed, but earlier periods remained largely ignored. To this end, quality books such as those of Fall (1993) and Lakroum (1982) can be mentioned, but nothing of the same amplitude exists in either anthropology or history of the period preceding the Western colonial period.

The same conclusion emerges as far as works about irrigated colonial perimeters are concerned, particularly that of the Office du Niger. Several studies have been done in this area, but they are confined to the colonial territory between the irrigation canals, which means very little. Until the interesting work of van Beusekom (2002), the close relationship between the populations of the irrigated zone and those that live beyond it was underestimated. The relationship is not one of simple economic interdependence; it is also social and human. The objective is not simply to recognize this obvious fact, but to adequately analyze it in relation to what takes place on both sides of the canals (Diawara 2005). Once the canals had been dug and the ditches built, the societies living on the other side were no longer studied. The studies confine themselves a bit too facilely to the lands that were developed, leading to a certain degree of insularity. Therein lies one of the main reasons for historians' inability to deal with rural history. Ironically enough, historians become victims of the development policy that they study. They not only repeat but also involuntarily perpetuate the divisions desired and practised by the colonialist mindset.

'Insularity' is not an empty word, applicable only to this situation. It is a structural term, since the history of slavery is written essentially from the perspective of the continent's coasts, although, as everyone knows, slaves came from the interior (Thioub 2004; Fall 2001). How can we be content with these spaces, deemed *illegible*, which are marked by and integrated into the system of exploitation (Scott 1998: 24, also Introduction and Chap. 1)? It is as if the only sources of the history of Africa were written ones.

Stephen Ellis (2002: 7, 8) exposes the limits of African historians, arguing that they contribute to the gloom of the discipline by not dealing with contemporary history of the continent in appropriate terms. He rightly adds that the lack of contemporary history impoverishes disciplines like political science that have difficulty dealing with a subject rooted in the historicity of the continent. This argument concerns political science as much as it does development studies, which are all too often satisfied by a synchronic perspective. Ferguson (1990: 45) goes further, arguing that modern writers, by ignoring history in their reasoning, are even more guilty than the colonialists themselves. We will cite the example of the colonial ethnologist Maurice Delafosse in due course. Achille Mbembe (2002: 240) takes a step further in his critique of the relationship between the past, the present and the future in the African context. He is of the opinion that several factors have inhibited the development of concepts that might have explained the significance of the past and the present of that continent, in relationship to the future. The key factor is 'historicism', which takes two forms: 'afro-radicalism' and 'nativism', both of which lead to this impasse. Afro-radicalism calls upon Marxist and nationalist categories, while nativism exalts the idea of a single African identity based upon 'race'. Both of these lines of thought have appropriated and, as it were, canonized three historical facts: slavery, colonization and apartheid. Such a tendentious and oversimplified view of the past is certainly not the appropriate response to Ellis's critique. It leads to the cult of the victimization of the continent (Grignon and Passeron 1989: 67, 117). This approach to history has nothing to offer towards an understanding of the thorny problem of local knowledge, which requires the insight afforded by historians.

The Local Knowledge Alibi, or Anthropology by Default

The ethnologist's interest in development has a very long history. Maurice Delafosse (1923) and Henri Labouret (1941) were a part of the farmers' lobby in the colonial administration (Spittler 1986). These authors' paternalistic compassion refers to 'African traditions', their integration into the administration and the colonial development policy (Amselle 1990 Conklin 1998; Michel 1998). Delafosse had trouble convincing his administrative hierarchy to accept his motto: to take what is good from local traditions (Conklin 1998). However, ethnological and French ethnographic interest in questions of development were limited. Those in charge ridiculed its application (Amselle 1990; Olivier de Sardan 1995). Despite related remarks to the farmers' lobby, one must not believe that French ethnology supported and actively served the colonial administration. Spittler (1986) recalls the deplorable relationship between colonial administrators and those who took an interest in local practices. The syndrome of the ethnographic present thus left its mark on classical ethnology. This syndrome reemerged among development experts, who seized local knowledge as a mine to be exploited without considering its history or dynamics and without addressing the issue of historical shackles.[6]

Local knowledge is more than just material to supplement the other factors necessary for development. It takes more than simple capital to supplement the missing funds from the World Bank and other lenders (Freud 2000). Considered within its social and temporal context, local knowledge should be the basis for the future. Jörn Rüsen (2001: 8) writes: 'The memory of the past and the historical awareness must prepare the ground for the future. In the words of Jan Assmann, they fulfill a "foundational function."' I will take up this formula by arguing that local knowledge (and its context of social and temporal production) is to development what historical knowledge is to the future: it cannot be artificially separated from what generates it. Thus, one must begin with a complex whole, not with its isolated elements, no matter how available and tempting they may be. This temptation is akin to the technocratic habit in scientific circles. Whether live or inanimate, matter is reduced to its simplest material expression. In the case of living beings, one extracts the active principle to meet a precise need. The problem is that development and development experts increasingly confront a social body. The living social body is made up of complex power and counterpower relationships that defy materialist logic. Examples are legion. I shall refer to two types, related to the realms of the present and the past. Let us begin with the former.

Local knowledge is the subject of one of the most important markets on the planet. In the fields of art, music, agronomy and pharmacy, large companies compete fiercely. Let us take the example of material culture. The most beautiful cult objects are reduced to museum artefacts, to art objects from which mass-produced, stylized copies are sometimes made. In this case, the objects become merchandise destined for the collections of famous brands (Dior, Louis Vuitton) or for the displays of merchants of airport art. Bits of music taken from the great sagas, or from tales both sacred and profane, cannot escape similar treatment and are often reduced to a rhythm that floods the world music market. Or again, one appropriates by force techniques a thousand years old for selecting local plants. In laboratories, the genomes are deciphered and patented, which is to say, confiscated. One could cite countless examples where the local social and historical context of specialized knowledge, which underlies the coveted information, is simply brushed aside. It is ignored because it is dispensable with regard to the marketing of the product.

To seek to understand these factors would take time, since one would have to go to the sources of the knowledge, and it would cost money. The hunt for profit forgoes such costs. All that remains of this local knowledge is an aftertaste, quickly converted into the flavour of the exotic, much sought after in the West. Simplified and viewed from this perspective, local knowledge is readily consumed. No need to recall a past that is daily forgotten, *simplified* (see Scott 1998: 65). But such an approach misses a historic opportunity to know the past, to explain some of its significance in a dynamic oriented towards the future.[7] In his contribution to this book, Patrick Harries highlights the same tendency in South Africa, where history has lost ground as scholars turn their attention from a hostile past to confront the problems of the present and future. He notes, for example, the closing and downscaling of history departments in several parts of the country.

Let us now consider the past, illustrated here by the case of the Office du Niger and an example from metropolitan France in the nineteenth century. At the beginning of the last century, Delafosse wanted the French colonizers to profit from a particular type of local knowledge: the familial solidarity and the authority of the family or village chief. Those who wanted to profit from the principle of extraction became disillusioned. To extract the active element of a local plant with curative value and to later sell it on the world market was one thing, but when this knowledge could not be reduced to a chemical formula, the task became more arduous.

Consider the Office du Niger and its director, Emile Bélime, who tried to exploit the knowledge once highlighted by Delafosse. First, in an effort to populate the zone to be appraised, Bélime took forceful measures to ensure the arrival of people considered to be experts in agriculture. When local agricultural experts were needed, they were brought in. This is the period when Delavignette actually recognized the farmers' expertise and titled his book *Les paysans noirs* (1931). African farmers were no longer referred to as 'barbarians' but as actual farmers, like those in France (a possible impact of the French *Front Populaire*). Second, to settle the problem of future resistance in the Yatenga colonies, it was found to be a good idea to force people in Upper Volta to emigrate to the Office. However, several conflicting questions were posed by this measure: was it necessary to force entire families to move, out of respect for the chief and to keep the familial structure intact? Or was it necessary to reduce the mass of 'useless mouths' (the administration's view of the elderly and the children)? Was it perhaps necessary to only accept able-bodied men, thus weakening the family left behind?

During the third phase, the administration decided to take a middle road: to force young families to emigrate to reduce the number of dependants to a minimum.[8] It was known that two men were needed to cultivate a hectare properly (Bernard 1922). Owing to this fact, thousands of workers arrived (Schreyger 1984; van Beusekom 2002). To cap it all, in order to solve the problems of flight and revolt by the young people transported to French Sudan, Bélime invited the king of Yatenga, the *naaba*, to come to the villages of the Office du Niger. Not only did this sham appoint the transplanted village chiefs as officials in the Office du Niger, but the Office's representative also became the person responsible for forced immigration. Ethnic management was instituted to extract the best of so-called traditional solidarity (Diawara 2005).

The Office du Niger project was a dismal failure. Why?

1. The bondage to the Office du Niger, the brutality of exploitation, and the injustice of uprooting people from their country of origin greatly compromised the project's expected goals.
2. On account of the resulting disintegration of the familial structure, the abandoned elders were compelled to refuse to give their daughters as

spouses to those whom they considered to be exiles and slaves of the White Man (van Beusekom 2002).

3. The remaining economic structures disintegrated following the departure of the able-bodied persons.
4. In addition, a labour crisis occurred, and maintenance of different categories of fields in the original homeland became difficult.

Most development experts rarely take into consideration local knowledge in its temporal framework. They barely mention the long history and influence of Western intervention in Africa, let alone other interventions, notably those by North Africans and Asians. The development experts, expatriated or not, cannot or do not *want* to consider it. This has nothing to do with their ability to take care of the here and now, to relieve human misery with technology. As in the case of the engineer, the same logic of catching up informs the plans of national and international development agencies: to make up for lost time, to develop. It is the same socio-evolutionism of the beginning of the last century. The future calls itself development.

Finally, local knowledge has to be used practically, as capital to be mobilized to fill in budget shortfalls. This was the case in the Office du Niger, where the Sarraut plan's substantial financing was cut off even before implementation. The financial crisis that followed the Second World War did not change matters. The subsequent crisis of the 1980s reminds us of the ones that preceded it (Freud 2000). Development planners consider neither the history nor the specificity of local knowledge. Local knowledge is consequently a minor parameter in development studies.

I therefore maintain that development experts do not have the time to consult the memory of recent, much less not-so-recent, development. And the academics? Until now, they have not felt particularly responsible, for the following reasons:

1. Fascination with precolonial history. For decades, this history rightfully interested key professionals. It was necessary to prove that the continent had its own history. The trendy oral tradition method did the rest. The great empires and other royal kingdoms of the past were celebrated, sometimes indiscriminately.
2. Preoccupation with the duty of denouncing colonialism in parallel with indulging the fascination mentioned above. To condemn the colonizer was an essential task, even if this meant building a historical monument in black and white that ignored the subtle details of history (Cooper 1999, Mbembe 2002).
3. Concentration on stories of the past stored in colonial archives, conveniently located in the cities, thus avoiding the eternal language question that always crops up when dealing with the local population. The need

to collect and analyze data at first hand was thus bypassed, sometimes in complete safety and comfort.

Even scholars who show an interest in the memory of development present it as a counterpart to colonial history, rather than as a local history with direct and charged implications for the local people. Under such conditions, the story of local rural history takes a long time to write.[9] The delay is even more pronounced because the historian, as the classical division of labor requires, hardly ever deals with the present, much less with the future. Historians find themselves in a position similar to that of the classical French ethnologists who turned their back on questions of development and all that it entails. They do not cross into the territory reserved for anthropologists, who in turn do not encroach on the territory of historians. Their work therefore remains literally a 'closed book', unknown to many people in the field of development who regard the past as distant and out of reach, and therefore too difficult or impractical to address. Moreover, who ever consults a historian when discussing problems of development and the future?[10] The disciplinary limits inherited from the eighteenth century are intact, as are the academic chairs, but the need to communicate beyond academic divisions is still urgent in the African context.

The Comparative and Metropolitan French Perspective

The development policies in the colonies did not originate ex nihilo but were preceded by numerous local experiments in Metropolitan France. It is important to be familiar with these experiments in order to draw lessons from them. These experiments are well known, but their relation to the colonial experience is not. I will briefly discuss one example, which could be multiplied at will.

Modernist colonialist ideology had its roots in Metropolitan France, which was already exerting its influence during the second half of the nineteenth century, as indicated by this example from Brittany (the province that, as fate would have it, would later welcome African birth certificates from overseas France). After a princess related to Napoleon II visited Brittany and the island of Ouessant, the local council launched a programme of modernization. The distinguished hostess, the prefect, the assistant prefect and local politicians were present at its inauguration. Gregor Dobler (2002), who recalls this story, compares it to a sort of Agenda 21 of a contemporary African village. One starts by disqualifying what exists (Cooper 1996: part 1), thus providing a pretext for modernization, which alone seems destined to save the souls and to assure the well-being of the population. In the words of the local council:

> Land cultivation on the island requires radical transformation. Barley, potatoes, and
> some oats and rows of peas and beans are basically the only plants being cultivated.
> Barley, which is the most important crop, is sown so frequently that it would be

ruinous, if the island were not fertile enough to ensure all the riches that are desired from it or would be submitted to reasonable cultivation, to crop rotation that would produce such wonders on the land of Ouessant that this island would surely become, in only a few years, the rival of the English Channel islands for the beauty and richness of its crops.

With this idea in mind, the municipal council asked the administrator to look into what kind of crop rotation would be best suited to Ouessant and to produce a statement in French and in Breton to be given to the head of each family. In order to enact the measure, the council expressed the desire that the municipal administration use its efforts and means of persuasion to apply this grand and fertile amelioration measure in the future (Dobler 2002: 181).

This quotation necessitates some comments. First, the transformation is meant to be radical, as will be seen with Bélime in the Office du Niger in the colony of the French Sudan. It promises all possible happiness to the country as long as it is developed according to the state-of-the-art rules, rationalization and modernization. It even promises that the island will compete with the British, just as the Office du Niger would compete with the British plantations of Anglo-Egyptian Sudan or the Southern United States. The administration must take steps to ensure rapid execution. It is a question of military-like training. Everything is justified: once existing practices have been disqualified as destructive, they must be replaced.

Commenting seven years later on the depressed state of Ouessant, the administrator noted:

> By making successive improvements over a period of several years, the administration brought about a veritable revolution in the situation of the previously abandoned island. … Attempts were also made to bring equal progress to the agricultural economic situation; they were not as well received, because they ran counter to ingrained habits. (Archives Départementales du Finistère, Quimper, 4, p. 344, Service des Iles 1836–1918, 'Letter from the Assistant Prefect to the Prefect,' June 8, 1868; quoted in Dobler 2002: 2–3).

As is often the case, the measures taken did not attain the desired results. Why? As was observed in the Office du Niger, since 'ingrained habits' were involved, they must necessarily be eradicated. Eugen Weber, a specialist in rural French history, also notes this scorn for farmers, whether they were from Lower Brittany, Lozère, Auvergne or Landes. If we are to believe this historian, central and western France did not experience technological changes in 1840. The actual changes occurred during the twenty years preceding the First World War, when it was necessary to replace tools that were so primitive as to be worthy of museums of prehistory (Weber 1977: 118). Despite this confession, Weber maintains that those farmers who were considered to be 'passive, stubborn and stupid' rightly refused the changes because they found them useless (479).

The municipal council of Ouessant was just like Emile Bélime, the engineer and general director of the Office du Niger, and the lobbies who supported him. The latter were full of modernist thought, convinced that humanity would be saved by technology and science. Here, the state, represented by the mu-

nicipality or the Niger Committee, becomes the active force of this modernization. Observing the attitude of the Breton farmers and the reactions of the
period's administration, one might almost believe oneself to be in any of today's
state development projects in Africa. The project proposed to the local Bretons
was so similar to those put forth by the colonial period's administration that it
is hard to tell the difference between what one says and does in Africa now and
what one said and did in Brittany then.

This distant past is not the only possible point of comparison. A recent
common past can serve as a substantial field of investigation. Further research
on the life stories of the first Europeans who moved to the colony could yield
interesting results. They were administrators, traders, extension workers, engineers, technicians of all sorts, irrigators, agronomists, animal breeders, house-
wives and children. There were also many who worked abroad and spent time
in postcolonial Africa before returning home. A focused investigation of their
experiences will greatly contribute to the completion of the historical pan-
orama of the continent. These men and women rarely wrote. An oral history
in reverse, that is to say, no longer in Africa, but in Europe, could bring clarity
to the archives.

To successfully complete this work, the anthropologist and the development expert must necessarily refer to the historian and vice versa.

The Case of the Office du Niger, French Sudan and Mali (1932 to the Present)

Three thorough studies on the introduction of industrial crops (cotton and
rice) in the French Sudan, in a large irrigated area called the Office du Niger,
are now available. I will not discuss here the studies of Magasa and Coulibaly.
Emil Schreyger (1984), Richard Roberts (1996) and Monica van Beusekom
(2002) illustrate the avatars of these two products as well as the problems of the
enterprise that promoted them. However, some fundamental reservations need
to be stated.

First, Roberts' study is, at best, removed from the reality of the farmers, as
Eric Sylla (1998) demonstrates. It remains anchored in the analysis of written
documents, which contain few accounts coming directly from the farmers.
All of them are related by the colonial administration or by the services of the
Office du Niger. Meanwhile, Schreyger's book, although it examines direct
and indirect accounts by the farmers, it is strictly limited to academia, for good
reason. The ethnologist, who conducted his doctoral research during the reign
of the military dictator, did not try to connect what he observed to what happened in the 1920s. Van Beusekom, on the other hand, describes those of the
farmers' strategies that gave a twist to the development policy that had been
formulated in Paris without any consent from the colonial administration, let

alone from the farmers. Consequently, by restricting herself to the irrigated zone, she neglected the farmers living beyond the canals in the dry zone. Colonial and postcolonial state fiction always separated the two zones; the historian also makes a de facto separation.

To each his own liability, to each his own discipline. We certainly cannot force the historian or the ethnologist – in a word, the academic – to become a development expert. Different fields have different perspectives. I believe it is important to refocus on the fieldwork even though van Beusekom and Schreyger have accomplished part of the task. What I call 'refocusing' is necessary to discuss the past in light of the challenges presented by this field of study. Without refocusing, recent history excludes professionals, who consequently become incapable of informing development experts obsessed with the present and in some cases even with the future.

In each of these three cases, history is written from the perspective of Metropolitan France. Why not invert this approach and consider the other point of view? The perspectives of the farmers and the employees of the irrigated area transcend nationalities, countries, and the period of intervention. This would lead to the consideration of the perspective of those who lived long ago, which is sometimes the perspective of the present. The result would be that the former Western employees of the Office du Niger and the local farmers, as well as local Voltaic, Sudanese and Malian extension workers, enter the picture. This will allow for a dual perspective including both Europe and Africa.

In Europe, the memory of still-living former workers of the Office du Niger or the Sudanese and Malian development enterprises is a valuable resource. Once they are deceased (which certainly applies to the majority of the role-players from the turn of the twentieth century), the memories of their descendants will still make a difference. Young European and African researchers can collect this information. Oral inquiries into the lives of former volunteers and colonists are necessary in the West. The German case is uniquely interesting, since the perspectives of both East and West Germany would be brought to light. Furthermore, the collection would be the most extensive in Germany and France, due to the history of many legionnaires who worked in the Office du Niger after the First World War. In Africa, the former farmers of the Office du Niger (the colonists, as they were called) are also mostly deceased by now. But their descendants are still alive, and their painful memories are sometimes vivid. These can be gathered in Mali and Burkina Faso following the works of Magasa (1978) and Coulibaly (1997).

Historians need to make an effort to look more carefully at data collected by such studies in order to question the past. This is an important task for history as a discipline. It is useless for history to deal only with the past. The past must be engraved in the present (Koselleck 1990; Cooper 2002). It is the framework of the present that must be clarified (Ellis 2002). Van Beusekom (2002: xix) makes a commendable effort by questioning not only the discourse of development, but also its practice. In this way she analyses the effects of local knowledge on the development policy. Schreyger, while inquiring about the Office du Niger as an ethnologist, constantly demonstrates the sensitivity of a historian in order to move beyond ethnography. In both cases, the challenge seems to be to move beyond the trenches of one's own discipline. The anthropologist takes on a historian's skill. The historian needs to be trained in anthropology in order to confront the classical borders dividing academic disciplines.

By refocusing in this way, the historians can nudge the development experts, who are not usually familiar with the context of intervention and tend to think of history as so far away that there is hardly time to integrate it as a parameter of development. Why not offer them this opportunity? It is not a question of being subservient, as certain anthropologists have become, when a legion of social science specialists turn into 'consultants.' It is not a question of abandoning scholarship to meet the demands of contracts, nor a question of submitting to demands made by donors and funding agencies. It is a question of producing fundamental, independent work following the rigorous standards required for basic research that can serve in this new domain. It is a question of responding to this pertinent need for an alternative contemporary history of Africa (as described by Ellis 2002: 24), without giving in to the temptation of the prophet historian, who, as if enchanted, solves all the problems of colleagues, including those from disciplines like political science and developmental studies.

Conclusion

I have tried to show how the social and historical context has been ignored, or relegated to parentheses, in development studies. The failure to consider the past for constructing a future has not concerned development specialists, and this counterexample will inevitably fail. It is high time for history to rise from its own ashes within the context of the search for local knowledge. *The Past of the Present* is the subtitle of Cooper's book (2002). Of what present are we speaking? To whom does this present belong? Cooper's book is inspiring in this regard. The theme of development that he has addressed (1996), furthermore, is the center of gravity for all political action in our countries. Why not write the history of this present so close to the interests and preoccupations of our interlocutors?

As for the Office du Niger, which I have mentioned here and elsewhere, the harvest looks promising when one begins with the present and returns methodically into the past, with the help of abundant accounts. The task will consist in retracing the history of developmental projects, slowly returning to the preceding century – a century that, in the case of the Office du Niger, is a black hole.

Take up your pens and write about the roots of the present!

Notes

1. I am grateful to Dr Ari Levine (the University of Georgia, Athens), Dr Peter Mark (Wesleyan University) and Ms Vasantha Ramaswamy-Wolter (Johann Wolfgang-Goethe Universität) for their comments and editing of the earlier draft of this essay.
2. I am grateful to Bogumil Jewsiewicki for calling my attention to this work.
3. In this volume, Bogumil Jewsiewicki attests to the presentist conception of time among African Christians in Pentecostal churches.
4. With regard to this fixation on the future, see Bernard Lategan's analysis in the present volume of 'types of future orientation'.
5. For a review, see Agrawal (1996) and Diawara (2000).
6. Olivier de Sardan (1995: chap. 4, p. 77 ff., p. 146), who recognizes the dynamic quality of popular technical knowledge, nevertheless avoids the sticky question of historical context, which he refers back to Richards (1985).
7. Achille Mbembé (2002: 240) echoes this tendency, which impedes the development of concepts that might have explained the sense of the past and present of the continent by reference to the future.
8. This question was often asked in the colonies (Cooper 1996: 110 ff.).
9. Charles van Onselen (1997) gives us an excellent example in his work on South Africa.
10. This assessment, which was not unique to the continent, is established by Jörn Rüsen (2001: 2) in reference to Germany.

Bibliography

Agrawal, A. 1996. 'Poststructuralist Approaches to Development: Some Critical Reflections', *Peace and Change* 21(4): 464–477.

Ajayi, J.F. 1969. 'Colonialism: An Episode in African History', in P. Duignan and L.H. Gann (eds), *Colonialism in Africa*. Cambridge: 497–509.

Amselle, J.-L. 1990. *Logiques métisses: Anthropologie de l'identité en Afrique et ailleurs*. Paris.

Amselle, J.-L. and E. Sibeud (eds). 1998. *Maurice Delafosse: Entre orientalisme et ethnographie: l'itinéraire d'un africaniste (1870–1926)*. Paris.

Bernard, F. 1922. 'La mise en valeur des colonies et le programme Sarraut', *Revue de Paris,* September: 365–394; October: 543–560.

Chazan, N., R. Mortimer, J. Ravenhill and D. Rothschild (eds). 1992. *Politics and Society in Contemporary Africa*. Boulder.

Conklin, A.L. 1997. *A Mission to Civilize: The Republican Idea of Empire in France and West Africa, 1895–1930*. Stanford.

Conklin, A. 1998. 'On a semé la haine: Maurice Delafosse et la politique du gouvernement général en AOF, 1915–1936', in J.-L.Amselle and E. Sibeud (eds), *Maurice Delafosse: Entre orientalisme et ethnographie: l 'itinéraire d'un africaniste (1870–1926)*. Paris: 65–77.

Cooper, F. 1994. 'Conflict and Connection: Rethinking Colonial African History', *American Historical Review* 99 no. 5: 1516–1545.

Cooper, F. 1996. *Decolonization and African society: The Labor Question in French and British Africa*. Cambridge.

Cooper, F. 1999. 'Divergences et convergences vers une relecture de l'histoire coloniale africaine', in M. Diouf (ed.), *L'historiographie indienne en débat: Colonialisme, nationalisme et sociétés postcoloniales*. Paris. 433–482.

Cooper, F. 2002. *Africa since 1940: The Past of the Present*. Cambridge.

Coulibaly, C. 1997. *Politiques agricoles et stratégies paysannes au Mali, 1910–1985, le règne des mythes à l'Office du Niger*. Bamako.

Delafosse, M. 1923. *Broussard ou les états d'âme d'un colonial suivi de ses propos et opinions.* Paris.

Delavignette, R. 1931. *Les paysans noirs, récit soudanais en douze mois.* Paris.

Diawara, M. 2000. 'Globalization, Development Politics and Local Knowledge', *International Sociology* 15(2): 365–375.

Diawara, M. 2005. 'L'Office du Niger ou l'univers sur-moderne (1920–)', in I. Mandé and B. Stefanson (eds), *Les historiens africains et la mondialisation -Actes du 3ᵉ congrès international (Bamako 2001).* Paris: 31–43.

Diop, C.A. 1955. *Nations nègres et culture.* Paris.

Diop, C.A. 1967. *Antériorité des civilisations nègres: mythe ou vérité historique?* Paris.

Diouf, M. (ed.). 1999. *L'historiographie indienne en débat: colonialisme, nationalisme et sociétés postcoloniales.* Paris.

Dobler, G. 2002. 'Lokale Ziele und das Wissen der Experten: Zwei Entwicklungsprojekte auf der Ile d'Ouessant', *Sociologus* 2: 165–190.

Ellis, S. 2002. 'Writing Histories of Contemporary Africa', *Journal of African History* 43: 1–26.

Fall, B. 1993. *Le travail forcé en Afrique-Occidentale française, 1900–1946.* Paris.

Fall, M. 2001. 'L'État national entre terroirs et territoire', in *Historisches Seminar Hamburg.* Hamburg.

Ferguson, J. 1990. *The Anti-Politics Machine: 'Development', Depolitization, and Bureaucratic Power in Lesotho.* Minneapolis.

Freud, C. 2000. La banque mondiale n'a plus d'argent, mais elle a des idées?, *Cahiers d'études africaines,* no. 157: 135–140.

Goerg, O. 1991. 'L'historiographie de l'Afrique de l'Ouest : tendances actuelles', *Genèses* 11 no. 6: 144–160.

Grignon, C and Passeron, J.-C. 1989. *Le savant et le populaire.* Paris.

Hartog, F. 1996. *Memoire d'Ulysse: recits sur la frontiere en Grece ancienne.* Paris.

Hartog, F. 2003. *Régimes d'historicité.* Paris.

Koselleck, R. 1979. *Vergangene Zukunft: Zur Semantik geschichtlicher Zeiten.* Frankfurt am Main.

Koselleck, R. 1990. *Le futur passé.* Paris.

Labouret, H. 1941. *Paysan d'Afrique Occidentale.* Paris.

Lakroum, M. 1982. *Le travail inégal: paysans et salariés sénégalais face à la crise des années trente.* Paris.

Magassa, H. 1978. *Papa, commandant a jeté un grand filet devant nous: les exploits de la rive gauche du Niger.* Paris.

Mbembe, A. 2002. 'African Modes of Self-Writing', *Public Culture* 14 no. 3: 239–273.

Michel, M. 1998. 'Maurice Delafosse et l'invention d'une africanité nègre', in J.-L. Amselle and E. Sibeud (eds), *Maurice Delafosse: Entre orientalisme et ethnographie: l'itinéraire d'un africaniste (1870–1926).* Paris: 78–89.

Moniot, H. 1995. 'L'histoire à l'épreuve de l'Afrique', *Cahiers d'Études africaines* 38–139, XXXV-2-3: 647–656.

Mudimbe, V.Y. and B. Jewsiewicki. 1993. 'Africans' Memories and Contemporary History of Africa', in V.Y. Mudimbe and B. Jewsiewicki (eds), *History Making in Africa: History and Theory.* Middletown: 1–11.

Olivier de Sardan, J.-P. 1995. *Anthropologie et développement: essai en socio-anthropologie du changement social.* Paris.

Richards, P. 1985. *Indigenous Agricultural Revolution: Ecology and Food Production in West Africa.* London.

Roberts, R.L. 1996. *Two Worlds of Cotton: Colonialism and the Regional Economy in the French Soudan, 1800–1946.* Stanford.

Rüsen, J. 2001. 'Die Zukunft der Vergangenheit', in J. Rüsen, *Zerbrechende Zeit: Über den Sinn der Geschichte.* Cologne: 131–141.

Sanneh, L.O. 1999. *Abolitionist Abroad: American Blacks and the Making of Modern West Africa.* Cambridge, MA.

Schreyger, E. 1984. *L'Office du Niger: la problématique d'une grande entreprise agricole dans la zone du Sahel.* Stuttgart.

Scott, J.C. 1998. *Seeing Like A State: How Certain Schemes to Improve Human Condition Have Failed*. New Haven.

Spittler, G. 1986. *Verwaltung in einem afrikanischen Bauernstaat: Das koloniale Französich-Westafrika 1919–1939*. Wiesbaden.

Spittler, G., H. d'Almeida-Topor and M. Lakroum (eds). 2003. *Le travail en Afrique*. Paris.

Sylla, E. 1998. 'Richard L. Roberts: Two Worlds of Cotton: Colonialism and the Regional Economy in the French Soudan, 1800–1946', *African Studies Review* 41(2): 160–161.

Thioub, I. 2004. 'Letture africane della schiavitù e della tratta atlantica', *Passato e Presente* no. 62 (May–August): 129–146.

Beusekom, M. van. 2002. *Negotiating Development: African Farmers and Colonial Experts at the Office du Niger, 1920–1960*. Oxford.

Van Onselen, C. 1997. *The Seed is Mine: The Life of a South African Sharecropper 1894–1985*. Oxford.

Weber, E.J. 1977. *Peasants into Frenchmen: The Modernization of Rural France, 1870–1914*. Stanford.

CHAPTER 6

Remembering Conflict
The Centenary Commemoration of the South African War of 1899–1902 as a Case Study

ALBERT GRUNDLINGH

Introduction

The wider significance and potentially contradictory impact of memory in divided societies has not gone unnoticed in the literature: 'Memory is a powerful
tool in the quest for understanding, justice and knowledge. It raises consciousness. It heals some wounds, restores dignity, and prompts uprisings' (Misztal
2003: 126). In South Africa this statement could be buttressed by numerous
examples. South Africa's divisive past is in no small measure responsible for
the multiplicity of ways in which memory functions in the country. Since
the advent of full democracy in 1994, the ways in which historical memories
operate in the public sphere have become more pronounced and are more contested than before. In a democratic society new emancipatory choices present
themselves and individual choices expand, and as a consequence the chances of
constructing a unified public memory recede.

   What follows is a case study of how, in the new context, an 'old war' was
remembered in various ways. Essentially it seeks to demonstrate the unavoidable 'contamination' that occurs when different groups seek to appropriate historical memory, not only for the immediate present but also as a way to ensure
its control in the future. By the same token it is equally germane to note the
permutations and gyrations of those who had inherited a particular memory
and had to defend it in a context of dramatically shifted power configurations.

Notes for this section begin on page 118.

Democracy opens up new opportunities, and rival claims to control historical memory can emerge in the process. The centenary commemorations of the South African War of 1899–1902 had all these ingredients.

The passage from the twentieth to the twenty-first century was an occasion to recall one of South Africa's most devastating wars. The scorched-earth policy of the British during the latter part of the conflict reduced the republics of the Transvaal and the Orange Free State almost to a wasteland. The Boer women and children who died by the thousands in British concentration camps, which were hastily constructed to house those being swept from the veld, far outnumbered republican battlefield casualties and constituted about 10 percent of the total Boer population. Moreover, the war involved all groups in South Africa and had a significant social and political impact on black people. It was indeed a war that had the potential to be remembered, even a hundred years later.

What has been called the 'cult of centenary' has become increasingly important in 'perpetuating, revising or creating public perceptions of past events and people' (Quinault 1998: 303). A centenary becomes even more potent if it deals with dramatic events such as wars. Much academic work relating to the processes of remembrance has focused on war and collective memory. Enquiries in this area have usually revolved around a cluster of questions, as Martin Evans and Ken Lunn (1997: 16) have indicated:

> What are the function and place of historical memories of war? How do they relate to concepts of national identity? How have the memories of war been constructed? What have been the contours of these memories and how have they altered over time? How do memories of war circulate and how are they transmitted from one generation to the next? How are memories of war constructed in terms of race, gender and class?

This chapter does not pretend to deal fully with such a formidable range of questions. Its main aim is to analyse the dynamics of commemoration, bearing in mind that the contours of remembrance have been substantially revised through major political changes in South Africa.

The State and Commemoration of the War

The advent of the centenary of the war was marked by considerable ambiguity in African National Congress (ANC) circles. The public representation of the war, as a seminal event in Afrikaner history, had a long association with sectarian nationalist politics. Moreover, it was not a war that was made to loom large in the memory of black oppositional groupings under apartheid; they had more than sufficient other armoury in their ideological arsenal to draw upon for historical legitimization (Nasson 2000: 150; Misztal 2003: 127). The question then arises why a new government should wish to help commemorate a war that has been a white public reserve for the greater part of the century.

For the predominantly white National Party, whose support base included many Afrikaners who could claim a direct historical interest in the war, there was no doubt that the event should be commemorated. Apart from the significance of the war for Afrikaners as such, it was argued that the war was the biggest colonial conflict in Africa and therefore had a significantly wider reach. Afrikaner spokespeople took umbrage that the ANC 'wants us to forget altogether. But we won't. It is an opportunity to place the country's history in perspective' (*Die Burger* 12 September 1998; Nasson 2000; Lodge 1990/1999). International interest in the event was mounting, it was claimed, whilst commemorations could not be properly planned owing to the inertia of the ANC government.

The initial indecision of the state on the matter led to some strange prohibitions. At Bloemfontein in March 1998 during a show to promote tourism in the Free State, a planned war exhibition was vetoed by the local legislature on the grounds that it was too 'sensitive'. The exhibition would have consisted of British uniforms, the Union Jack, the old Free State republican flag and, for the sake of inclusivity, a variety of African drums. The person responsible for the exhibition deliberately refrained from portraying a Boer fighter, as she was apprehensive that it might be regarded as offensive. She was too timid: it was not, it transpired, the nature of her exhibition that irked the local authorities, but the fact that at the time no official decision was taken as to whether the state would put its weight behind the commemorations (*Die Volksblad* 11 March 1998; *Die Burger* 12 May 1998; *Beeld* 10 September 1998; *Rapport* 3 May 1998).

It was only towards the end of 1998 that the state decided, through a cabinet decision, to support the centenary. For the Department of Arts, Culture, Science and Technology (DACST), an alternative was to play down or officially ignore the event. The risk, however, it was argued, was that the commemorations might have developed their own dynamics, not unlike the 1938 Voortrekker centenary celebrations, which saw a massive mobilization of Afrikaners across class and other divides. Given the dramatically different circumstances between 1938 and 1999, such a possibility was rather remote, but the spectre of spirited right-wing Afrikaner resistance kept preying on the minds of those in power. The other option was that the decision should be left to the individual provinces, but a strong counter argument was that the provinces lacked the necessary capacity to undertake a project of this kind. The possibility of embarrassingly contradictory interpretations emerging from the provinces as to what the centenary was supposed to mean in a new dispensation, was considered a further risk. The decision then was to adopt the commemorations as a national legacy project alongside other initiatives such as the Nelson Mandela Museum, the Constitutional Court in Johannesburg and Freedom Park in Pretoria (Dominy and Callinicos 1999: 389–391; *Rapport* 18 June 1998).

Besides these considerations it also has to be borne in mind that the centenary was the first major heritage event to be marked under an ANC government. Moreover, it promised to attract international attention, particularly as the advent of commemorations was to overlap with the Commonwealth Conference, which was to be held in South Africa at much the same time. Many commonwealth countries, of course, had participated in the war, which provided further impetus for the ANC to highlight the passing of a colonial world and to put the spotlight on the new incumbents of power.

Over the years the years the memory of the war has congealed into a particularly solid body of cultural and historical understanding, and the government might well have wished for more pliable material to work with. The timing of the centenary could obviously not be changed, but the state could still try to leave its imprint on the commemorative proceedings. Ministers and directors of arts and culture in the various provinces were advised to take a particular interest in the event so as 'to broaden its representation' (Dominy and Callinicos, 1999: 396). Government also made its influence felt by renaming the war the Anglo-Boer South African War (DACST 1999), a clumsy composite of names that had little chance of being generally accepted. The Anglo-Boer War, a more traditional name for the war, proved difficult to dislodge in the public mind. Most scholars, though, preferred the term 'South African War' to indicate that all groupings in the country were affected.

The National Party, in pressuring the ANC in 1998 to take a stand on the centenary, had hoped that the state would be involved as a facilitator in supporting the event yet would refrain from exerting control (*Die Burger* 12 September 1998). The arrangement was not to be that simple. Although civil society was to be allowed a certain latitude, once the state had decided to participate it could not afford to be outflanked and had to give a particular emphasis to proceedings.

This much became clear when the War Museum of the Boer Republics in Bloemfontein (which since 1994 had played a leading role in planning the commemorations), suddenly found itself under siege. Advisors close to DACTS had some appreciation for the fact that the institution was aware of the need for a reinterpretation of the war and that it had also sponsored research into black participation in the war, but ultimately, 'given the previous ethos and uncertain institutional positioning of the museum, it is perhaps not the most effective institution to drive the process' (Dominy and Callinicos 1999: 396).

With little regard for the museum work that had been patiently and assiduously performed since 1931, much of it voluntarily, the state moved in under the banner of restructuring and transformation. As the museum received a subsidy from the state, it was financially vulnerable. But the state did not use an economic weapon; rather, it targeted the museum council. The existing council was not opposed to adjusting their composition after consultation, but that was not enough. With the stroke of a pen the entire composition was swiftly and drastically changed. Predominantly Zulu speakers, with no or little knowledge of the war, were imported from Kwa-Zulu Natal to fill six of the nine positions on the council. The original council was decimated; only three members from the Free State who had a direct and long-standing interest in the work of the museum were allowed to remain (*Beeld* 22 and 29 April 1999). Not surprisingly, this development gave rise to considerable dissatisfaction on the part of the museum establishment. The impression was created, it was argued, that the state 'wished to deny Afrikaners even their own memories and sentiments related to key events in their history' (*Beeld* 19 April 1999):

> The museum hierarchy decided to retaliate. Having their representation on the council slashed to an absolute minority and having members without the necessary expertise unilaterally foisted upon them on the eve of the commemorations, were considered ill advised if not perverse. They prepared a court interdict against the relevant minister, Ben Ngubane, in which he was accused of not applying his mind to the matter and being unduly influenced by officials with irrelevant, ideological and prejudiced motives. Wiser counsels then prevailed and the matter was settled out of court with a new board consisting of seven members appointed by the minister and seven by the museum.

The official launch of the centenary commemorations was planned to take place in the Free State. Initially a large sports stadium in Bloemfontein was considered as a venue. However, the plan was rejected, and the reasons for not following through reflected the state's anxiety about publicly moving into uncharted cultural waters. DACST advisors made these reservations clear:

> There is a strong possibility that a public event will not turn out the way the organizers designed it. The ABSAW is not yet seen by the majority of black South Africans as a significant event in their history and there is a strong possibility that the crowd in the stadium will be very small, despite the presence of the president. Another possibility is (particularly if there is little black participation) that the event may be used as a rallying focus for right wing minorities.

In the light of this, a 'more appropriate form for the launch' was considered to be a 'small elite event with a high media presence' (DACST 1999). The masses, so it seemed, could not always be relied upon. Eventually it was decided to have a launch just outside Brandfort, a small town north of Bloemfontein. It was ostensibly a suitable place, as it housed the graves of Boer and British combatants, as well as (it was claimed) of a black concentration camp victim. Brandfort is also the town where Winnie Mandela, the former wife of Nelson Mandela, was held under house arrest by the apartheid government, but whether this also fed into the choice of venue is conjectural (WOZA 1999).

The launch indeed turned out to be a grand affair as seven luxury air-conditioned buses left Bloemfontein on Saturday 9 October, followed by a cooling truck with refreshments, cool drinks and mineral water for the hordes of ambassadors, politicians, invited guests and hangers-on (*Die Volksblad* 11 October 1999). Clearly, the launch was not meant to be a reenactment of events a century ago, when a solitary Boer fighter might have left his family and homestead on his trusty steed with provisions for thirty days to join his comrades on commando.

The crowd that gathered at Brandfort was predominantly black, comprising many schoolchildren. They gathered some distance from the dignitaries congregated at the fenced-off podiums. Conspicuous by their absence were the whites who traditionally attended public ceremonies of this kind in the halcyon days of Afrikaner nationalism. As one journalist observed:

> Nary to be seen were the bearded, solid pipe-smoking Afrikaners of yore in *velskoens*, slouch hats and colourful 'kappies' and Voortrekker dresses. Nowhere in sight was a *Vierkleur* or even a venerable ox-wagon. Instead, virtually the only white men in view were the substantial numbers of uniformed police and military personnel who lined the perimeters of the various ceremonial sites – and, of course, a smattering of gorgeously attired members of the diplomatic community. (*The Citizen* 11 October 1999)

The appearance of President Thabo Mbeki was met with calls of 'Amandla Baba' and shrill ululation. Not everything proceeded as planned. There were shouts of glee when a burly white sergeant-major slipped and fell as he clambered to a vantage point on a rocky outcrop. But this was followed by a respectful silence as 'Baba' himself raised an admonishing hand (*The Citizen* 11 October 1999). It is somewhat doubtful how many of the crowd had a fair grasp as to what they were supposed to commemorate. Many had just come to see Mbeki; others, holding placards, thought it was the opportune time to make known some more pressing concerns: 'We beg our second black president to alleviate the poverty in Brandfort' (*Die Volksblad* 11 October 1999).

A distinct African flavour was added to the occasion in an unmistakable attempt at symbolic inversion by having young black girls dressed up in white bonnets and Voortrekker dresses to represent Boer women, while black boys were put on display in red coats and bobby helmets to represent British soldiers. 'While one must presume that the intention was not to be comic,' a bemused historian commented, 'this outlandish spectacle certainly took some planning imagination' (Nasson 2000: 155–157).

Mbeki's oratory was to be the high point of proceedings. In a speech finely crafted for the occasion he hit all the right notes, paying homage to all those who had fallen, emphasizing the importance of black participation and dwelling on the need to use the past in a positive way for nation building purposes. Complete with a couple of Afrikaans sentences added in praise of the '*dapper boerevegters*' (brave Boer fighters), his pleas for reconciliation in the aftermath of strife were well received by the Afrikaans press (*Business Day* 11 October 1999; *Beeld* 12 October 1999; *Die Burger* 12 October 1999). Equally well received was the duke of Kent's speech on behalf of the British government. It came as close as British reserve would allow to presenting South Africans with a public apology for the loss of women and children in the camps (Africa News 1999).

The potential impact of these speeches, however, was somewhat blunted by planning oversights, deliberate or otherwise, that contrasted badly with the nation building rhetoric of Mbeki. The organizers neglected to invite an Afrikaner representative to the podium, ostensibly because the Boer republics no longer existed and therefore a suitable representative could not be found. This questionable defence only rankled Afrikaners further; it was like having a wedding without a bride, they retorted. When wreaths had to be laid on Boer graves, the director of the War Museum had to be hastily summoned (*Die Volksblad* 9 and 11 October 1999; *Die Afrikaner* 15 October 1999). It was for this reason, it was claimed, that the white inhabitants of Brandfort stayed well clear of proceedings. A spokesman said:

> The government hijacked the commemoration of the war between Boer and Brit. The Duke of Kent passed by, giving us a royal wave and was afforded the opportunity to speak. A descendant of the Boers, however, was not allowed to pay tribute to the Boers. The descendants of the Boers feel that their faces have been pushed in the mud. Some of them even regarded it as the final victory for the British. (*Die Volksblad* 11 October 1999)

The launch was not only less inclusive and representative than history would have dictated, but also more carefully stage-managed than what it appeared. It transpired that the grave of what was supposed to be the black concentration camp inmate whom Mbeki paid tribute to, was actually that of a farm worker buried at the time of the war. Authentic black concentration camp graves were two kilometres away. The director general of DACST virtually admitted that they were aware of this, but 'that it would have spoiled the ideal of single commemorative event in one place' (*Cape Argus* 15 October 1999). The matter gave rise to considerable controversy, but ultimately it was glossed over by emphasizing the symbolic nature of the grave as representing all black victims, regardless of the historical accuracy of the particular gravesite (*Die Volksblad* 2 and 9 February 2000; *Beeld* 2 February 2000).

This was not the final embarrassing note to the official launch. During February and March 2000 rumours started to surface about financial irregularities related to the government allocation for commemorative events. A former National Party member of parliament, Leon de Beer, who had been imprisoned for electoral fraud in the 1980s in Hillbrow, was fingered in the subsequent inquiries, and an audit firm was called in to investigate matters (*Mail and Guardian* 17–23 March 2000; *Die Volksblad* 9 February and 4 November 2000).

These subterranean currents had little overall effect on the first wave of commemoration. Despite omissions, inaccuracies and allegations of fraud, the state had succeeded in staking its official claim in the moulding of the war heritage. This was to be carried over into the public arena.

Public Discourses on Black Participation in the War

On the eve of the centenary, R.W. Johnson, a scholar with a long-standing interest in South Africa, commented in the British press:

Given the ANC's endless invocation of a 'non-racist, non-sexist South Africa', there is nothing more politically incorrect in the new South Africa than a white male. Accordingly, it seems certain that whatever remembrance of the war takes place, a great effort will be made to stress that this was essentially a conflict between white males. There is also a tremendous keenness to seek out the role played by blacks ... (*Times* 2 October 1999)

Such an emphasis did indeed occur. As far as general awareness of the nature of participation in the war was concerned, the issue of black involvement made a long overdue entry onto the public stage. It was somewhat misguided, though, to claim as one journalist did that historians had 'torn out the page' on black vicissitudes during the war (*Saturday Star* 14 September 1996). On the contrary, progressive historians working on the war had all but exhausted the topic during the previous thirty years (cf. Nasson 2000). That the issue only surfaced in the public arena after such a lapse of time, had all to do with an altered climate of public opinion and little with the alleged neglect of professional historians.

Once in the public sphere, the question of black fatalities became a matter of considerable interest. A salient feature in the discourse of the commemoration of the war was the discovery of an increasing number of black war graves, especially concentration camp victims. Both the Afrikaans and the English-language press announced these findings in banner headlines.[1] The keenness to report on this prompted one reporter to take a rather jaundiced view:

Some ... newspaper coverage seems to have been reduced to only one aspect of the war: the participation of black compatriots, and some journalists have without a hint of irony turned to serial gravediggers. So caught up are they in this new assignment that they can't see the war for the graves. (WOZA 1999)

The rate at which black graves were claimed to be discovered caused a measure of concern for certain Afrikaner groupings. They saw in this a deliberate intention to inflate black casualties so that, for political reasons, these could surpass the number of whites who had perished in the camps. With this accomplished, ran the argument, the Afrikaner history of suffering could be proportionally reduced and presented as of lesser importance than before (*Die Afrikaner* 17 January 1999; *Rapport* 17 October 1999). This, however, was somewhat of a minority view. Less suspicious and more pervasive was a pragmatic attempt on the part of Afrikaner cultural brokers to welcome the new development and to project, under the rubric of nation building, a common bond of suffering between Afrikaners and black people. The British could now be put in the dock, and on the basis of a conveniently constructed 'common' anti-imperialist past the old white elite could try and speak to the new black elite (*Financial Mail* 2 October 1999; *Die Burger* 9 October 1999; *Rapport* 17 October 1999; cf. Cuthbertson and Jeeves 1999).

Such an interpretation, which failed to take into account the subsequent apartheid interlude, was just too ingenuous to make much headway. It also underestimated the extent to which the new black elite sought to manoeuvre itself onto the moral high ground and preferred to conduct exchanges on nation building on its own terms. Ben Ngubane, opening an exhibition at the War Museum in Bloemfontein on 8 October 1999, started his speech off cautiously enough by genuflecting to the notion of mutual suffering, but could not restrain himself for too long before he had to claim 'that notwithstanding the general suffering across the colour divide blacks suffered even more' during the war (Ngubane 1999). The tragedy of a hundred years ago was now recast as an almost tawdry spectacle, an Olympics of suffering. Afrikaner nationalists, of course, were past masters of invoking the concentration camp catastrophe for political purposes, particularly in the 1930s and 1940s. Sixty years later, a 'new set of skeletal people were to rise up from those terrible days' of the war to participate in the séance of a new round of politicians (Nasson 2000: 163).

Although there can be no doubt as to the tribulations of black people in the war, it is an oversimplification to emphasize this to the exclusion of much else. Black people were not only victims. Some tried to be master of their own fate as far as circumstances allowed; there were those who decided to join the fighting forces on specific terms if possible, while others profited from increased agricultural markets brought about by the need to feed British troops. In certain areas of the Transvaal there was also an awareness that as a result of the war the props of colonial society were being loosened, and that this offered new opportunities to try and reclaim land that had been lost before (Nasson 2000: 163; cf. Warwick 1983).

These specific and more varied dimensions of black involvement failed to enter into the public arena during the centenary. A partial explanation for this may simply be that the full extent and nuances of black participation were not that widely known at the time of the centenary. However, a more convincing argument is probably that even if such information was more readily available, the 'suffering' dimension would still have surfaced as the prime commemorative aspect. While the other angles were not completely without the potential to be codified into useful ideological constructs to be used in the present, there is little to compete against 'suffering'. Having already laid claim to the high moral ground as a result of the iniquities of apartheid, the additional revelation of black vicissitudes a century ago was a bonus to be timeously deployed, if so required, in the public sphere. The discourse of victimhood is a powerful one; particularly when there is a convenient and rich fund to draw upon (cf. *New York Review of Books* 8 April 1999). Moreover, 'suffering' also allowed for competition with the erstwhile Afrikaner rulers for the highest honour, whilst the other dimensions, even if they demonstrated African initiative and resilience, still had the drawback that they ultimately reduced black participants to a marginal role in the conflict that did not quite square with the assertiveness of a new elite in power.

The enthusiastic endorsement of 'suffering', however, was not welcomed across the board. In certain unreconstructed Africanist circles, it was argued 'that the obsessions of black politicians to claim the Anglo-Boer War reflects, if any-thing, the extent of psychological damage suffered by black people as a result of colonialism' (*Mail and Guardian* 15 October 1999. See also *Sunday Times* 17 October 1999; *Sunday World* 17 October1999). In this view the war was held to be merely a squabble between colonial overlords, while black people 'couldn't even sit down comfortably and watch the fight, because they no longer owned any land to sit on'. Since neither side asked black people to enter the conflict on equal terms, 'there is nothing in this centenary for their descendants to cel-ebrate' (*Mail and Guardian* 15 October 1999). Any association with the war was accordingly inappropriate and showed an 'unhealthy identification with the master', and 'to emulate him is a pathology that afflicts the oppressed all over the world' (*Sunday World* 17 October 1999).

Both discourses had their own internal political logic, but in terms of the impact and cultural purchase, it is probably safe to claim that despite the media prominence given to black participation and the jockeying for moral positions, the centenary failed to stir the imagination of black people to a significant de-gree. 'The vast majority of ordinary black South Africans has little knowledge as far as the Anglo-Boer War is concerned', one black commentator noted (Sekete 2002: 41). It was after all a war that had taken place well outside living memory, and even if some oral recollections survived, as they certainly did,[2] it was too much to expect, given the tumultuous twentieth century and the pre-dominant effect of apartheid, that one distant event amongst many other more recent ones would be etched in collective memory. Neither was it necessary, beyond the ritual incantation of a superior moral position, for those in power to invoke a particular legacy of the war to bolster their political legitimacy. With an overwhelming majority in the 1999 election, the ANC hardly needed such an unlikely platform as a war between whites a hundred years ago to ce-ment its position.

Afrikanerdom and the Commemoration of the War

While the war was deeply woven into the fabric of Afrikaner national con-sciousness during the first half of the century, it did not present itself as an oc-casion to celebrate. After all, the Boers had lost the war, and one does not celebrate defeats. This was in contrast to the Great Trek centenary commemo-rations in 1938 – which had much more of a celebratory ring – linked to the successful nineteenth-century Boer settlement of the interior of South Africa. The fiftieth anniversary of the outbreak of war in 1949, a year after a narrow National Party victory at the polls, allowed some respite from the historical legacy of loss that had permeated so much of Afrikaner thinking after the war. Afrikaners could now start to put the war behind them; in 1948 they had re-gained what they had lost in 1902 (Grundlingh 2002: 29). The future seemed

bright and so inviting that the historian D.W. Kruger could confidently proclaim on the anniversary of the war in 1949 that 'the sun has risen for the Afrikaner and now it was Africa for the Afrikaners' (Kruger 1969: 67).

In 1999, with a black government in power, this vision had all but evapo-
rated. Nor was it possible to rekindle the embers of the memory of a war that had
helped to stoke the Afrikaner nationalist fires of the 1930s and 1940s. Whereas
impoverished whites had formed a substantial section of Afrikanerdom at the
time and political hostility was mainly directed at imperialistic English speakers, sixty years later Afrikaners had become predominantly middle-class and no
longer felt inferior to English speakers (Giliomee 1999: 2). Symbolically there
were parallels between an emasculated Afrikanerdom of 1999 and the defeated
Boer republics of a hundred years ago. However, in terms of realpolitik in 1999
only the foolhardy would have thought of invoking a receding memory as a
viable political rallying point.

Nevertheless, it was in the arena of cultural politics that the war could still
speak to Afrikaners in a meaningful way. Much of this had to do with the rene-
gotiation of identity. The commemoration of the war coincided with a period
of considerable drift in Afrikaner society; besides the loss of political power old
cultural sureties had disappeared or were under threat, while the future looked
increasingly uncertain. One Afrikaner commentator summed this up:

> Since the election of 1994 there was a notable escapist tendency among Afrikaners.
> Some escaped into the other worldly idea of nation-building, others fled overseas,
> whilst a larger number sought their salvation in individualistic ... economic pros-
> perity and personal enrichment. (Goosen 2001: 63)

To this can be added that the commemoration allowed some Afrikaners
another escape hatch – that of the past. In the run-up to the centenary, Afrikaners as a group had to come face to face with disturbing presentations of their
immediate apartheid past. Unsettling revelations from the Truth and Reconciliation Committee, reflecting Afrikaner excesses during apartheid, added to
a sense of unease and disillusionment. Under these circumstances, the coming
centenary of the war was viewed in some circles as an opportunity to showcase
a heroic period in Afrikaner history for which they did not have to apologize
(Grundlingh 2002: 34; *Southern Cross* 6 October 1999). More generally, the
commemoration provided an opportunity to withdraw from a present where
tensions between black and white seemed to persist, and to find relative solace
in what now may appear as an almost brotherly conflict between white and
white that had already fully exhausted itself and no longer presented a threat of
any kind (Louw 1999: 15).

Woven into this mode of remembrance was a certain strand of nostalgia.
The conditions, indeed, were conducive for the emergence of nostalgic thinking. A sociologist, writing in general on nostalgia, has noted:

> In its collective manifestations nostalgia thrives – on the rude transitions rendered
> by history, on the discontinuities and dislocations wrought by such phenomena as

war, depression, civil disturbance … , in short these events cause masses of people to feel uneasy and to wonder whether the world and their being in it are quite what they always took it to be. (Davis 1979: 49)

In the Afrikaans press a noted Afrikaans author, aptly observed that circumstances were ripe for nostalgic indulgence and that the centenary offered a mythological space where ethnic nesting could take place (*Die Burger* 1 October 1999).

Particularly for an older generation with longer historical memories, remembering the war was a process that incorporated much of the trials and tribulations of the Afrikaner in twentieth-century South Africa. Thus one elderly correspondent to the *Beeld* newspaper used the war as a point of departure to explain:

> The damage which the war did a century ago to our development was incalculable and unthinkable. … We were a true example of how a disadvantaged nation could recover; and half a century after the worst form of degradation achieved a position of strength from which we could dictate. But in the meantime our fellow citizens have awoken; and we were too jealous to share the wonderful infrastructure of our country with them and we thought that the best way out would be to establish homelands and we invested millions in this, only to witness how these noble attempts were total failures . … And now our fears have become true and there is not a single aspect of our country's administration which is properly maintained. (*Beeld* 21 August 1998)

Recalling the war and extrapolating from that in such a way allows for the juxtaposition of a somewhat idealized yet troubled past, with a foreboding present.

Centenaries present themselves as crafted occasions for the merging of past and present, and nostalgia is one binding element in this process. As such, the commemorations of the war, as we have seen, involved a fair amount of nostalgia. Yet it was not unthinking, uncritical, non-reflective immersion in nostalgia that marked the way in which Afrikaners remembered the war. There was a strong awareness that the apartheid past had failed and that Afrikaners now had to adapt to a new order. In line with this realization, for the most part a deliberate attempt was made to acknowledge the role of black people and view the conflict not only in local but also in international terms (Jacobs 2002: 3–10).

There were, however, select groupings clustered together as the 'Volkskomitee vir die herdenking van die Tweede Vryheidsoorlog', which harked backed to distant memories of a time when the war explicitly provided an ideological arsenal to promote the Afrikaner ethnic politics of the day (Agten 2002: 93–94). The basic message stayed the same, even if it was dressed up in a more modern idiom than that of fifty years ago (*Rapport* 2 June 2002).

Such exceptions apart, overall there was a tendency to downplay the potential political ramifications of the war and to steer away from active public promotions of such agendas. The trend, in fact, was towards personalizing and privatizing the memory of the war – a notion that involved safeguarding a realm of experience from being appropriated and moulded by agencies with overt political aims (cf. Bailey 2000: 384). The war was not expected to perform a specific wider function. The politics of the personal took a cultural form; for example the re-recording, recollecting and preserving of material related to the war. Many of these narratives were of a purely anecdotal nature and were devoid of explicit messages that could be construed to have a meaning in the present.[3] Of course, the very act of collecting can in itself be seen as ideological, as it is often, at times quite unwittingly, spurred on by wider pressures in society. Essentially, though, the intention was not to make a grand political statement but to accomplish memory work in a space specifically carved out for the retention and reworking of remembrances. 'When memory is no longer everywhere, it will not be anywhere unless one takes the responsibility to recapture it through individual means,' the French historian Pierre Nora has aptly noted (quoted in Gillis 1994: 14). What also prompted the cautionary salvaging mode of memory was the implosion of much of the earlier Afrikaner ethnic constructs of history. Cultural entrepreneurs now had to dig carefully among the debris to recover and reconstruct those building blocks that were considered worth retaining and that could be reused in the overall construction of a new identity.

In form and content, the commemorations often bore a local character. Families visited gravesites of relatives or battlefields where ancestors fought, while many small towns used the opportunity to recall specific events that took place in the vicinity. The format of the commemorations varied: mock battles, community barbecues and dances, torch processions, marathon running, exhibitions and lectures or a combination of these activities (see for example *Rapport* 6 June 1999; *Die Volksblad* 9 October 1999; *Die Volksblad* 12 October 1999; *Die Volksblad* 19 January 2000; *Die Volksblad* 23 November 2001). Unlike the 1938 Great Trek centenary celebrations, when the symbolism of the trek was clearly defined and spelt out in a very deliberate manner way in every town (cf. Grundlingh and Sapire 1989: 19–27), in 1999 the commemorative proceedings of the war were not marked by an all-encompassing single cohesive message of memorialization.

Each town gave its own imprint to proceedings. Nor were all these gatherings sombre and solemn occasions. At Machadodorp, which during the war had been a temporary capital for the Transvaal republic after the fall of Pretoria in June 1900, the high point of the proceedings was supposed to be the symbolic arrival of Paul Kruger. Once 'Oom Paul' was duly received, the attention shifted to the tent where liquor was served. Before long the townspeople turned the occasion into a festive one. The footstomping rhythms of American country and western music blared across the town square as Machadodorp made merry. Traditional Afrikaans music, once standard fare at such occasions, seemed to have been forgotten. A reporter noted wryly: 'Not the "Hartseerwals". Not "Ou Ryperd". No, it was "Hand me down that bottle of Tequila, Sheila!"' (*Rapport* 11 June 2000)

What was particularly remarkable during the commemorations was the considerable growth in Afrikaans literature on the war. At least a hundred titles, some of them reprints, appeared and sold well in a market not known for huge sales (*Die Burger* 27 September 1999; *Rapport* 17 October 1999). The literary explosion not only mirrored a revitalized interest in the conflict, but also a probing and questioning attitude. One bestseller was a novel (Coetzee 1998) dealing with the darker side of Boer treachery and war crimes (*The Sunday Independent* 2 August 1998; Van der Merwe 1999; *Beeld* 11 May 1998; Renders 1999: 117–121). Besides literary works, several plays were produced, of which some focused on the ethnic and racial tensions spawned by the war (*Die Burger* 1 April 1999). In addition, the South African Broadcasting Corporation produced a television documentary, 'Verskroeide Aarde' (Scorched Earth), that covered a variety of angles and drew much praise as well as a considerable number of viewers (Binge 2002). Certain artworks also sought to rework traditional themes. In an exhibition in Pretoria a bronze statue depicted a young Boer woman on horseback, wearing only a Voortrekker bonnet and what was described as a 'very sado-erotic corset covered in sharp pins reminiscent of something between a punk and a porcupine' (*Pretoria News* October 1999). This statue was seen as a way of crossing old boundaries and merging fashion, historical memories and eroticism into a new form. Overall these developments reflected intensive memory work in a designated cultural space and a creative engagement with identity through the reframing of remembrance.

Under the twin impact of the disintegration of apartheid and the declining power of the National Party, a gradual erosion of traditionally constructed Afrikaner culture was long in evidence before the centenary (O'Meara 1996: 368–372). This assisted in opening the way for a more varied approach. The commemorations, then, provided Afrikaners with an opportunity to reevaluate a particularly dramatic period in their history and to rework it, relatively free from previous political agendas and restraints, into a more kaleidoscopic whole without necessarily translating this into a fixed leitmotif for the future. Of course, some renditions of the war preferred to be rooted in an earlier period, but perhaps the outstanding feature of the commemorations was the cultural dynamism released to find new answers to abiding questions in a non-prescriptive way.

Conclusion

The object of this chapter is to try to explore the different considerations that fed into the commemorating memory of the war. It is not, in essence, concerned with the 'accuracy' of historical renditions: such an investigation is more than likely to produce predictable results showing that 'history' was distorted. Commemorations by their very nature give their own shape and form to public understanding of the past. Debates over commemorations are not primarily intended to pit one version of the past against another or to assert the authority of academic scholarship, but are geared to invite inquiry in an attempt to explain the way in which commemorations as such are constructed to derive maximum benefit from the past in the present (cf. Carrier 1996). In this respect Ian Buruma (1999: 34) has made the salutary point that 'memory is not the same as history and memorializing is different from writing history'.

In reviewing the construction of the commemoration, the apogee of the state's involvement was probably the official launch at Brandfort. For the rest of the almost three years the state only sporadically genuflected in the direction of the centenary. It would appear that once it had exhausted whatever political mileage it could get out of the occasion, it left civil society to its own devices. In public, a significant discourse turned on black participation in the war, and it was conducted along lines designed to establish the high moral ground. For Afrikanerdom the commemoration of the war involved much memory work as earlier received memories of the war ceased to have the same purchase for a new generation in a changed environment. The nuances and differences that emerged during the commemorations served to underline the general assertion that historical memory is 'always contextual, partial and subject to self-interested manipulation and obfuscation' (Kenny 1999: 425).

Notes

1. For example *The Star,* 'Search for Site of Black Camp', 14 September 1999; *Cape Argus,* 'How Blacks Died', 11 October 1999; *City Press,* 'South Africa's Forgotten POW's', 18 April 1999; *Cape Argus,* 'Graves Rewrite History of Blacks in Boer War', 26 September 2000; *Sunday Independent,* 'Deaths of Thousands of Africans Come to Light', 16 May 1999; *Die Volksblad,* 'Nog swart grafte ontdek', 26 May 1999; *Beeld,* 'Speurtog na Anglo-Boereoorlog se swart konsentrasiekampe', 17 April 1999; *Die Burger,* 'Nog swart graftes', 11 November 1999; *Die Volksblad* 'Nog ABO begraafplase kan later ontdek word', 9 February 2000.

2. See for example *Die Volksblad* 19 January 1997 and *Die Volksblad* 28 March 1999. These articles contain evidence of black recollections of the war.

3. *Die Volksblad* in the Free State and *Die Burger* in the Western Cape published such material on a regular basis throughout the commemorative period. Some of those in the Free State were collected in two volumes edited by Nieman (2001, 2002).

Bibliography

Africa News. 1999. 'Text of speech'. <http//www.afrika.nl/news/09.10.99.html>.
Agten, S. 2002. *Een veranderende oorlog: de Geschiedschryving van de Anglo-Boereoorlog, 1899–1902.* Leuven.
Bailey, J. 2000. 'Some Meanings of the 'Private' in Sociological Thought', *Sociology* 34(3): 384–401.
Beeld. 1998. 'NP wil regering betrokke hê by oorlog'. 10 September.

Beeld. 1998. 'Wat ongedaan gemaak is, weer opgebou?' 21 August. (Letter from Dr W.F. te Water, Standerton, translation).

Beeld. 1999. 'Speurtog na Anglo-Boereoorlog se swart konsentrasiekampe'. 17 April.

Beeld. 1999. 'Twyfel heers oor maghebbers se siening van Afrikaners' (Translation). 19 April.

Beeld. 1999. 'Nuwe herrie oor museum'. 22 April.

Beeld. 1999. 'Minister, oorlogsmuseum skik oor raad'. 29 April.

Beeld. 1999. 'Versoening'. 12 October.

Beeld. 2000. 'Monument se ligging is beslis verkeerd'. 2 February.

Binge, H. 2002. Interview with producer. Stellenbosch. 2 March.

Burama, I. 1999. 'The Joys and Perils of Victimhood', New York Review of Books, 8 April.

Business Day. 1999. 'Mbeki praises Boer fighters'. 11 October.

Cape Argus. 1999. 'How blacks died'. 11 October.

Cape Argus. 1999. 'Row over black Boer War monument'. 15 October.

Cape Argus. 2000 'Graves rewrite history of blacks in Boer War'. 26 September.

Carrier, P. 1996. 'Historical Traces of the Present: The Uses of Commemoration', *Historical Reflections* 22(2): 431–445.

The Citizen. 1999. 'SA War remembered in different style'. 11 October.

City Press. 1999. 'South Africa's forgotten POW's'. 18 April.

Coetzee, C. 1998. *Op soek na Generaal Mannetjies Mentz*. Cape Town.

Cuthbertson, G. and A. Jeeves.1999. 'A Many-Sided Struggle for Southern Africa', *South African Historical Journal* 41(1): 21-39.

DACST. 1999. Notes on government programme for the commemoration of the centenary of the Anglo-Boer War. In private possession.

Davis, F. 1979. *Yearning for Yesterday: A Sociology of Nostalgia*. London

Die Afrikaner. 1999. 'Segsman vir die swartes'. 17 January.

Die Afrikaner. 1999. 'Net Swartes by herdenkingsfees'. 15 October.

Die Burger. 1998. 'Wes-Kaap sal oorlog herdenk'. (Translation.) 12 May.

Die Burger. 1998. 'Regering moet nou alles insit om ABO herdenking te laat slaag'. 12 September.

Die Burger. 1999. 'KKNK herdenk ABO met die opvoerings'. 1 April.

Die Burger. 1999. 'ABO steeds gewilde tema'. 27 September.

Die Burger. 1999. 'Oppas vir goedkoop nostalgie'. 1 October.

Die Burger. 1999. 'Oorlog skep band Afrikaners en Swartes'. 9 October.

Die Burger. 1999. 'Oorlog en versoening'. 12 October.

Die Burger. 1999. 'Nog swart grafte'. 11 November.

Die Volksblad. 1997. 'Dinamiese wêreld gaan oop toe navorsing oor oorlog begin'. 19 January.

Die Die Volksblad. 1998. 'Anglo-Boereoorlog is te sensitief vir Bloemfontein'. 11 March.

Die Volksblad. 1999. 'Nog swart grafte ontdek'. 26 May.

Die Volksblad. 1999. 'Oorlog te sensitief'. 28 March.

Die Volksblad. 1999. 'Fakkels in Bethlehem'. 9 October.

Die Volksblad. 1999. 'Onmin in herdenking'. 9 October.

Die Volksblad. 1999. 'Party bly weg omdat regering herdenking kaap.' (Translation.) 11 October.

Die Volksblad. 1999. 'Herinneringe aan die oorlog word 'n werklikheid'. 12 October.

Die Volksblad. 2000. 'Colesberg wedloop'. 19 January.

Die Volksblad. 2000. 'Regte begraafplaas van ABO slagoffers opgespoor'. 2 February.

Die Volksblad. 2000.'Vrae oor ABO geld'. 7 February.

Die Volksblad. 2000.'Besluit oor begraafplaas geregverdig'. 9 February.

Die Volksblad. 2000. 'Nog ABO begraafplase kan later ontdek word'. 9 February.

Die Volksblad. 2000. 'Bekende firma ondersoek ABO herdenking'. 4 November.

Die Volksblad. 2001. 'Louw familie hou saamtrek'. 23 November.

Dominy, G. and L. Callinicos. 1999. 'Is There Anything to Celebrate? Paradoxes of Policy and Examination of the State's Approach to Commemorating South Africa's Most Ambitious Struggle', *South African Historical Journal* 41(1): 389–391.

Evans, M. and K. Lunn (eds). 1997. *War and Memory in the Twentieth Century*. Oxford.

Financial Mail. 1999. 'A congress of anti-colonial victims'. 2 October.

Giliomee, H. 1999. 'Streef na onafhanklikheid van gees', *Afrikaans Vandag* 6(4): 2.

Gillis, J.R. (ed.). 1994. *Commemorations: The Politics of National Identity.* New York.

Goosen, D. 2001. *Voorlopige aantekeninge oor Politiek.* Orania.

Grundlingh, A. and H. Sapire. 1989. 'From Feverish Festival to Repetitive Ritual? The Changing Fortunes of Great Trek Mythology in an Industrialising South Africa, 1938–1988' *South African Historical Journal* 21(1): 1–19.

Jacobs, F. 2002. 'Die herdenking van die Anglo-Boereoorlog in oënskou', *Knapsak* 14(1): 3–10.

Kenny, M. 1999. 'A Place for Memory: The Interface between Individual and Collective History', *Society for Comparative Study of Society and History* 41(4): 425.

Kruger, D.W. 1969. 'Die Tweede Vryheidsoorlog in ons nasionale ontwikkeling 'soos die son uit die môrewolke', *Koers* 17(2): 67.

Lodge, T. 1990/1999. 'Charters from the Past: The African National Congress and Its Historiographical Traditions', *Radical History Review* 46(7): 161.

Louw, P. 1999. 'Gee swaarkry van die oorlog nuwe sin', *Afrikaans Vandag* 6(4): 15.

Mail and Guardian. 1999. 'It was a white man's war'. 15 October.

Mail and Guardian. 2000. 'Boer War events turn to farce'. 17–23 March.

Misztal, B.A. 2003. *Theories of Social Remembering.* Maidenhead.

Nasson, B. 2000. 'Commemorating the Anglo-Boer War in Post-Apartheid South Africa', *Radical History Review* 78(3): 150.

Ngubane, B. 1999. Address of Ben Ngubane. 8 October 1999. In private possession.

Nieman, N. (ed.). 2001 and 2002. *Ons lesers vertel.* Bloemfontein.

O'Meara, D. 1996. *Forty Lost Years: The Apartheid State and the Politics of the National Party, 1948–1994.* Johannesburg.

Pretoria News. 1999. 'A different angle on history'. October.

Quinault, R. 1998. 'The Cult of the Centenary, c.1784–1914' *Historical Research* 71(176): 303.

Rapport. 1998. 'Staat erken nog nie eeufees'. 3 May.

Rapport. 1998. 'Regering en oorlogsherdenking'. 18 June.

Rapport. 1999. 'Feesprogram in 2001 en 2002'. 6 June.

Rapport. 1999. 'Erken Swartes se rol in die oorlog'. 17 October.

Rapport. 1999. 'Oorlogsboeke verkoop soos soetkoek'. 17 October.

Rapport. 1999. 'Moenie boere uit die oorlog skryf nie'. 17 October.

Rapport. 2000. 'Paul Kruger ruk-en-rol op Machadodorp volksfees'. (Translation). 11 June.

Rapport. 2002. 'Heft burgers! Hoor Brandfort'. 2 June.

Renders, L. 1999. 'Tot in die hart van boosheid: twee resente Afrikaanse romans oor die Anglo-Boereoorlog', *Literator* 20(3): 117–121.

Saturday Star. 1996. 'How Boer war historians tore out the page on blacks'. 14 September.

Sekete, A. 2002. 'The Black People and the Anglo-Boer War: How Did They See It?' *Knapsak* 41.

Southern Cross. 1999. 'A century on'. 6 October.

The Star. 1999. 'Search for site of black camp'. 14 September.

Sunday Independent. 1998. 'Anglo Boer War spawns milestone in new fiction'. 2 August.

Sunday Independent. 1999. 'Deaths of thousands of Africans come to light'. 16 May.

Sunday Times. 1999. 'Boer War had nothing to do with blacks'. 17 October.

Sunday World. 1999. 'Victims of the white man's war'. 17 October.

Times. 1999. 'Bitter legacy of the "white man's war"'. 2 October.

Van der Merwe, C 1999. 'Die verstommende verskietende ster ooit' Online at <http//www.mweb.co/litnet/leeskring/mentz/>.

Warwick, P. 1983. *Black People and the South African War of 1899–1902.* Cambridge.

WOZA. 1999. Online at <http//woza.za.forum2/Oct 99.boer war25.html>.

CHAPTER 7

From Public History to Private Enterprise
The Politics of Memory in the New South Africa

PATRICK HARRIES

The political shifts in South Africa in the early 1990s initiated a sea change in the way the country looked at its past. Scholars became less concerned with the causes of apartheid than with the consequences of the ideology that, since 1948, had dominated South Africa. One of the consequences of the apartheid period was a landscape of memory that reflected deep communal divisions and reinforced entrenched social identities. The roots of these divisions go back to the nineteenth century, when the Cape and Natal developed a sense of 'Britishness' through an architectural tradition and display that, like naming practices, monuments, social pageants and commemorations, frequently recalled the colonies' ties with the metropole and its royal family. This heritage tradition became more assertive as British capitalism developed South Africa into an industrial nation in the years after the conquest of the Boer republics (Merrington 1997, 1998; Mylam 2005; cf. du Plessis 1987 and Prinsloo 1995). At the time of union in 1910, a new (white) 'South Africanism' found expression through the building of monuments, the preservation of relics and the conservation of archives that aimed to 'awaken ... and foster ... a national consciousness' (Botha 1921, 1924). This national consciousness excluded the black population and forced many Afrikaners into a subsidiary role.

The divisions within the white population quickly produced opposing heritage traditions that were easily visible in the country's two capitals. In Pretoria, Sir Herbert Baker's Union Buildings reflected an imperial past that sat uneasily with Fort Klapperkop (erected to withstand imperial invasion) and the

Notes for this section begin on page 139.

nearby Voortrekker monument (which bore witness to the rebirth of Afrikaner nationalism). Church Square in Pretoria recalled the republican inheritance of Afrikaner nationalism, while the Rhodes memorial in Cape Town harked back to a British past. At the University of Cape Town (UCT), the Jameson Memorial Hall was named after the prime minister of the Cape colony who, as a younger man, had attempted to overthrow the government of the sovereign Transvaal Republic. The hall looks across the Cape Flats to Stellenbosch University, where the Majuba residence celebrates the Boer victory over the British in 1881, which laid the basis for the rise of the Transvaal as an independent state. The Smuts Hall residence at UCT is met, at Stellenbosch University, by a memorial hall named after the field marshal's bitter political opponent, D.F. Malan. On occasions these assertive naming practices opened old wounds, for instance, when the headquarters of the South African Defence Force, called 'Robert's Heights' after the British general responsible for the defeat of the Boers in the 1899–1902 war, was renamed 'Voortrekker Hoogte' (Voortrekker Heights), or when the mixed-race Sophiatown was cleared of its black population and renamed 'Triomf' (Triumph).

Intense and bitter conflicts divided the white population over the composition of the flag that would represent the Union of South Africa, and for many years arguments continued to simmer over the place to be occupied by this flag alongside the Union Jack (Saker 1980). Disputes arose at the same time over the content of a common national anthem, and over whether this should be sung alongside 'God Save the King'. These divisions were particularly reflected in the governing United Party and contributed to the resignation of General Hertzog and his followers when South Africa entered the Second World War. After the electoral victory of the Nationalist Party in 1948, South Africans' war memories were excluded from the public sphere and confined to the private spaces occupied by individuals, their families and institutions. Village and town councils argued increasingly bitterly over the names given to schools, hospitals, mayoral complexes, theatres, streets, public squares, airports and even telecommunications towers. During this time, the National Party worked assiduously to represent itself, through a sectarian imagery, as the party of all 'true Afrikaners'. A national holiday was established on 16 December to celebrate the vow to God taken by a group of Boers on the eve of the battle of Blood River in 1838. First celebrated in 1864, this day commemorated the victory of the Boers, God's chosen people, over the Zulu army of king Dingane. Another public holiday on 31 May both celebrated the establishment of the Republic of South Africa in 1961 and erased the memory of the Boer surrender at Vereeniging on the same day in 1902. On these sacred days Afrikaners met in large numbers at 'their' historical sites to listen to speeches that recalled their separate, historical identity as a clearly visible 'people' (du Toit 1983; Thompson 1985). At these pageants and festivals, often marked by the flags and folk songs of the old republics, Afrikaner leaders frequently recalled moments in an antagonistic past in ways that strengthened the bonds of community and contributed to their victories in the whites-only elections held after 1948.

As the National Party grew in strength and power, it increasingly dominated the country's landscape of memory. This reconfiguration of the mnemonics of memory took various forms. The meaning of the Women's Monument outside Bloemfontein, erected to commemorate the victims of the concentration camps of the South African War, changed from reconciliation to retribution as the monument became an icon of Afrikaner suffering and fortitude under the leadership of men (Grundlingh 2002). In 1968 the National Party prime minister unveiled a memorial outside the small northern Cape town of Calvinia to mark the site of the last hostilities in the South African War. The spirit of reconciliation behind the monument was, however, offset by its representation of a Boer warrior and by an inscription calling for a vigilant defense of Boer republican traditions. In the same year the Group Areas Act divided Calvinia along racial lines, which, four years later, led to the demolition of a chapel in the town dedicated to the memory of Abraham Esau, a 'Cape patriot' of mixed race, executed by Boer forces in 1901 (Nasson 2004c). By the early 1970s, few South Africans knew the English version of the national anthem.

Other symbols served to unite the white population in a common front that implicitly excluded the black majority from membership of the South African nation. In natural history museums the organization and exhibition of human artefacts according to the evolutionist principles of 'civilized' and 'uncivilized' was replaced in the 1930s by formal categories of race and tribe. During the era of segregation the museums became time capsules in which Africans were fixed in primitive tribal categories whose exotic cultures attracted a large public. The racialization of museum displays was entrenched in the 1960s when European and Asian artefacts in the South African Museum in Cape Town were moved to a new Cultural History Museum occupying the premises of the old Supreme Court (a.k.a. the Slave Lodge) and the African exhibits were left with the animals. Visitors to these major museums in the heart of Cape Town were led to compare the primitive nature of African culture, particularly in the museum's Stone-Age Bushman diorama, with the advanced cultures of European and Asian peoples displayed in the Cultural History Museum. This led visitors to return home with a reinforced belief in the racial superiority of the peoples of European descent who, despite their differences, constituted a national group with a clear duty to uplift the native tribes and, following the ideology of apartheid, bring them to independence. The nearby National Gallery produced the same impression, as it displayed only European works of art and left the exhibition of African art to smaller, private galleries.

Sections of the black population challenged the jaundiced or insulting way in which they were portrayed in – or excluded from – national museums, monuments, festivals, anthems, flags and commemorations. Chief Mangosotho Buthelezi proclaimed 24 September to be the day on which the Kwazulu homeland would remember King Shaka, the founder of the Zulu nation; every year on Shaka Day, Buthelezi delivered blistering speeches on Zulu history at the memorial to the king at Stanger (Forsyth 1992; Harries 1993; Klopper 1996). At the same time, the glorious Zulu past was brought alive by the rebuilding of the residences of the kings and the establishment of viewing sites and other facilities at historic battlefields (Laband 1986). The government of the independent homeland of Ciskei played on similar historical origins when, in 1978, it repatriated the bones of Chief Maqoma, who had died on Robben Island a century earlier, to a Hero's Acre built in the Amatola Mountains. This ceremony, held at Ntaba ka Ndoda, Sandile's stronghold, was attended by representatives of the Australian and French governments and by 15,000 participants, all honouring the Xhosa dead of the Frontier Wars (Mostert 1992; Peires 1989; Hodgson 1987). Others used the tools of memory to recall their heritage of resistance and to assert their place in the nation. From its foreign exile, the ANC chose to establish its armed wing, Mkhonto we Sizwe, on 16 December 1961, adopting its own flag, colours and anthem, the Christian hymn 'Nkosi Sikelel' iAfrika'.

The reforms brought to apartheid by P.W. Botha led to conflicts within the Afrikaner community that quickly affected the symbolism of the *Volk*. In 1979 a leading Afrikaner historian was actually tarred and feathered by right-wing extremists when he suggested publicly that some of the tenets of the Day of the Vow were historical myths (van Jaarsveld 1980; Liebenberg 1985; Thompson 1985; see. Ndlovu 2000; Dlamini 2001). In the years that followed, Afrikaner nationalism attempted to reshape an uncomfortable past by infusing sites of memory with new meanings. Public celebrations of the Day of the Vow, held annually at the Voortrekker monument outside Pretoria, declined as Afrikaners took on new, more functional identities or celebrated their nation in isolated spots such as Schoemansdal outside Makhado (formerly Louis Trichardt) or Paardekraal near Krugersdorp. When P.W. Botha attempted to bring the reformed apartheid state back into the world community, he reactivated memories of South Africa's participation in the world wars that had so divided the white population. Forgotten memorials took on a new, public importance as government officials joined veterans in public services commemorating the dead of two world wars alongside those killed in apartheid's 'border wars' (Nasson 2004b). The sense of racial trusteeship developed at this time and could still be seen in the P.W. Botha section of the George Museum, where a poster confronted visitors with the information that 'first as prime Minister and then as State President, Mr Botha was closely involved in the government's initiatives to improve relations with black communities, to raise their standard of living and to accommodate them politically.' It also noted Mr Botha's role in bringing reforms to apartheid, most notably the shift in the early 1980s towards a form of power-sharing government between the different racial groups. This 'implied an undivided country', the poster stated unambiguously, 'one citizenship for all, equal opportunities and participation in government'. No mention was made of the bloody uprisings that accompanied this change in policy, which almost entirely ignored the black majority, or the brutal methods needed to implement it (South African Press Association 1998). One of Botha's reforms was to reorganize the structure of museums in a clearly segregationist manner that, in the 1980s, placed historical museums under 'own affairs' (which were the concern of the separate Indian, Coloured or White Chambers of Parliament) while natural history museums fell under the ambit of non-racial 'general affairs'.

As this racial dispensation excluded the black population, 'its' museums and official commemorations were confined to the tribal homelands. In the meantime, some museums started to employ various devices in an attempt to break the 'time machine' nature of their tribal displays and to include black Africans in their representation of urban life and the broader South African nation (Davison 1993, 1998; Coombes 2003; Gore 2004, 2005). Many black South Africans used the same tools of memory to define and recall their separate heritage and to assert their place in the nation. Leslie Witz has recently documented the counter-memories mounted in opposition to the 1952 festival marking the tercentenary of the arrival at the Cape of Jan van Riebeeck, the first Dutch governor (Witz 2003; Rassool and Witz 1993). The struggle against apartheid created other memories through which local communities forged new identities. In Sharpeville an illegal memorial recalled those killed in the massacre of 1960 and the uprising of 1984. By the 1980s three annual commemorations took place in Vaal Triangle townships, memorializing the events of 21 March 1960 (the Sharpeville massacre), 16 June 1976 (the Soweto uprising) and 3 September 1984 (the uprising in Sebokeng that quickly spread to other townships of the Vaal Triangle). These were emotional days for embattled communities, and observations frequently were held in churches that themselves became symbols of the struggle against apartheid (Noonan 2003). Young revolutionaries in Alexandra systematically renamed the streets, parks, sections and schools during the uprising in the township in the mid 1980s (Bozzoli 2004).

These sharp changes and challenges to the politics of memory accompanied the political upheavals of the last decade of apartheid. In this chapter I now want to turn to some of the ways in which the post-apartheid state in South Africa, at national and local levels, has employed public history to produce a new, more consensual history; and how these changes are registered and received by different communities. In the following section I look at the role of the state in the celebration of memory. In the next part I turn to the impact of community museums before examining the influence of the market, and tourism in general, on the public history of post-1994 South Africa. In the conclusion I comment on the difficulty of balancing the needs of South Africans to forget not their duty to remember. In the process I focus on the tensions between public and professional history and suggest ways in which these may be resolved.

Memory and Reconciliation: The Role of the State

South Africa boasts seven World Heritage sites, of which three celebrate unique natural environments. The others recognize the possibility that life began in what is today the Free State (the Vredefort Dome), that Gauteng houses the Cradle of Humankind (centred on the remains of early hominids found in the Sterkfontein Caves) and that South Africa produced a complex political kingdom a thousand years ago (at Mapungubwe). While these historical statements pursue a tradition established by Jan Smuts, Robben Island marks a break with the past (Gordon 2003). Several members of the South African government, and many of their political ancestors, spent lengthy periods incarcerated on the island that has become a showcase and foundational cornerstone of the new South Africa (Coombes 2003). Great care has been taken to balance the dark history of the island, centred on the penitentiary, with an image of the triumph of the spirit (represented by the unspoilt coastline, wild animals and open vistas). But the positive attributes of this premier site of national memory are balanced by some problematic aspects. There were no women or white political prisoners on Robben Island, for instance, and the men were divided into different and often disputatious political factions. The prison, as a symbol of brutal incarceration and suffering, stands in an uneasy juxtaposition with the freedom of nature and the wild game that represent the triumph of the human spirit. Vestiges of earlier struggles are also visible on the island, such as the remnants of the fortifications erected during the Second World War and the earlier leprosy hospital. The Red Location Museum of Struggle in New Brighton is modelled on the Robben Island complex. In both museums there is a strong tension between the need to appeal to local and international interest to holiday-makers and struggle aficionados. As we will see, the conflict between public history and private enterprise has produced an ambiguous and sometimes confusing image.

Freedom Park is the most ambitious site of memory to be established in the country. It is being erected, at a cost of over R560 million, on 52 hectares of Salvokop that overlook the Union Buildings, Church Square and the Voortrekker Monument. The first phase of the park, a garden of remembrance for freedom fighters, was opened in March 2004. On this site the heroes of the struggle against apartheid will be recalled – alongside the victims of genocide, slavery, the wars of conquest and resistance, the South African and world wars, and the struggle for national liberation. In this way, individuals from different, even historically hostile, communities will find a shared sense of commemoration in Freedom Park. A similarly inclusive perspective drives the Constitutional Hill project. This complex, opened on 21 March 2004, is built around Johannesburg's old fort, once used as a transit jail for political and other prisoners, irrespective of race or gender, which today houses the constitution of South Africa.

The Truth and Reconciliation Commission has created another powerful archive of memory in South Africa. The evidence produced by the commission has confronted many South Africans with the violence of the system needed to maintain apartheid. It has served a healing function by allowing victims to express their pain in public and by getting perpetrators to ask for forgiveness. But the brief of the TRC was shaped by the context in which it was created: a negotiated transfer of power, the continued presence of the white community and the need to effect 'transformation' (i.e. a transfer of power at the institutional level) without endangering the structure of the economy or the various branches of the state (from the judiciary, police and prisons, via the armed forces, to the civil service and state industries). No less a figure than Nelson Mandela outlined this path when, on leaving prison, he met very publicly with the prosecutor responsible for his life sentence, the wife of 'architect of apartheid' Hendrik Verwoerd, and the warders who had overseen his imprisonment on Robben Island. This attitude of reconciliation was extended to the private sector of the economy when ANC leaders attended the funeral of Harry Oppenheimer, a beneficiary, perhaps even a draftsman, of the 'cheap labour system' that stood at the heart of apartheid. The symbolism of the ANC's new attitude to private enterprise was particularly caught by the image of Mandela at the New York Stock Exchange. Mandela would eventually call on South Africans to 'forget the past' (and build the future). As several historians have shown, this focus on reconciliation strongly influenced the landscape of memory produced by the TRC's archive (cf. du Toit 2005; Posel 2002; Alexander 2002; Thelen 2002; Bundy 2000; Cherry 2000; Maier 2000).

Unlike the historical commissions established by several European countries to investigate their actions during the Second World War, the TRC drew none of its senior commissioners from the historical profession. The confinement of the TRC brief to 'gross human rights violations' justly directed public attention to the torturers and created a magnificent archive on the brutality required to enforce apartheid. But the archive, the major site of memory covering the period of struggle from 1960 to 1993, is silent on many issues. It says little about apartheid as a changing and dynamic system and, in the process, hides from public scrutiny the intellectuals and politicians who conceptualized, mounted and administered the system of 'separate development'. It particularly overlooks the profiteers who benefited from a system defined by the UN in 1973 as 'a crime against humanity'. The TRC also failed to examine the campaign of violence and destruction waged against South Africa's neighbours as the government attempted to reform apartheid in the 1980s. By stressing the individual nature of the violence of apartheid and by limiting its brief to the post-1960 period, the TRC has underplayed the widespread, systemic nature of racism in South Africa. This has tended to hide the deep historical roots of apartheid and, when combined with the therapeutic nature of the TRC, has obscured the everyday, venal ways in which most people (mainly white, but also black) accommodated apartheid or actively collaborated in its implementation. These ranged from everyday actions, such as catching a train, standing in a queue or crossing a railway line, to accepting the ineligibility of blacks for certain occupations or accepting that people defined as 'black' by the Population Registration Act received inferior education and salaries (Finnegan 1994). The TRC's concentration on the testimony of victims and perpetrators has created a dichotomous evidence that, many argue, hides the essential nature of – and responsibility for – apartheid. At the same time, it has been careful not to create individual heroes or commemorate events that might disturb the policy of reconciliation; nor has it even attempted to describe the ambiguous position of those good men caught within an evil system (Friedländer 1969; Good 2006).

The German case has shown that, as companies become global, or appeal to a multicultural market, they are required to conform to international standards of morality. In South Africa the relationship between apartheid and capital accumulation has been a major subject of study for the last thirty years, yet the TRC and the government have overlooked studies that clearly show how apartheid exploited and impoverished many black South Africans even as it contributed directly to the development of some of the country's major corporations (Innes 1983; O'Meara 1983). During the late 1980s this relationship was clear to many foreign corporations that, rather than compromise their international standing, chose to withdraw from the country. As business enterprises and political leaders refused to take responsibility for apartheid, the TRC portrayed the apartheid system as the product of Afrikaners as a 'nation' or whites as a racial group. In his testimony before the TRC, Desmond Smith, the general manager of Sanlam, the financial giant at the heart of Afrikaner nationalism, expressed his regret for the pain caused by apartheid but failed to show how his company benefited from, and supported, this 'crime against humanity'. 'Sanlam as a member of a privileged group benefited from Apartheid in one way or another', he stated before the commission, 'relative to members of disadvantaged groups.'[1] Attempts to attribute apartheid to a group in this manner effectively serve to hide the institutions and individuals responsible for the invention and implementation of the policy.

While the TRC hesitated to investigate companies, or to call on them to pay reparations, it has pressed the government to compensate victims of gross human rights violations. In some quarters the TRC's failure to confront the origins of and responsibility for violence has been condemned, as it is feared that a culture of impunity, will merely cause conflict to reignite at a later date. From this perspective, forgetting aspects of the past will reassure local and international investors and mollify groups marginalised by political change. However, there is concern that this policy will bring neither truth nor justice, and that in the long run it will undermine both respect for the rule of law and the authority of the state (Taylor 2002).

Mr Mbeki's oration at the reburial of Sarah Baartman (the 'Hottentot Venus') at Hankey in the Eastern Cape in August 2002 provided an opportune occasion for an attack on one strain of the racism overlooked by the TRC (Mbeki 2002). In a speech delivered before 10,000 listeners, the president showed an admirable familiarity with the pseudoscientific writings of the eighteenth and nineteenth centuries, and condemned a fundamental evil in public life. But in the process, he came close to portraying racism as an inherent, almost physical, attribute of Europeans and their descendants. This led him to overlook the long history of violence between the San and Bantu-speaking agriculturalists and, from one perspective, caused him to miss an opportunity to criticize the universal nature of racism.[2] His speech seemed particularly provocative as Hankey holds the remains of Dr John Philip, the early nineteenth-century missionary figure at the heart of the South African liberal tradition. But the ensuing heated discussions succeeded in placing the question of racism squarely in the public domain. Baartman's elevation, from an entrepreneurial figure compelled to capitalize on her physiognomy, into a symbol of colonial exploitation and national humiliation, has been remarkable. By July 2004 she had become 'a Khoisan woman enslaved and paraded in Europe as a sexual freak' and her burial place a national heritage site (*IOL* 2004; for accounts of Baartman's history see Fauvelle-Aymar 2002; Gordon 1992; Abrahams, 2004; Strother 1999).

The ANC government's attempt to use Heritage as a means of constructing a utilitarian history was particularly visible during the commemorations marking the outbreak of the South African War. At events held at memorials in Gauteng and elsewhere, politicians portrayed the ancestors of Afrikaner and African nationalism as the victims of British imperialism (Brink and Krige 1999). This idea, built upon Archbishop Tutu's ruminations at the Women's Monument in Bloemfontein, tried to reconcile the two hostile nationalisms in a common, historical victimhood. Despite howls of protest from the historical profession, this reinterpretation of the past led president Mbeki to recall, in March 2004, 'the cruel war waged' by the British 'against the people of South Africa' (Mbeki 2004; for historians' criticisms see Smith 1999; Grundlingh 2004; Brink and Krige 1999; Nasson 2004a). Mbeki's purpose, of course, was to reconcile historically hostile communities in a common experience as victims of external aggression. But this requires not only a convenient forgetting of the deep hostility that existed between Boers and blacks in the old republics; it also requires that the many black and white South Africans who fought on the side of the British in that war be stripped of their idealism and national identity. For many this opens old wounds, as Afrikaner nationalist historians not only forgot the service of 'freeborn English Natives', black 'Cape patriots' and colonials in what they called the 'English War'; they also suppressed the memory of their sons' military service in two world wars (Nasson 2004b).

Reconciling communities divided by a war that took place over a century ago has proved difficult. In September 2003 a monument to Abraham Esau, now identified on the accompanying plaque as 'a martyr', 'fell over' a month later. A new hospital in Calvinia has been called Abraham Esau and the monument has been reerected there. The theme of reconciliation has also, somewhat surprisingly, been attached to Church Square in Pretoria, where the statue of an African chief now faces that of Paul Kruger, the president who mounted long and brutal wars of conquest and led the Transvaal Republic against British imperialism. The square, a former icon of Afrikaner nationalism, has become the home of the local ANC-dominated government and, in the eyes of one Afrikaner historian, has become a symbol of reconciliation between Africans and Afrikaners (Tempelhoff 1998).

The government has reinforced its strategy of reconciliation by placing neutral symbols such as plants and animals on banknotes and coins and by fusing Die Stem and Nkosi Sikelel' iAfrica into a common national anthem. While the ANC has not adopted an anonymous nomenclature, such as Britain's 'bank holidays', it has avoided politicizing the calendar in ways that will resuscitate the memory of a painful and hostile past. The Sharpeville massacre of 21 March 1960 is celebrated as 'Human Rights Day', when the population is encouraged to reflect on 'human life, liberty and well-being' rather than the brutal killing of sixty-nine unarmed protesters that marked a new phase in the struggle against apartheid (*Cape Argus* 21 March 2000). The Soweto uprising of 1976 is commemorated on 16 June, named 'Youth Day' in an attempt to turn it into a 'color blind' day on which young people dance to rock bands and, somewhat incongruously, reflect on problems affecting their generation (such as high levels of unemployment and HIV/AIDS). But while this form of celebration draws large numbers of young people, it is sufficiently anonymous to suppress the memory of the revolt of black youth in 1976 that changed the history of South Africa (Ndlovu 1998; *Cape Argus* 16 June 2000). Shaka Day, 24 September, has been claimed as a national Heritage Day rather than a narrower, exclusively Zulu day of commemoration. Women's Day, 9 August, recalls the mass march on the Union Buildings in 1956 to protest the imposition of pass laws on African women. Freedom Day, 27 April, commemorates the first fully democratic elections held in South Africa.

Perhaps most remarkable is the transformation of the Day of the Vow into Reconciliation Day, an act that, perhaps, encourages people to forget, rather than confront, the past. In 1998 the government threw its weight behind a 'counter-memory' when it unveiled a monument to the Zulus killed in the battle of Blood River and paid for a feast that attracted some 10,000 people. Afrikaners and Zulus attended separate ceremonies on the two sides of the drift that played a central role in the battle (Carter 1998). This policy of creating a dialogue between two opposing memories has been counterpoised, in the case of the Voortrekker monument, by a determined attempt to change the meaning of the site by downplaying its political associations and mounting events that open it to a wider public (Kruger and van Heerden 2005; Vally 2004; Grundlingh 2001; Marx 1988; Delmont 1993).

National monuments have been erected to the contribution of women in the struggle (in Pretoria), to Hector Peterson (the first scholar killed on 16 June 1976) in Soweto, and to those killed in the Sharpeville massacre near Vereeniging. Nelson Mandela has become the nation's premier icon, with a statue erected to him in Santon, museums in his honour at Mveso, Qunu and Umtata, and the home in Soweto he shared with his second wife Winnie has become an important site of memory. A statue has been erected to Steve Biko in Mdantsane, and his home in Ginsburg, near King William's Town, has become a site of national memory. There are plans to erect statues to the Zulu kings Cetshwayo and Dinizulu alongside the statue of Louis Botha on the Berea in Durban.

There is an obvious ambivalence in the ranks of government over the question of the renaming of towns. While the ANC accepted Tzaneen's refusal to adopt the name of Mark Shope, the party has been more assertive about the renaming of most of Pretoria as Tshwane or in calling Pietpotgietersrus after Mokopane, the chief responsible for the death of the Voortrekker leader. On the other hand, changes to the names of provinces have been geographical rather than hagiographical, recalling locations rather than fallen heroes, and towns have generally been renamed in such a way as to avoid causing injury. The renaming of streets has sometimes caused offense when imposed on communities. But this renaming is fitful and driven by local interests. In Cape Town it is still possible to find oneself on streets named after Antonio Salazar (the Portugues dictator) and the brownshirt Oswald Pirow.

In general the government has not taken down monuments erected under white supremacy. Its policy has rather been to erect alternative sites in the vicinity that dilute, break the monopoly or enter into dialogue with the original site. Otherwise, it has encouraged museums to transform their message by incorporating material relating to local black communities. Sometimes this means leaving exhibitions largely untouched as a corner is cleared for the new display or, perhaps, a new room added to the structure. Both communities and government have erected monuments and memorials to celebrate the fallen heroes of the struggle against apartheid, yet there is no equivalent of the Heroes' Acre in Harare and Windhoek (Rassool, Witz and Minkley 2000). On the other hand, the monument erected by the old Ciskei government to encourage the growth of Xhosa identity, Ntaba ka Ndoda, has been allowed to fall into ruin (*Mail and Guardian* 4 May 2004).

Community

The heavy investment of government in public history has been paralleled by an upsurge of community memory. The authors of the *Lonely Planet Guide to South Africa* advise their readers, on returning from Robben Island, to embark on a tour of the District Six Museum. This remarkable community museum is filled with aural, tangible and textual memories of a section of Cape Town destroyed by apartheid's Group Areas Act in the late 1960s and 1970s. Few exhibits are under glass or locked away from the viewer, and multiple voices replace the single, authorized view normally encountered in state museums. As the museum raises its own funds and is run by members of the community, it provides a particularly democratic outlet for social memory (Coombes 2003; for background on District Six see Soudien 2001³). But although the museum is an exemplary 'location of learning' about apartheid, it is not always clear who constitutes 'the community', and there is a tendency to portray the history of District Six before the removals as a golden age occupied by a creole population that stood as the antithesis of apartheid. This view poses few questions about the historical process of 'creolization' or the divisions within the community. It particularly omits any reference to the individuals and agencies that participated in, and benefited from, the destruction of District Six. This general concern with the evidence of victims, and frequently with their triumph over adversity, has coloured historians' attempts to recount the experience of forced removals under the Group Areas Act. While laudably bringing the memories of the victims of the act into the mainstream of national history, this form of history-from-below tends to leave out the hidden, dark sides of community life, such as family violence, sexual molestation and crime. It particularly leaves out the moral question of who formulated the Group Areas Act and who profited from its implementation – a question that could be answered without much trouble by combining the archives of memory with those found in the Deeds' Office.⁴

In many cases, memory has fuelled group identity in post-apartheid South Africa. The Khoisan have particularly emerged in a newly invented form to claim their rights as a constituent part of the rainbow nation. This identity was given particular prominence when an exhibition at the National Gallery in Cape Town, held significantly in 1995, the year after the change in government, attempted to include in an exhibition on the San the violence perpetrated against these hunter-gatherers by the immigrant white settlers. Criticisms of the exhibition ranged from comments on the negative image of the San – exposed as victims of genocide rather than as a proud people facing adversity – to concerns over the social propriety of organizing an exhibition without consulting 'local communities'. The ensuing public debate contributed to the removal from the South African Museum of the plaster casts of 'racially pure' Bushmen, in the setting of a Stone Age diorama, that were so dear to the heart of Cape Town's schoolchildren (Skotness 2002; for criticism see Schrire et al. 1996; Lane 1996; Kashfir 1997; Douglas and Law 1997; for the political context of the exhibition, Skotness 2002; on the diorama question, Davison 2001).

Various other mnemonics of memory have also served to reinforce – or reinvent – this Khoisan community. These include the return to South Africa of the remains of Sarah Baartman from the Musée de l'homme in Paris and the ongoing debate over whether the museums should repatriate the skeletal remains of 'Bushmen' and other 'inferior' or 'dying-out races'. In the late nineteenth and early twentieth centuries, several physical anthropologists were engaged in the dubious acquisition of these remains. The racial studies of these scientists seemed valid in those days but, with the march of time, are no longer deemed acceptable, and many are now calling for the bones of their subjects to be returned to their areas of origin (*Cape Argus* 20 July 2002; Legassick and Rassool 2000). These demands – and the ensuing 'debate' – publicize the oppression suffered by the Khoisan people and, by stressing their existence in the past, make the general public aware of their situation in the present (for some of the political issues, see Bank 1997; Caliguire 1996; more broadly, Sharp 1997).

At the same time a wider, 'coloured' identity has been encouraged by memories tied to sites such as the chapel and memorial dedicated to Abraham Esau in Calvinia. The rediscovery of slavery and its material vestiges has also served to recall the origins and growth of this particularly South African community. During the struggle against apartheid, individuals repressed the memory of their slave origins for various reasons. For some, slavery was a social stigma best forgotten; for others, the memory of slavery threatened to divide the opposition to apartheid along racial lines. For whites who could be associated with the old slave-owning class, the memory of slavery was a source of guilt and pain that merely served to push 'coloureds' into an alliance with African nationalism (Ward and Worden 1998; Coombes 2003; on the wider politics of memory associated with slavery see Klein 1989; Akyeampong 2001). The recovery of slave identities took place slowly after 1994, when it was encouraged by the incorporation of South Africa into the UNESCO slave route (in 1996) and by the renaming of the Cultural History Museum as the Slave Lodge (in 1999). The mounting of exhibitions on slavery at the Slave Lodge and on various wine estates (most notably Groot Constantia) has also brought the memory of slavery more clearly into view (*Quarterly Bulletin of the National Library of South Africa* 1999; *IOL* 27 April 2002).

The Slave Lodge, a two-storied, whitewashed building, is at the head of Cape Town's main thoroughfare, a street gratefully named Adderley after the politician who, in the mid-nineteenth century, prevented the colony from being turned into a convict station. The building is a site of multiple memories: it first served as the Dutch East India Company Slave Lodge but, soon after the second British occupation of the Cape, was occupied by various government offices, including those of the South African Museum, the Surveyor General, the Vice-Admiralty Court (engaged in the suppression of the slave trade after 1808) and the governor's Advisory Council (1827–1834). For the next twenty years it housed the Nominated Council and then, in 1854, became the site of the Legislative Council voted into office on the basis of a low and non-racial qualified franchise (Mountain 2004). After the establishment of responsible government, the House of Assembly moved to new premises in the neighbouring Company Gardens; eventually the Supreme Court occupied the building that, in the 1960s, became the Cultural History Museum. The point is that recent political changes have drawn attention to the slave history of the lodge in a way that obscures the other important voices represented by this building. The debate over the Prestwich Street burial ground in Cape Town provides another example of the heightened public concern to celebrate and honour communities marked by a long history of suffering and discrimination. During construction on the western Foreshore, the old District One of the city, the discovery of a series of shallow graves, believed to be those of slaves, stopped work at Prestwick Street. The costly halt to development only ended with a promise to develop a site of memory to the slaves buried in the area (Weeder 2004).

Various other communities are also calling for recognition, particularly through their portrayal of their role in the struggle against apartheid. Members of the Mamelodi community have asked for 21 November to be recognized as a day on which to remember the KwaNdebele Youth massacre in 1985. In Sebokeng the chosen date is the start of the rent and service boycotts that initiated the Vaal Triangle uprising (3 September 1984). Others have called for memorial parks and stones to be laid, or libraries to be built, in honour of those killed or injured in the struggle. In 1998 the Mamelodi ANC and the local civic organization erected a stone memorial to Stanza Bopape, whom they saw as a symbol, like Hector Peterson, of the struggle against apartheid in the 1980s and early 1990s. At the same time a board, soon to be vandalized, was erected near the gate of the local hospital, bearing the names of fifty victims of the struggle in Mamelodi. In October 1999 Thabo Mbeki and Mangosuthu Buthelezi unveiled a memorial at Thokoza bearing the names of victims of the struggle in the area between the followers of their two organizations, the ANC and the Inkatha Freedom Party. The local Council of Greater Germiston unveiled a monument at Katlehong on Human Rights Day (21 March) 1998. IFP and ANC supporters gathered to chant slogans and watch the unveiling of a two-metre high wall with a plaque recalling the memory of those killed in the fighting between the two organizations. This temporary monument aims to foster reconciliation and will later include the names of victims. Other communities hit by the fighting during the last decade of apartheid have erected monuments at Sebokeng and Kagiso (Kgalema 1999). In general, these memorials conform to the TRC's expressed wish that communitarian memorials should not foster hurt and hostility in a way that will detract attention from nation-building and reconciliation.[5]

In the Western Cape a museum to migrant labour has been established at the Lwandle informal settlement outside Somerset West (Mgijima and Buhelezi 2006; Witz 2005). The Langa pass office has been preserved as a memorial to the vicious system of internal passports that controlled the movement of black Africans to the cities. A simple memorial was erected on Human Rights Day 2000 at the site, at the corner of NY1 and NY111, where the Gugulethu Seven had been murdered by police some fourteen years earlier. Five years later, after the mothers of the young men expressed their belief that it was an unfitting tribute to their sons, the monument was removed and replaced by seven granite blocks bearing the images of the victims. Another memorial has been erected at the place in Thornton Road, Athlone, where young stone-throwers were gunned down by police hidden in the back of a truck (the so-called Trojan Horse incident).

Political conservatives have also commemorated their losses in ways that call for recognition and justice. They maintain a strong presence on the Internet, where viewers can read books, consult articles and enter chat groups. They have erected a memorial in Ventersdorp to mark the site of a crucial clash between the militia of the Afrikaner Weerstandsbeweging (AWB) and the Security Forces in August 1991. Three AWB members died and fifty-eight others were injured in a bloody confrontation, 'forgotten' by most historians today, that destroyed the last vestige of Afrikaner unity.[6] In the small, informally segregated village of Orania in the dry northern Cape, Betsie Verwoerd's home is preserved as a monument to her husband and his achievements. On Youth Day (16 June) 2005, leaders of the conservative Freedom Front youth movement walked from Pretoria to the Constitutional Court in Johannesburg, where they handed in a memorandum calling for equal treatment for all young people in the country. The year before, hundreds of white crosses had been erected on 16 June, at Rietvlei on the N1 highway near Polokwane, to commemorate and protest against the widespread killings of white farm owners and managers.

Market

If the politicians wish to forget the violence behind so many of South Africa's public holidays, the business sector would like to forget the holidays themselves, at least partly because each of the fourteen holidays costs the nation R2.9 billion. Yet the origins of at least one very popular museum lie in a business venture, for Solly and Abe Krok were only able to obtain the licence to construct a theme park, Gold Reef City and Casino, by agreeing to open a museum devoted to apartheid. The Apartheid Museum is the natural remedy for those uneasy with the TRC's treatment of apartheid. Contrary to the TRC, this museum displays the segregationist origins of apartheid and closely examines its historical links with business and labour, British imperialism and Afrikaner nationalism. Cognitive methods of understanding are strongly exhibited but are accompanied by emotive ones as the museum confronts the viewer with the everyday hurt and pain inflicted by apartheid, as well as the extreme and pervasive violence used to maintain this system in power. However, even here there is no naming of perpetrators or beneficiaries, Western support for apartheid in the context of the Cold War goes unremarked, criticism of apartheid by liberals is glossed over and, again, the responsibility for the creation and administration of apartheid seems to lie entirely with whites as a racial group (Bonner 2004; Vuckovic 2002). Here and elsewhere, the tourist industry is responding to a market-driven demand for a South Africa constructed out of fragments of memory that transform places into destinations that are packaged into branded products. Aimed at very specific sectors of the tourist market, from sun addicts to culture lovers or political activists whose geographical provenance is as varied as their gendered or generational experiences, these tours could almost be franchised. They include tribal villages, township tours, slave routes, freedom trails and, in Cape Town, a local theme park (Ratanga Junction) (Schutte 2003; Tomaselli 2001; Witz, Rassool and Minkley 2001; Witz 1998; Robins 1998; Mountain 2004; Bremner 2004). Tour operators devise these products – stretching from a picture of primitive Africa to a monochrome view of the anti-apartheid struggle or an examination of Cape Dutch architecture – in response to very specific demands from a paying public. This commodification of heritage is particularly visible in the battlefield tours that stress the glamour and glory of war and suppress its costs and cruelties (Couzens 2004; Guy 1998). At Isandlwana, the site of a major Zulu victory over the British in January 1879, a luxury lodge has been cut into the iNyoni Rock overlooking the hillside where, every year, people from the surrounding districts reenact the battle for visitors. The local community has a share in this package: the lodge provides employment and sells their curios, and it is locals who reenact the battle. 'Guests also get an opportunity to observe life in an authentic Zulu village', reports a newspaper belonging to the Independent group, 'where they can meet the residents and experience how they live and learn about their customs.' At the time of this report, guests were entertained in the evening by a group irreverently named 'the Real Isandlwana heroes' (*IOL* 24 November 2003; *IOL* 21 January 2006). Professional historians may decry this crude marketing of the past; but it has become both a resource and a means of empowerment for individuals and communities. In a neoliberal age of precarious employment, this form of public history generates a financial income for marginalized communities; perhaps most importantly, it also creates self-worth and identity in the face of the cultural homogenization brought by globalization.

In Conclusion

In this chapter I have attempted to investigate the importance of the mnemonics of memory for the way in which South Africans construct the past. The state has been particularly important in introducing forms of remembrance that recall the experiences of sectors of the population once ignored and forgotten. These changes have not always been accepted unequivocally. The statue of chief Tshwane on Church Square has been painted in the colours of the old South African flag and the statue of Steve Biko, the plaque to Hector Petersen and the memorial board in Mamelodi have all been vandalised. Various institutions lie behind the forms of public history I have outlined. The Mayibuye Centre at the University of the Western Cape (UWC) played a major role in the development of Robben Island as a site of national memory. The South African Heritage Resource Agency, the Department of Arts and Culture and the Department of Environmental Affairs and Tourism are responsible for the implementation of a government policy deeply concerned to bring memory into the national narrative of the past. The paradigm of 'people's history' developed at UWC in the 1980s aimed to equip communities with the resources needed to write their own histories. This perspective served to challenge racist views of the past, but it also sought to defy the guild approach to the past held by professional historians. The subversive, deeply democratic nature of 'people's history' informed the development of the District Six and other community museums. Local communities have entered into these undertakings as a way of constituting and empowering themselves (Witz 2005; Marschall 2005; Hamilton 1992). But as I have tried to show, most of these histories turn around the community as a racial or ethnic group. Through this focus on the community as the predominant social unit memory tends to constitute the nation as a patchwork of interests and experiences that share few common threads. A community based history also keeps the focus firmly on victims and their experience rather than on those responsible for their plight. This is a view reinforced by the commodification of Heritage. In 2006 South Africa's main Sunday newspaper recognized this broad appeal of heritage when it launched a major project aimed at marking historical sites in Johannesburg and other urban centres.[7]

As I have tried to show in this chapter, much of public history has been directed at reconciling formerly hostile groups and at recognising the victimhood and final triumph over adversity of once-ignored communities. This form of feel-good history has developed at a time when the historical profession, for a range of reasons, is undergoing a period of crisis in South Africa (Nuttall and Wright 2000; Cobley 2001). As professional history shrinks in status and authority, public history has released the past from the grip of the academic profession in ways that empower individuals and communities.

The appeal and strength of public history rests on a series of signifiers or free floating resources that, as in the case of the Women's Monument, or Van Riebeeck, or the South African War, may be pressed into service by any cause. The meaning given to objects are not static or hegemonic and may, in time, suffer neglect and disappear. More concerned with the consequences of apartheid than with its causes, this form of history creates the picture of a country at peace with itself, and in the process serves to stabilize state structures and the economy. But its disregard for division and discord in the past creates a space for the emergence of starkly revisionist views of the past. This is perhaps most notable in Herman Giliomee's recent reconsideration of apartheid. By rooting apartheid in the structural problems confronting a specific generation of Afrikaners, he portrays the ideology as as the defensive reaction of a besieged people – rather than as the product of an aggressive, acquisitive nationalism. This point of view is reinforced when, by comparing the 'achievements' of the apartheid regime with its 'failures', or by praising the strong state it created, Giliomee shifts attention from the racial exploitation that accompanied the rise of Afrikaner nationalism (2000; cf. Combrink 1998). This revisionist view of apartheid took on a new potency when, in November 2006, president Mbeki expressed his understanding of P.W. Botha's vision of 'the apartheid system as a protective wall, a laager, intended to ensure the very survival of the Afrikaner people' (Mbeki 2006). In his search for the consensual history needed to bind Afrikaner and African communities in a common understanding, Mbeki seems ready to substitute the UN's definition of apartheid as 'a crime against humanity' with Giliomee's perspective of it as 'a radical survival plan' for the Afrikaner people. A recent edition of South African 'key words' simply leaves out the word 'apartheid'.

This serviceable malleable history might further the TRC's view that South Africans should 'come to terms with the past'. But it runs against the claims of professional historians who see the past as something we have to live with and that we need to incorporate, warts and all, into our daily lives. Only by focusing the steady gaze of history on the mnemomics of the past can the fleeting and uncertain remembering of public history be turned into a resource on which to build a lasting, collective identity. But the last word can usefully be given to Frank Eloff, the medical doctor in Damon Galgut's novel *The Good Doctor* (2003). Shrugging his shoulders, Eloff remarks laconically that, in a country like South Africa where democracy is shaky and little more than a decade old, 'the past has only just happened. It's not past yet'.

Notes

1. Dr Ally's attempt to examine the relationship between apartheid and Sanlam's economic development was cut short, albeit in a jocular manner, by the chairman of the commission.

2. In the speech, Mbeki made no mention of the contradictions within the pseudoscientific writings on racism, nor of the writings of opponents of these ideas who effectively triumphed in the years after WWII. This was also perhaps a lost occasion on which to raise the wider question of xenophobia by referring to the uneasy relationship between Bantu-speaking agriculturalists and San hunter-gatherers (Mbeki 2002).

3. See also District Six Museum website. <www.districtsix.co.za>. (consulted 22.10.2007)

4. Some of the best work on the memory of forced removals under the Group Areas Act is found in Field 2001.

5. See particularly the TRC follow-up workshops in June–August 1997.

6. It is not mentioned in Mandela's *Long Walk to Freedom* or in the chronology attached to Allister Sparks' *Beyond the Miracle: Inside the New South Africa*.

7. The state of construction of these places of memory may be viewed on the Heritage Project attached to the *Sunday Times* website (www.sundaytimes.co.za).

Bibliography

Abrahams, Y. 2004. 'Gender and locating Sarah Baartmann in the present', in A.W. Oliphant, P. Delius and L. Meltzer, *Democracy X: Making the Present, Re-shaping the Past.* Cape Town.

Akyeampong, E. 2001. 'History, Memory, Slave-Trade and Slavery in Anlo (Ghana)', *Slavery and Abolition* 22(3): 1–24.

Alexander, N. 2002. *An Ordinary Country: Issues in the Transition from Apartheid to Democracy in South Africa.* Pietermaritzburg.

Bank, A. 1997. *Khoisan Identities and Cultural heritage Conference.* Cape Town, 12–16 July.

Bonner, P. 2004. 'History Teaching and the Apartheid Museum', in S. Jeppie (ed.), *New Histories for South Africa.* Cape Town.

Botha, C.G. 1921. 'The Preservation of our National Monuments', *South African Journal of Science* 18(1–2): 7–35.

Botha, C.G. 1924. 'The Public Archives: Their Value to Scientific Research', *South African Journal of Science* 21:177–185.

Bozzoli, B. 2004. *Theatres of Struggle and the End of Apartheid.* Johannesburg.

Bremner, L. 2004. *One City, Colliding Worlds.* Johannesburg.

Brink, E. and S. Krige. 1999. 'Remapping and Remembering the South African War in Johannesburg and Pretoria', *South African Historical Journal* 41: 404–421.

Bundy, C. 2000. 'The Beast of the Past: History and the TRC', in W. James and L. van de Vijver (eds.), *After the TRC: Reflections on Truth and Reconciliation in South Africa.* Athens and Cape Town.

Caliguire, D. 1996. 'Voices from the Communities', in W. James, D. Caliquire and K. Cullinan (eds.), *Now That We are Free: Coloured Communities in a Democratic South Africa.* Cape Town.

Carter, C. 1998. 'No Unity on Day of Reconciliation', *Mail and Guardian,* 4 December.

Cherry, J. 2000. 'Historical Truth: Something to Fight For', in C. Villa-Vicencio and W. Verwoerd (eds.), *Looking Back Reaching Forward: Reflections on the Truth and Reconciliation Commission of South Africa.* Cape Town: 134-143.

Cobley, A. 2001. 'Does Social History Have a Future? The Ending of Apartheid and Recent Trends in South African History', *Journal of South African Studies* 27(3): 613–625.

Combrink, N.L. 1998. 'History and the Commission on Truth and Reconciliation: The Problem of Collective Guilt', *Journal for Contemporary History* 23(2): 101–119.

Coombes, A. 2003. *History after Apartheid: Visual Culture and Public Memory in a Democratic South Africa.* Durham.

Couzens, T. 2004. *Battles of South Africa.* Claremont.

Davison, P. 1993. 'Human Subjects as Museum Objects: A Project to Make Life-Casts of "Bushmen" and "Hottentots", 1907–24', *Annuals of the South African Museum* 102(5): 165–183.

Davison, P. 1998. 'Museums and the Reshaping of Memory', in S. Nuttall and C. Coetzee (eds), *Negotiating the Past: The Making of Memory in South Africa*. Cape Town.

Davison, P. 2001. 'Typecast: Representations of the Bushmen at the South African Museum', *Public Archaeology* 2(1): 3–20.

Delmont, E. 1993. 'The Voortrekker Monument: Monolith to Myth', *South African Historical Journal* 29: 79–101.

Dlamini, N. 2001. 'The Battle of Ncome Project: State Memorialism, Discomforting Spaces', *Journal of Southern African Studies* 13(1): 125–138.

Douglas, S. and J. Law. 1997. 'Beating the Bush(man!): Reflections on "Miscast: Negotiating Khoisan history and culture"', *Visual Anthropology* 10: 85–108.

Du Plessis, M. 1987. 'Space, Story and History: Reading Gold Reef City', *English Studies in Africa* 30(2): 105–114.

Du Toit, A. 1983. 'No Chosen People: The Myth of the Calvinist origins of Afrikaner Nationalism and Racial Ideology', *American Historical Review* 88(4): 920-952.

Du Toit, A. 2005. 'Experiments with Truth and Justice in South Africa: Stockenström, Gandhi and the TRC', *Journal of Southern African Studies* 31(2): 419–448.

Fauvelle-Aymar, F.X. 2002. *L'Invention du Hottentot: Histoire du regard occidental sur les Khoisan*. Paris.

Field, S. (ed.). 2001. *Lost Communities, Living Memories: Remembering Forced Removals in Cape Town*. Cape Town.

Finnegan, B. 1994. *Crossing the Line: A Year in the Land of Apartheid*. Berkeley.

Forsyth, P. 1992. 'The Past in the Service of the Present: The Political Use of History by Chief A.N.M.G Buthelzi, "1951–1991"', *South African Historical Journal* 26(1): 74–92.

Friedländer, S. 1969. *Kurt Gerstein: The Ambiguity of Good*. New York.

Friedländer, S., N. Frei, T. Rendtorff and R. Wittmann. 2002. *Bertelsmann im Dritten Reich*. Munich.

Giliomee, H. 2000. *The Afrikaners: Biography of a People*. Cape Town.

Good, M. 2006. *The Search for Major Plagge: The Nazi Who Saved Jews*. New York.

Gordon, R.J. 1992. 'The Venal Hottentot Venus and the Great Chain of Being', *African Studies* 51(2): 185–209.

Gordon, P. 2003. 'Early Social Anthropology in South Africa', *Journal of African History* 34(3): 3–27.

Gore, J.M. 2004. 'A Lack of Nation? The Evolution of History in South African Museums, c. 1825–1945', *South African History Journal* 51(1): 24–46.

Gore, J.M. 2005. 'New Histories in a Post-Colonial Society: Transformation in South African Museums since 1994', *Historia* 50(1): 75–102.

Grundlingh, A. 2001. 'A Cultural Conondrum? Old Monuments and New Regimes: The Voortrekker Monument as Symbol of Afrikaner Power in a Post-apartheid South Africa', *Radical History Review* 81 (Fall issue): 113-132.

Grundlingh, A. 2002. 'The National Women's Monument: The Making and Mutation of Meaning in Afrikaner Memory of the South African War', in A. Grundlingh, G. Cuthbertson and M. Suthie (eds), *Revisiting the South African War of 1899–1902*. Athens and Cape Town.

Grundlingh, A. 2004. 'Reframing Remembrance: The Politics of the Centenary Commemoration of the South African War of 1899–1902', *Journal of Southern African Studies* 30(2): 359–375.

Guy, J. 1998. 'Battling with Banality', *Journal of Natal and Zulu History* 18: 156–193.

Hamilton, C. 1992. 'The Poetics and Politics of Public History', *South African Historical Journal* 27(1): 234–237.

Harries, P. 1993. 'Imagery, Symbolism and Tradition in a South African Bantustan: Mangosothu Buthelezi, Inkatha, and Zulu History', *History and Theory* 32: 105–125.

Hodgson, J. 1987. 'Ntaba kaNdoda: Orchestrating Symbols for National Unity in Ciskei', *Journal of Theology for Southern Africa* 58(1): 18–31.

Innes, D. 1983. *Anglo-American and the Rise of Modern South Africa*. New York.

IOL. 2002. (Independent News and Media Website. www.iol.co.za). Consulted on 27.03.2003).

Kasfir, S. 1997. 'Cast, Miscast: The Curator's Dilemma', *African Arts* 30(1): 1–9.

Kgalema, L. 1999. 'Symbols of Hope: Monuments as Symbols of Remembrance and Peace in the Process of Reconciliation', unpublished paper, Centre for the Study of Violence and Reconciliation.

Klein, M. 1989. 'Studying the History of Those Who Would Rather Forget: Oral History and the Experience of Slavery', *History in Africa* 16: 209–217.

Klopper, S. 1996. '"He is my King, but he is my child": Inkatha, the African National Congress and the Struggle for Control over Zulu Cultural Symbols', *Oxford Art Journal* 19(1): 53–66.

Kruger, C. and M. Van Heerden. 2005. 'The Voortrekker Monument Heritage Site: A New Statement of Significance', *Historia* 50(2): 237–260.

Laband, J. 1986. *Fight Us in the Open.* Pietermaritzburg.

Lane, P. 1996. 'Breaking the Mould? Exhibiting Khoisan in Southern African Museums', *Anthropology Today* 12(5): 3–10.

Legassick, M. and C. Rassool. 2000. *Skeletons in the Cupboard: South African Museums and the Trade in Human Remains, 1907–1917.* Cape Town and Kimberley.

Liebenberg, B.J. 1988. 'Mites rondom Bloedrivier en die Gelofte', *South African Historical Journal* 20(1): 17–32.

Maier, C.S. 2000. 'Doing History, Doing Justice: The Narrative of the Historian and the Truth Commission', in R.I. Rotberg and D. Thompson (eds), *Truth v. Justice: The Morality of Truth Commissions.* Princeton.

Mail and Guardian. 2004. 'A Question of Reconstructing History'. 4 May.

Marschall, S. 2005. 'Making Money with Memories: The Fusion of Heritage, Tourism and Identity Formation in South Africa', *Historia* 50(1): 103–122.

Marx, C. 1988. *Im Zeichen des Ochsenwagens.* Berlin.

Matshikiza, J. 1999. 'The War That Dispossessed Me', *Mail and Guardian,* 16 November.

Mbeki, T. 2002. 'Speech at the Funeral of Sarah Baartman'. 9 August.

Mbeki, T. 2004. 'Address at the Ceremony to Hand Over the Garden of Remembrance Freedom Park'. 8 March.

Mbeki, T. 2006. 'May the Groot Krokodil, P. W. Botha, Rest in Peace', *ANC Today* 6(43): 3–9.

Merrington, P. 1997. 'Masques, Monuments and Masons: The 1910 Pageant of the Union of South Africa', *Theatre Journal* 49(1): 1–14.

Merrington, P. 1998. 'History, Pageantry and Archivism: Creed System and Tropes of Public History in Imperial South Africa, c. 1919', *Kronos. Journal of Cape History* 25: 129–151.

Mgijima, B. and V. Buthelezi. 2006. 'Mapping Museum-Community Relations in Lwandle', *Journal of Southern African Studies* 32(4): 795–806.

Mostert, N. 1992. *Frontiers: The Epic of South Africa's Creation and the Tragedy of the Xhosa People.* London.

Mountain, A. 2004. *An Unsung Heritage: Perspectives on Slavery. Including a Guide to Slave Heritage Sites in the Western Cape.* Cape Town.

Mylam, P. 2005. *The Cult of Rhodes: Remembering an Imperialist in Africa.* Cape Town.

Merrington, P. 1998. 'History, Pageantry and Archivism: Creed System and Tropes of Public History in Imperial South Africa, c. 1919', *Kronos. Journal of Cape History* 25: 129–151.

Nasson, B. 2004a. 'Anglo-Boer War Commemoration in Post-apartheid South Africa, in D. J. Walkowitz (ed.). *Memory and the Impact of Political Transformation in Public Space.* Raleigh: 277–294.

Nasson, B. 2004b. 'Delville Wood and South African Great War Commemoration', *English Historical Review* 119(480): 57–86.

Nasson, B. 2004c. 'Why They Fought: Black Cape Colonists and Imperial Wars, 1899–1918', *International Journal of African Historical Studies* 37(1): 55–70.

Ndlovu, S. 1998. *The Soweto Uprising: Counter Memories of June 1976.* Johannesburg.

Ndlovu, S.M. 2000. 'Johannes Nkosi and the Communist Party of South Africa: Images of 'Blood River' and King Dingane in the Late 1920s–1930', *History and Theory* 39(1): 11–32.

Noonan, P. 2003. *They're Burning the Churches: The Final Dramatic Events That Scuttled Apartheid.* Bellevue.

Nuttall, T. and J. Wright. 2000. 'Probing the Predicaments of Academic History in Contemporary South Africa', *South African Historical Journal* 42(1): 26–48.

O'Meara, D. 1983. *Volkskapitalisme: Class, Capital and Ideology in the Development of Afrikaner Nationalism 1934–1948.* Johannesburg.

Peires, J.B. 1989. 'Ethnicity and Pseudo-ethnicity', in L. Vail (ed.), *The Creation of Tribalism in Southern Africa.* London.

Plenel, E. 2002. *La Découverte du Monde.* Paris.

Posel, P. 2002. 'The TRC Report: What Kind of History? What Kind of Truth?' in D. Posel and G. Simpson (eds), *Commissioning the Past; Understanding South Africa's Truth and Reconciliation Commission.* Johannesburg.

Prinsloo, I. 1995. 'South African Syntheses', *Architectural Review* 197(1): 32–34.

Quarterly Bulletin of the National Library of South Africa. 1999. 'Editorial', 54(1):42.

Rassool, C. and S. Prosalendis (eds). 2001. *Recalling Community in Cape Town: Creating and Curating the District Six Museum.* Cape Town.

Rassool, C. and L. Witz. 1993. 'The 1952 Van Riebeeck Tercentenary Festival: Constructing and Contesting Public National History in South Africa', *Journal of African History* 34(3): 447–468.

Rassool, C. 2000. 'The Rise of Heritage and the Reconstitution of History in South Africa', *Kronos,* 26: 1–26.

Rassool, C, L. Witz and G. Minkley. 2000. 'Burying and Memorializing the Body of Truth: The TRC and National Heritage', in W. James and L. Van de Vijver (eds.), *After the TRC: Reflections on Truth and Reconciliation in South Africa.* Athens and Cape Town.

Robins, S. 1998. 'Spicing up the Multicultural (Post-)Apartheid City', *Kronos* 25: 280–293.

Saker, S. 1980. *The South African Flag Controversy 1925–1928.* Cape Town.

Schrire, C. et al. 1996. Reviews of "Miscast Exhibition"', *South African Review of Books* 44: 13–39.

Schutte, G. 2003. 'Tourists and Tribes in the "New" South Africa', *Ethnohistory* 50(3): 473–487.

Sharp, J. 1997. 'Beyond Exposé Analysis: Hybridity, Social Memory and Identity Politics', *Journal of Contemporary African studies* 15(1): 45–66.

Skotness, P. 1996. Miscast. Neogotiating Khoisan History and Material Culture. Exhibition in the African National Gallery, Cape Town. Curated by Pippa Skotness.

Skotness, P. 2002. 'The Politics of Bushman Representation', in P. Landau and D. Kaspin (eds.), *Images and Empires: Visuality in Colonial and Postcolonial Africa.* Berkeley.

Smith, I. 1999. 'Making Up History As We Go Along'. *Mail and Guardian,* 10 November.

Soudien, C. 2001. 'District Six and Its Uses in the Discussion about Non-racialism', in Z. Erasmus (ed.), *Coloured by History, Shaped by Place: New Perspectives on Coloured Identities in Cape Town.* Cape Town.

Sparks, A. 2003. *Beyond the Miracle: Inside the New South Africa.* Johannesburg.

Strother, Z.S. 1999. 'Display for the Body Hottentot', in B. Lindfors (ed.), *Africans on Stage: Studies in Ethnological Show Business.* Cape Town.

Sunday Times website. www.sundaytimes.co.za (consulted on 12.13.2004).

Taylor, R. 2002. 'Justice Denied: Political Violence in Kwazulu-Natal after 1994', *African Affairs* 101(405): 473–508.

Tempelhoff, J.W.N. 1998. 'Omvormings van 'n Afrikaanse kernsimbool: 'n hede-geskiedenis van Kerkplein, 1989–1997', *Journal of Contemporary History* 23(2): 120–147.

Thelen, D. 2002. 'How the Truth and Reconciliation Commission Challenges the Way We Use History', *South African Historical Journal* 47(1): 162–190.

Thompson, L. 1985. *The Political Mythology of Apartheid.* New Haven.

Tomaselli, K.G. 2001. 'Semiotics of the Encounter: The Staging of Authenticity via Cultural Tourism, Theme Parks and Film and TV Series in the Kalahari Desert and KwaZulu Natal,

South Africa', *Bulletin of the International Committee on Urgent Anthropological and Ethnological Research* 41(1): 93–100.

Vally, R. 2004. 'Histoire, mémoire, reconciliation en Afrique du Sud: Le Monument aux Voortrekkers, cinquante ans plus tard. Histoire d'une auto-réconciliation', *Cahiers d'études africaines* 44(1–2): 173–174.

Van Jaarsveld, F. 1980. 'A Historical Mirror of Blood River', in A. Koning and H. Keane (eds.), *The Meaning of History.* Pretoria.

Vuckovic, N. 2002. 'Du musée ethnographique au musée de l'Apartheid, aujourd'hui', in M. Ferro (ed.), *Le livre noir du colonialisme.* Paris.

Ward, K. and N. Worden. 1998. 'Commemorating, Suppressing and Invoking Cape Slavery', in S. Nuttall and C. Coetzee, *Negotiating the Past: The Making of Memory in South Africa.* Cape Town.

Weeder, M. 2004. 'The Forced Removal of the Prestwich Dead', in A. Oliphant, W. Andries, P. Delius and L. Meltzer (eds.), *Democracy X: Marking the Present, Re-presenting the Past.* Pretoria.

Witz, L. 1998. 'From Langa Market Hall and Rhodes Estate to the Grand Parade and the Foreshore: Contesting Van Riebeeck's Cape Town', *Kronos Journal of Cape History* 25: 187–206.

Witz, L. 2003. *Apartheid's Festival: Contesting South Africa's National Past.* Indiana.

Witz, L. 2005. 'Transforming Museums on Postapartheid Tourist Routes', in I. Karp, L. Szwaja and T. Ybarra-Frausto (eds.), *Museum Frictions.* Durham.

Witz, L, C. Rassool and G. Minkley. 2001. 'Repackaging the Past for South African Tourism', *Daedalus* 130(1): 277–296.

CHAPTER 8

Remembering with the Future in Mind

BERNARD LATEGAN

Introduction

How does one remember 'with the future mind'? What exactly is the 'future potential' of memory? One of the main assumptions of this book is that the presence or absence of a perspective on the future affects the way in which historical memory functions. The conceptual, methodological and hermeneutical claims inherent in such an assumption need to be clarified and substantiated in the context of the present project.

   Is it possible to speak of the future potential of memory? Is memory not per definition oriented towards the past in its attempt to recall what has already happened in order to make sense of the present? The interest in the future potential of memory is aroused exactly by the observance of the ambivalent nature of memory, which becomes especially visible during major social transformations. It would seem that memory can fulfill more than one function in times of transition. On the one hand, it can strengthen individual and collective identity by emphasizing links with the past. On the other hand, it can provide a basis on which to deal with change and to construct the future. In the first case, historical memory is often used to justify entrenched positions, to reinforce existing stereotypes and to resist change, rendering it impossible for individuals and groups to envisage themselves as part of a positive future. In the second case, historical memory serves as a point of orientation in a time of uncertainty, providing direction and a sense of continuity. In this role, it has the potential to mediate between conflicting positions and to transcend existing differences, thereby facilitating change. It doing so, it enables individuals and groups to anticipate a constructive future and to participate in the process of bringing this about.

The preceding chapters provide ample evidence of this ambiguous nature of historical memory and its apparently unpredictable outcome. It both enables and restricts. Examples include an ahistorical view of Africa's past inhibiting the africanization of sociology, the emphasis on space rather than on time providing unexpected creative possibilities for interpretation, oral traces providing the basis of performative utterances in the present, the loss of a link with the past simultaneously preventing a link with the future, the anachronistic use of past events to serve contemporary political ends, and the need for memory itself to evolve through certain stages before catastrophic experiences can lead to a deeper discovery of humaneness. Especially with the recurring theme of forgiveness, all the variations are demonstrated: forgiving and forgetting, forgiving but not forgetting, forgetting but not forgiving, not forgetting and not forgiving, forgiving on condition of confession, forgiving without confession.

At the same time, many of the chapters in this volume – explicitly or implicitly – do associate historical memory with some kind of orientation towards the future. To mention a few examples: Bisanswa refers to a dynamic 'memory of crossing' that is characterized not by fixed locations and certainties, but by mobility and openness towards the future. Joubert insists that invoking oral memory is not meant as a retreat into the past, but an urgent attempt to make sense of the present. Diawara's whole point is that without recalling the past, there is no way out of the misunderstanding and misrepresentations of the present and no hope to open perspectives on the future. Despite these allusions to the future dimension of historical memory, the concept remains vague.

There is clearly a need for a more nuanced and more satisfying understanding of the role of the future in the process of memory. The mantra 'remembering the past with the future in mind' should not be misunderstood as the articulation of an ethical imperative or the expression of a preferred attitude. It is simply the recognition that the interaction between past and future is more complex and more unpredictable than it would appear at first sight.

From the perspective of historiography, perhaps no one has examined and described the interaction between past and future more intensely that Reinhart Koselleck. His main focus was on how in any given present, the time dimensions of past and future are brought to bear on each other (Koselleck 1995: 11). The object of his enquiry was texts in which experiences with time were implicitly or explicitly articulated. He was especially interested in texts where the relation between a specific past and its future was expressed, either explicitly or implicitly. On the basis of his investigation, Koselleck comes to his well-known formulation of historical time as '*vergangene Zukunft*'. (The parallel between this 'realized future' and other concepts of future already present in time will be discussed in due course.) For the purpose of our investigation, it is important to constantly keep in mind the limitations Koselleck has set for himself. He is not interested in the interaction between past and future in general but restricts himself to instances where the future that was anticipated at a certain point in time has become past through the passage of time (1995: 12). The reason for this restriction is his hypothesis that this is the very place where we come to grips with what 'historical time' is. The qualification of the past by the present and vice versa, or, in anthropological terms, the interaction between experience and expectation, is where historical time is defined in the first place.

Despite his different focus, the views of Koselleck are of special significance for our theme. Firstly, he insists that future and past can only be understood as part of the same historical horizon. Secondly, he shows how (at least from the period from 1500 onwards) the present (or 'own' time) was experienced as a 'new time' (*Neuzeit*) with open possibilities for the future. Thirdly, he presupposes a link between historical time, natural time and biological time. We shall not discuss these views in detail, but use them as basis for our own investigation of the future potential of memory.[1]

Koselleck's insights force us to rethink our use of categories of time, but also to be aware to what extent our concept of the future is influenced by changes in the perception of time and space – changes that are the result of the historical process itself. What exactly do we mean by 'historical time'? It is not easy to find a convincing answer as soon as we consider other forms of time – 'physical' or 'astronomical time', 'biological time' or 'narrative time', to mention just a few alternative concepts of time. It is not difficult to see the links: the dating of sources and the verification of the exact occurrence of events, that feature so prominently in historiography, rely on concepts that have their origin in astrophysical systems of time measurement. The historiographer who deals with the lives and times of his subjects is also well aware of the realities of biological time. And every historian who records and describes events does so in narrative form and therefore has to choose between different time perspectives from which to present his or her narrative. But to fully grasp the essential characteristics that differentiate 'historical time' from other concepts of time remains a challenge (see Koselleck 1995: 9).

We have to resist the temptation to pursue this intriguing question further at this stage. Significant for our own theme is the recognition that changes in other concepts of time and space influence in due course what we understand as 'historical time' (1995: 11). Even more, the relationship between the different forms of time – whatever their origin (for example the natural sciences) – has to be defined in historical terms or in historical form (cf. the 'story' of the Big Bang). We shall eventually return to this interrelationship.

The aftermath of the Reformation provides a good example of how concepts of time in one sphere inevitably influence concepts of time in other spheres. The Reformation generated a tremendous interest in the future. Although this interest was initiated by eschatological expectations as part of a specific theological tradition, the church in the end was able neither to control the upsurge of interest in the future nor to contain it within the ecclesiastical domain. It soon spilt over to the secular terrain and assumed a life of its own. In fact, the development of secular concepts of the future was stimulated precisely by what was perceived as the failure of Christian eschatological expectations. The latter were unconvincing on at least two counts. The first was the classic disappointment that all forms of overexpectation must face, namely, the realization of the delay of the *parousia* or the non-coming of the end of the world. The second (directly related to the first) was that the continuation of history, as a result of the delay of the end, necessitated alternative forms of understanding reality and alternative forms to anticipate the future. We shall come back to the strategies the church employed to keep eschatology alive (of which the concept of *realized* eschatology is the most prominent). The disenchantment with what was perceived as the unfulfilled expectations of faith gave rise to secular scepticism and alternative approaches to deal with a future that did not materialize. Koselleck discussed two prominent examples: rational forms to predict future events, and a more coherent and comprehensive philosophy of history. The important insight for our present purpose is that the scope and the nature of future expectations cannot be regulated. The church could perhaps influence developments in the secular sphere, but it could not control them. By the same token, concepts of time and of the future that emerge in the context of historical thought or are employed by historians are inevitably influenced to a larger or lesser degree by concepts of time and the future in other contexts.

Recently, Jörn Rüsen has approached the future potential of memory from a different perspective in his reflections on the question: 'Can yesterday become better?' While Koselleck focuses on how an anticipated future played itself out in the passage of time, Rüsen insists that an orientation towards the future is a *constitutive* element of the historical process itself (Rüsen 2003: 26, cf. also Rüsen 2000: 77–82). This orientation does more than relativize a seemingly hopeless present: it is the primary factor that sets the process of history-making in motion in the first place. But on an even more fundamental level, the process is driven by the inescapable need for *sense-making* – a need that can only proceed within the horizon of expectation.[2] Memory in itself can generate no sense but needs the perspective of the future to become understandable and to stimulate further reflection and action. Historical awareness is thus based on a synthesis of experience and interpretation (2003: 20). This enables Rüsen to navigate between what he considers to be the one-sidedness of both the modern and the postmodern position: there is no historical experience that is free from interpretation, but also no historical awareness without experience.

The important point for our topic is the fact that Rüsen sees a direct link between the future orientation of historical memory and its sense-making function. From the perspective that it is not (yet) the end, human acts and suffering are placed in a narrative framework, becoming part of a 'biography' that not only opens new perspectives on the past, but inevitably calls for further action. In this sense, yesterday can not only become better, but historical memory becomes '*handlungszielkompatibel*' (2003: 27). This means that historical memory is in essence teleological in nature.

Rüsen's position is not uncontroversial, especially when he declares his intention to explicate history as the 'Ort des Utopischen' (2003: 20). The connotations associated with utopian expectations make the concept problematic in the context of historical memory (as I will discuss further below). The same applies to the notion of teleology, although Rüsen attempts to salvage the positive from the negative by distinguishing between 'theoretical' and 'practical' teleology, as we shall see. But these criticisms do not distract from the importance of Rüsen's recognition of the *constitutive* role of an orientation towards the future for the generation of historical memory in the first place. The crucial question now becomes: What kind of future orientation is the most suitable to fulfill this constitutive role? Before exploring this question in more detail, we first have to take note of recent developments that are changing our understanding of the concepts of time and space in significant ways.

Changes in Time (and Space)

When we examine the future potential of memory against the background of recent social transformations, we cannot assume that concepts of the future have remained constant. A disenchantment of a different kind has taken place. World events since 1989 have generated a deep scepticism with regard to grand narratives and comprehensive 'solutions'. The Cold War's ultimate reliance on military power has made way for other, less violent ways to deal with conflict and inequalities. We experience the effect of this change of attitude in our own present circumstances. One of the deep roots of the opposition to the United States' war on Iraq is the conviction that the Bush administration used an outdated way to deal with conflict, acting in terms of a paradigm that belongs to a previous era.

But what is achievable in history and politics is also influenced by new developments in science and technology and by the way the world is understood. This is nowhere more visible than in the so-called 'network society' (Castells 1996). When considering the future potential of history in our day and age, we have to take into consideration the basic shifts in the understanding of time and space that underlies the present understanding of reality.

Time and space provide the basic coordinates for three important types of configuration: the way we define and understand reality, the way we write history and the way we construct narratives. In the case of the third type of configuration, for instance, the narrative structure is created by making use of spatial strategies like distanciation (contrasting the familiar with what is strange, or using the technique of foregrounding or backgrounding) and by using temporal markers like sequence (differentiating between beginning, middle and end). It is inevitable that changes in our concept of time and space will influence our understanding of all three configurations. In recent years, dramatic changes have taken place in both the physical and historical concepts of space and time. These changes were the direct result of ongoing research into the origins of the universe and the explosive growth of the network society.

Recent theories in physics no longer work with three or four dimensions of space, but with more than ten. The dramatic expansion of space has led to the concept of hyperspace.

> It is assumed that the rapid expansion of the universe was just a rather minor aftershock of a much greater cataclysmic event, the cracking of space and time itself. The energy that drives the observed expansion of the universe is then found in the collapse of ten-dimensional space and time. According to the theory, the distant stars and galaxies are receding from us at astronomical speeds because of the original collapse of ten-dimensional space and time. (Kaku 1994: 27)

The 'collapse of ten-dimensional space and time' means that they are taken up in an even more inclusive concept – that of 'hyperspace'. Kaku (1994: 306) explains:

> If all of space-time is collapsing into a fiery cataclysm, then the only way to escape the Big Crunch is to leave space and time – escape via hyperspace. This may not be as far-fetched as it sounds. Calculations performed with Kaluza-Klein and superstring theories have shown that moments after Creation, the four-dimensional universe expanded at the expense of the six-dimensional universe. Thus the ultimate fate of the four- and the six-dimensional universes are linked. Assuming that this basic picture is correct, our six-dimensional twin universe may gradually expand, as our four-dimensional universe collapses. Moments before our universe shrinks to nothing, intelligent life may realize that the six-dimensional universe is opening up, and find a means to exploit that fact.

But as space becomes relative, so does time. For Einstein and many of his colleagues, the distinction between past, present and future is only a stubbornly persistent illusion.

These changes in the concepts of time and space in the domain of physics are reinforced by equally dramatic changes in social time and space. In his penetrating analysis of the network society, Castells argues that both space and time are being transformed in the digital age. But this transformation does not proceed along logical lines, as the sudden and apparently random appearance of new technological centres illustrates.

The dominant features of the new age are what he calls 'spaceless space' and 'timeless time'. Distance, the traditional marker of space, is eliminated in the network society. Instead, our society is constructed around flows: flows of capital, technology, organizational interaction, images, sounds and symbols. Flows are not just one element of the social organization. They are the expression of processes *dominating* our economic, political and symbolic life. 'The space of flows is the material organisation of time-sharing social practices that work through flows' (Castells 1996: 412). These flows undermine traditional systems of regulation and control. 'Thus, the more a social organization is based upon ahistorical flows, superseding the logic of any specific place, the more the logic of global power escapes the socio-political control of historically specific local/national societies' (1996: 416).

Like space, the concept of time is also transformed into what Castells calls 'timeless time'.

> Timeless time belongs to the space of flows, while time discipline, biological time, and socially determined sequencing characterize places around the world, materially restructuring and destructuring our segmented societies. Space shapes time in our society, thus reversing a historical trend: flows induce timeless time, places are time-bounded. The idea of progress, at the roots of our culture and society for the last two centuries, was based on the movement of history, indeed on the predetermined sequence of history under the lead of reason and with the impulse of productive forces, escaping the constraints of spatially bounded societies and cultures. The mastery of time, the control of rhythmicity colonized territories and transformed space in the vast movement of industrialization and urbanization accomplished by the twin historical processes of formation of capitalism and statism. *Becoming* structured *being,* time conformed to space. (1996: 466–467)

One of the consequences of this development is a 'systematic mixing of tenses' that leads to a blurring of distinctions and to the emergence of undifferentiated time. The vital point is that the *sequential* nature of time is lost. Time as linear, irreversible, measurable and predictable is being shattered in the network society, in a movement of extraordinary historical significance. It is important to remember that the claims of Castells relate only to time in the network society, which forms only a part (and a relatively small part at that) of reality. Nonetheless, a new temporality is emerging – a temporality where the distinctions between before and after and the sequential link between cause and effect become blurred. Even though this temporality functions only within the network society, the concept as such could have consequences for concepts of time in other contexts – for example, for the maintaining of a historical consciousness, let alone a hermeneutics of historical consciousness à la Ricoeur. Not only is ethical responsibility undermined by severing the link between deed and consequences, but disorientation is inevitable – a disorientation where continuity with the past is lost and direction for the future cannot be found.

Underlying the interaction between time and space are in fact the basic notions of distance and sequence. According to Bloch, there exists a primordial tension between the two. Space is associated with stability, time with change. An ideology of order prefers the first, an ideology of change the latter.[3] It is not difficult to guess where Bloch's own sentiments lie: the 'God of time' has no option but to take on the demon of the static ideology of order, and the false myth of the perfect state of original creation sees no need for the cry for liberation.

These developments have specific implications for our theme. Not only do they have a detrimental effect on historical consciousness as such, but the deterioration of the basic coordinates of space and time also threatens the very cohesion, orientation and sense-making that history is supposed to provide. The concept of the future becomes problematic again. We will have to rethink what kind of orientation to the future is still viable and whether we can indeed speak of the 'future potential' of historical memory.

Types of Future Orientation

What are the elements and attitudes needed for a memory that can indeed move beyond itself and engage the future?

The Priority of the Possible

The most basic requirement is that the openness of the future remains open.

In this context, Jüngel (1969) has argued convincingly that possibility has priority over reality. The ontological priority that Aristotle ascribes to reality implies that what is possible is always defined in terms of what is (already) real. The possible is at most reality that has not (yet) materialized. Consequently, there is a difference in status between the possible and the real. Authenticity (*Eigentlichkeit*) is a quality that can only be ascribed to reality – in this sense, the possible is not real (*nicht eigentlich*). This difference forms the basis of the 'already – not yet' antithesis that plays an important role in theology, as we shall presently see. Once reality has been accorded (ontological) priority, nothingness becomes a meaningless concept, and especially the idea of *creatio ex nihilo* is totally incomprehensible. However, Jüngel shows that the idea of both creation and re-creation presupposes a contrast not between the real and the non-real, but between what is possible and what is not possible. If this is the case, the reinterpretation of the past is not restricted to what has (already) happened, but becomes open to new possibilities. It is exactly when events do *not* follow the anticipated course or do *not* comply with the expectations of common (that is, historical) wisdom, that the future potential of history becomes visible. This happens when reality is no longer the determining factor.

This highlights a very important aspect of the future potential of memory, namely the element of 'exteriority' (*Externität*) that accompanies it. It might provide an important key to our attempt to understand the ambiguous nature of historical memory. If what is possible is determined by what is real, it is very unlikely that individuals and groups will be able to break free of (past) reality and even less likely that they will be able to transcend it. This is the basic structure of the historical memory of those who remain the captives of their own past and are unable to conceive of a future that is different from what they have already experienced. Once the situation is assessed not in terms of what is real and not real, but in terms of what is possible and not possible, it also means that what is then expected of the future is not the *im*possible. The future potential of memory does not expect the impossible but refuses to be restricted to what is real in terms of what has already happened.

This is a subtle but critical difference. It has far-reaching implications for understanding the role of historical memory in different contexts, as will be pointed out in the last section with reference to recent South African examples. Openness towards the future and the recognition of the priority of the possible are necessary but not sufficient conditions for a future-oriented memory. The exact content of future expectations needs to be analyzed critically, as do their underlying assumptions. One contemporary example is the ideal of a *volkstaat* as propagated by the Freedom Front in South Africa. They envisage a (relatively small) demarcated geographical area within the wider South Africa where Afrikaners who prefer this option will be allowed to rule themselves as an autonomous state. The qualification for citizenship is the identification with the cultural and political ideals of the Afrikaner. Because this state does not yet exist, it is an ideal that is strongly oriented towards the future and driven by a messianic zeal:

> Believing Afrikaners understand their nationhood as a calling. But a nation with such a calling must continue to exist, must be free and therefore must have land where it can fulfill itself.
>
> A state is only a *volkstaat* when the majority of its population consists of fellow members of the *volk* .... This state will have to be liberated by the hard work of Afrikaners themselves. In the long run their language and culture will survive only in a *volkstaat* under their own government.[4]

Although the Freedom Front, as a marginalized group in the present political dispensation, is resolved to work out its own salvation and is strongly oriented towards the future, the content of its ideal is wholly determined by the past. It continues the dream of territorial segregation and cultural hegemony (with strong racial undertones) – exactly the notions that the struggle against *apartheid* tried to overcome in order to create a dispensation free from this kind of exclusivist and separatist thinking.

In contrast, the 1996 constitution of South Africa gives evidence of a much more constructive future expectation. It envisages an inclusive and open society, based on democratic values, social justice and fundamental human rights where the rights of every citizen are equally protected by law and where the quality of life of all citizens is improved.

Teleological Notions

The classic formulation of a teleological approach to history comes from Droysen. According to him, the relentless thrust of historical events towards a goal is only discernible within the context of the 'Komos der sittlichen Welt':

> From observing the progress in the movement of the moral world, from recognizing its direction, from seeing goal after goal fulfilled and revealed, the contemplation of history argues to a goal of goals, in which movement is perfected, in which

all that moves and motivates this world of men and makes it hasten restlessly on becomes rest, eternal present. (Droysen 1977: 435)

All development and growth is movement towards a goal that seeks to attain its fulfillment in the movement.

Although formulated in secular terms, Droysen is using almost theological language. He even talks of the 'theodicy of history', without which history would be meaningless repetition, and of the 'proofs' of the existence of God that can be found in the way history unfolds. (He is careful, however, to put these 'proofs' between quotation marks – 1977: 443.) The goal of goals cannot be determined empirically, but lies nonetheless hidden behind observable events. This enables him to link the causal cosmos to the moral cosmos. 'The place of the causal cosmos of the natural sciences, however, is taken by a teleological cosmos which has its culminating point of metaphysical unity in the highest final goal, the goal of all goals' (Moltmann 1993: 252). The intention of Droysen is of course to tie the idea of 'meaning' in history to a stable and reliable anchor point. But in the process, the very nature of historical events as the 'restless movement of changing appearances' (1977: 421) is deprived of its constitutive dynamic. It is replaced by the longing for the perfect, the one, the eternal. Movement becomes rest.

More recently, Rüsen (2003) has returned to the concept to explain the directedness of memory towards the future. His intention is, however, the opposite of what Droysen had in mind. Rüsen wants to honour the dynamic nature of the historical process and keep possibilities for the future open. The thrust to act, to realize the possibilities that an understanding of the historical process generates, is for him what demonstrates the teleological intent and logic of the process (2003: 27). At the same time, he is very much aware of the negative aspects of a teleological approach, especially of the danger that teleological expectations can easily degenerate into master narratives. This will jeopardize openness towards the future – the very attitude that he considers to be constitutive for historical consciousness. Rüsen is therefore forced to distinguish between 'theoretical' and 'practical' teleology (2003: 28) in order to salvage his idea of a teleology that stimulates action. But this is an artificial distinction that does not overcome the negative connotations associated with teleology. Furthermore, is the ideal of a *telos* still tenable in a disenchanted world? Will it provide the shifting power needed to move memory from a past to a future orientation? We are obliged to consider other alternatives.

Apocalyptic Mindsets

In contrast to teleological notions, the apocalyptic mindset at first sight lacks neither dynamism nor future orientation. The distinctive feature is the sense of *crisis* – a crisis in the *present* circumstances of the individual or group that renders the future uncertain. Often the crisis is precipitated by suffering and intensified by feelings of hopelessness when the victim is bereft of political power or part of a marginalized group. It is important to remember that it takes its point of departure in the existential situation of the individual or group. It is this situation that triggers apocalyptic notions. As Blei (1986: 39) indicates, it is under circumstances of great personal and societal stress that the apocalyptic becomes the preferred genre.

The book of Daniel is an early example of apocalyptic literature, but the genre reached its peak in the period 200 BCE to CE 100 and found its classical expression in numerous Jewish and Christian writings of this time. (Both Judaism and Christianity were minority groups in a world dominated by Rome – a situation that changed only with the emergence of the *Holy* Roman Empire, in the case of Christianity.)

What interests us here is not apocalypticism as such, but the kind of future orientation that is at work here. As is well known, the term literally means to take away a lid or veil, thereby disclosing what is about to happen. The function is not prediction in the ordinary sense of the word, but the revelation of the end game of history. It is therefore often presented in dramatic terms, featuring the decisive battle between good and evil, involving both natural and supernatural beings and forces. Invariably and inevitably it concludes with the final judgement of the living and the dead. In the end, evil is defeated and the victory of the good is certain.

The decisiveness of the apocalyptic vision explains part of its attractiveness, also and especially in non-theological circles. Uncertainty in terms of the final outcome is to be eliminated, but – perversely, in the view of some – this mindset also legitimizes the causing and even the deliberate provocation of crises. The ultimate secular example is the French Revolution, the spirit of which has been emulated by all forms of revolutionary movements ever since. In this context, as Moltmann shows (1993: 232), history is understood as a permanent state of crisis, that is, as permanent, irresistible and unrestrained revolution. The task of history as science is to bring order to chaos and catastrophes, to manage the crisis. This idea is taken up even in non-revolutionary circles. The George W. Bush administration's self-defined mission to continue the war against evil after the conquest of Iraq is a recent example.

The apocalyptic mindset accepts the inevitability of change and is certainly future-oriented. But in terms of the specific needs of our present project, it is hampered by at least three problems. Firstly – despite appearances to the contrary – the future in the apocalyptic paradigm is not open but closed. The end is known before the final battle starts; good will triumph over evil. As Moltmann points out, 'the "science" of history, too, which arises in the shadow of revolution and the permanently smoldering crisis, acquires a positivistic, apocalyptic sense. ... Historical science thus becomes an instrument for the mastering of history' (1993: 236). Secondly – and what is not always noticed – the focus switches from future to present. It is the *present* situation that calls forth the apocalyptic vision in the first place, and it is the *present* situation that is interpreted in terms of apocalyptic expectations. The place of a world-orientation in terms of cosmology and metaphysics has been taken by a fixation on the present. The future is proleptically drawn into the present and judged, not changed, in terms of the anticipated future, whose outcome is already known. Thirdly, the basic undertone of the apocalyptic mindset is pessimistic, even fatalistic. Resolution comes through judgement and destruction. The new heaven and new earth imply the destruction of the present world. The future can only build on its ruins.

Utopian Ideals

In contrast to the pessimism of apocalypticism, utopian ideals are associated with positive expectations of the future.[5] The object of criticism is the *present*. Because no continuation with the present can be imagined, the utopian dream takes shape. Unlike in other movements in history, the criticism is not combined 'with a retrospective dream, with regeneration, reform, renaissance or reformation of the corrupt present, but with the category of the new – new age, new world, *novum organon, scienza nuova,* progress, final age' (Moltmann 1993: 224).

Such a schema, which presupposes a radical break with the present dispensation, is of little value if historical memory is expected to play a constructive role in transforming a concrete historical situation. For the latter it is important to retain a sense of continuation with the past, not only for reasons of identity, but also for the difficult task of reconsidering and reconstituting the memories that have the potential to put the fragile transition in jeopardy. Among the most valuable contributions of the TRC in South Africa were the instances where such memories were revisited and constructively transposed to a future context. The most painful experiences were where such attempts at 'to make yesterday become better' did not succeed.

Eschatological Expectations

The final variety of future-oriented memory we shall consider here is the basic pattern of eschatological thinking. In some respects it is closely related to apocalypticism, but there are also some significant differences. The most important difference for our purpose is that the rigid dualism of apocalypticism, which requires the destruction of the present dispensation before salvation can be achieved in a new dispensation, is replaced by the eschatological expectation of a new order unfolding within the realities of the present world (Hanson 1992: 279–282). This difference is of critical importance in distinguishing between 'realistic' and 'escapist' variations of future-oriented thinking.[6]

Eschatology is both the most radical and the most consistent future-oriented way of thinking within the horizon of history. What interests us at this point is not the content of eschatological thinking but its structure. Its uniqueness lies in the fact that its point of departure is not the specific outcome that is anticipated in the future. What unfolds in the future is rather the (secondary) result of a primary orientation. This primary orientation is the consistent attempt to *think from the end backwards*. It represents the opposite of all types of archaeological thinking, that is, the type of thinking that seeks explanation primarily in terms of the origins of things and events. Eschatological thinking is therefore a controversial procedure, in many ways the opposite of what is traditionally understood as the nature of historical consciousness. 'The real category of history is no longer the past and the transient, but the future' (Moltmann 1993: 260). However, such an approach is not unproblematic, as we shall see.

The primary orientation to think from the end backwards activates a series of supplementary attitudes that are typical of eschatological thinking. A strong emphasis on hope, the tension between promise and fulfillment, a positive attitude towards the future, the capacity to deal with adversity and suffering, the ability to overcome trauma, the magnanimity to forgive, the propensity to reconcile and the willingness to accept change are some of these characteristics and aptitudes.

The potential of the Judeo-Christian tradition for this kind of thinking has been developed by modern exponents like Ernst Bloch (1959) and Moltmann (1993). It had a marked effect on both theological and secular notions of history – including Marxist thinking. As Moltmann indicates (1993: 259), the Hebrew prophet does not dwell on the past. He is primarily a *seer*, not in the sense of predicting the future, but in the sense of articulating a future perspective on events. Time becomes future, and the future is the primary content of this reflection on history.

The way this orientation has been articulated in the Judeo-Christian tradition exhibits both similarities and differences. The Hebrew notion of *shalom*, which entails concepts like the hope for justice, the humanizing and socializing of humankind and peace for all creation, is taken up again in the Christian concept of the kingdom of God with similar notions of righteousness, peace, freedom and humanity. But these ideals are of course not foreign to other humanistic traditions, which are to be found in many other cultures and societies around the globe. The major difference between the Judaic and Christian traditions is the belief in the primary realization of messianic hope in the person of Jesus of Nazareth, which alters the structure of eschatological expectations in a pronounced 'already – non-yet' dichotomy.

Despite these differences, the main contours of an eschatological way of thinking are clear. It operates within a horizon of expectation and is directed towards what in every respect lies *ahead* of it. This forms the basis of the eschatological tension in the sense that these expectations are valid to the extent that they are made valid. But the horizon of expectation also provides the framework for sense-making. 'Meaningful action is always possible only within a horizon of expectation, otherwise all decisions and actions would be desperate thrusts into voids and would hang unintelligibly and meaninglessly in the air' (Molt-mann 1993: 327).

At the same time, the formative effect on the present of this type of think-ing becomes abundantly clear. In fact, eschatological tension is at the same time a source of disquiet with, and disturbance of, the present state of affairs. The inherent and very powerful revolutionary potential of eschatological think-ing – in both its theological and secular versions – cannot be overlooked. The disjuncture between reality and expectation lies at the root of all revolutionary ideals and movements of the past. Both Reformation and Revolution are his-torical demonstrations of the power of revolutionary ideas. It is therefore also not strange that the powers of the day have tried to control or at least contain this energy. In the history of the Christian church, this led to a campaign on two fronts. On the one hand, the delay of the *eschaton* was initially a source of embarrassment. It had to be explained in some way why the imminent end did not materialize. One of the most effective ways to do this was the notion of *realized eschatology* (of which C.H. Dodd was a prominent exponent.) The real end of history has already taken place (either in the event of the cross or of the resurrection), and in principle, nothing new is to be expected. But this 'solu-tion' robs eschatology of its most important asset, namely the ability to affect the present under the influence of an intensely awaited future.

On the other hand, unbridled eschatological fervour can lead to all kinds of excesses. Asocial behavior, the rejection of (ecclesial) authority and inaction had to be brought under control (Koselleck 1995: 22). These attempts at con-trol had the same outcome as realized eschatology: the future was effectively sanitized and defused.

An eschatological way of thinking has much to commend itself for the type of future orientation that we are looking for. In fact, it comes closest to the configuration needed to achieve a constructive transition from past to fu-ture. Nonetheless, it has two weaknesses. The first is the tendency to 'domes-ticate' the future, in the sense that the unknown is turned into the familiar, and thereby neutralize its power to change attitudes and to shift people and perceptions. The second is the limited applicability of a paradigm that is essen-tially theological and transcendental. Can this effectively and convincingly be translated into secular terms?

How Do We Then Remember 'with the Future in Mind'?

To conclude our theoretical speculations: if historical memory is to play a role in assisting individuals and groups to leave the captivity of the past and to embrace a new dispensation, it will have to offer more than just 'coherence in historical knowledge and historical presentation' (Rüsen 2002: 11). It must provide both the basis to go forward and the courage to reconsider the past in view of the movement towards the future. It entails more than the passive awaiting or the mere acceptance of the future as inevitable, but also the imagining of the future as the transcendence of the past. It should be pursued not with hubris or messianic fervour, but with the painful realization of how fragile the human condition is, and how seemingly boundless its capacity for destruction. Trauma and mourning consequently form an inherent part of memory of this kind. Even more so, it must have the capacity both to remember *and* to forgive.[7] These are the prerequisites for self-healing and for the healing of the other. The one without the other cannot provide the basis to sustain any transition in the long run.

For a true openness for and towards the future, the point of departure has to be the conscious choice for the priority of what is possible in contrast to what is real. As we have seen, the contrast between real and not real does not make provision for what is new. The not real is (merely) not yet realized reality and is determined by the reality that already exists. The contrast between possible and not possible is not determined by the past or by what already exists. It therefore has the capacity to deal both with risk and with what is new.

The capacity to anticipate what is new is another way of describing an attitude that is open for the *unexpected* and the *contingent*.[8] More often that not it is the experience of the unexpected that triggers the belief that the (present) reality can be overcome. In the case of South Africa, it was no doubt the unexpected un-banning of the ANC and release of Mandela, the unexpected absence of bitterness and the desire for revenge on his part, the unexpected non-violent transition of power and the peaceful first elections that gave rise to the belief that a constructive future might be – against all odds and expectations – a real possibility.

Recent Examples

When moving from theory to the actual dealing with the past, recent South African history provides several examples where the future potential of memory has influenced not only how the past is remembered, but also how the present is shaped and how the future is anticipated. Space does not allow a fuller discussion here, and we conclude by listing just a few examples:

- Bringing to the surface what was previously hidden or obscured. Example: The uncovering of the participation of blacks in the South African War as discussed elsewhere in this volume.
- Finding memories with future potential in sectional traditions. This usually requires going back much further than the immediate or even recent past. Examples: The revival of anti-colonial sentiment/experiences to provide a shared basis against a common opponent; the search for inclusive sentiments in former exclusivist national symbols.

- Finding memories that are in line with current ideology. Examples: Affirming an African identity, e.g. turning 'Ek is 'n Afrikaner' into 'Ek is 'n Afrikaan'; appropriation of *ubuntu* concepts.
- Attempts at crossover memories, trying to imagine the 'other'. This might range from a tentative venture into totally unfamiliar territory to active commemoration of the other on its own terms. Example: An underlying trend in 'alternative' Afrikaans literature, ranging from Joubert's (*Poppie Nongena*), via Brink's extensive contribution, to Krog's skilful presentation of the TRC process from an Afrikaner perspective (*Country of my Skull*).
- Creative and imaginative transformations of sectional memories. Example: The remarkable (and controversial) transformation of 16 December as the Day of the Covenant into the Day of Reconciliation.
- Remembering in the presence of the other. Attempts at reworking the past in a communal or inclusive context are a distinct feature of recent South African history, exemplified by the TRC process. The results are unpredictable. In some cases, new and alternative perspectives emerged; in others, existing memories were entrenched. The communal element is important for acceptance by both sides – where it is missing, the tendency is towards unsustainable restoration. Example: some of the abortive attempts at name-changing.
- Mediating the divergent and often conflicting memory streams with regard to land use and land possession – potentially a most explosive topic and perhaps one of the real tests for the future potential of memory.

The key to a constructive approach to our individual and collective memories is therefore the ability to include in the process of remembering a future dimension. This future dimension in itself can take various forms and function in different ways. Being serious about the past implies being even more serious about the future.

Notes

1. To illustrate how Koselleck applies his technique in practice: his analysis and discussion of Altdorfer's painting of the battle of Issus makes clear how extensively the artist incorporates aspects of the outcome of the struggle already in his presentation of the prelude to the great event (Koselleck 1995: 17–28). But this conscious form of anachronism is intensified by yet another, even more striking example: the Persians of the ancient battle resemble unmistakably the Turks, who, at the very time when Altdorfer was painting the scene (1529), were attempting (unsuccessfully) to lay siege to Vienna. Not only is the outcome of the battle of Issus included in its preparations, but the events of Altdorfer's own time are projected back to the year 333. As Koselleck shows, this conscious use of anachronism was not intended to obliterate the difference between past, present and future. Rather, the significance of each level is enhanced by the effect of the other two. This is achieved by placing them within one historical horizon. When the painting was

scrutinized by a contemporary of Altdorfer (who was the intended viewer), he or she looked at it with the benefit of twelve centuries of knowledge of how the future unfolded after the battle. But if the viewer shares the painter's Christian perspective, he or she also sees the victory of Alexander over the Persians as the transition from the second to the third world empire, to be followed by the fourth and last, namely the Roman Empire. The battle is part of the struggle between light and darkness and a preparation for what is to follow in the Christian era. Not for nothing has Altdorfer painted the sun above a ship whose mast unmistakably takes the form of a cross. It is one of those decisive moments in time between the beginning and end of history. The Greek and Roman empires were important milestones in a chain of events of which the most important were still to follow. 'Das Tafelwerk Altdorfers hatte, mit anderen Worten, eschatologischen Rang. Die Alexanderschlacht war zeitlos als Vorspiel, als Figur oder Typus des Endkampfes zwischen Christ und Antichrist; ihre Mitkämpfer waren Zeitgenossen all derer, die in Erwartung des jüngsten Gerichts lebten' (Koselleck 1995: 20).

The painting reflects a hallmark of the age of the Reformation, namely a heightened level of eschatological expectation. At the same time, the horizon to the future was shortened, not only in the sense that there was again an expectation of an imminent end, but also in the sense that prominent historical personas of the day were directly identified with end figures and end roles like Gog and Magog, the whore of Babylon and the Antichrist. This direct link between the present and the end time unleashed powerful forces and opened up the future in ways that were hardly imaginable in pre-Reformation times. As Koselleck shows, these energies also affected secular concepts of the future, especially the ideals of the Revolution that followed in the wake of the Reformation. In terms of, for example, Robespierre's expectation of the future, it was freedom and human happiness that would herald the coming of the golden age. How the Christian faith and especially the church tried to control the forces that it itself unleashed as result of its eschatological expectations is another matter. See the section on 'eschatological expectations' below (p. 156–158).

2. Rüsen talks in this regard of the 'Orientierungsfunktion des historischen Wissen' (2003: 26), which is in essence a sense-making operation (*Sinnbildung*).

3. See also Sauter (1973: 315–316) who reminds us how dominant the spatial aspect can be – to the point where concepts of time are explained in terms of spatial images: time as linear, as an axis, as continuous flow.

4. Policy statement on the website of the Freedom Front: www.vryheidsfront.co.za on 11.10.2004.

5. For a useful overview of utopian concepts and thinking, see G. Sauter (1973: 129–145).

6. In an interesting formulation, Calvin writes that in the contrast between the word of promise and experiential reality of suffering and death, hope 'hastens beyond this world'. He does not mean the fleeing of this world, but the straining after the future. Hope does not 'overstep these realities into a heavenly utopia, does not dream itself into a reality of a different kind. It can overstep the boundaries of life, with their closed wall of suffering, guilt and death, only at the point where they in actual fact have been broken through' (Moltmann 1993: 19).

7. See the moving account of Eva Moses Kor included in this book,

8. See R. Koselleck (1995: 159): 'Der Zufall is vielmehr geeignet, das Bestürzende, das Neue, das Unvorhergesehene und was immer dieser Art in der Geschichte erfahren wird, zu umschreiben.'

Bibliography

Association Catholique Françoise pour l'Etude de la Bible. 1977. *Apocalypses et théologie de l'esperance.* Paris.

Blei, K. 1986. *Christelijke toekomstverwachting.* The Hague.

Bloch, E. 1959. *Das Prinzip Hoffnung.* Frankfurt am Main.

Bühler, P. 1981. *Kreuz und Eschatologie.* Tübingen.

Castells, M. 1996. *The Rise of the Network Society. The Information Age: Economy, Society and Culture*, vol. 1. Oxford.

Droysen, J.G. 1977. *Historik*. Text edition by Peter Leyh. Stuttgart.

Hanson, P.D. 1992. 'Apocalypses and Apocalypticism', in *Anchor Bible Dictionary*, vol 1. New York: 279–282.

Jüngel, E. 1969. 'Die Welt als Möglichkeit und Wirklichkeit: Zum ontologische Ansatz der Recht-fertigungslehre', *Evangelische Theologie* 29: 417–442.

Kaku, M. 1994. *Hyperspace: A Scientific Odyssey through Parallel Universes, Time Warps, and the Tenth Dimension*. Oxford.

Kilian, R,, K. Funk and P. Fassi (eds). 1981. *Eschatologie: Bibeltheologische und philosophische Studien zum Verhältnis von Erlösungswelt und Wirklichkeitsbewältigung*. St. Ottilien.

Koselleck, R. 1995. *Vergangene Zukunft: Zur Semantik geschichtlicher Zeiten*. Frankfurt am Main.

Kreck, W. 1966. *Die Zukunft des Gekommenen: Grundprobleme der Eschatologie*. Munich.

McGinn, B. 1994. *Apocalypticism in the Western Tradition*. Aldershot.

Moltmann, J. 1993. *Theology of Hope*. Minneapolis.

Moltmann, J. 1995. *Das Kommen Gottes: Christliche Eschatologie*. Gütersloh.

Oblau, G. 1988. *Gotteszeit und Menschenzeit: Eschatologie in der Kirchlichen Dogmatik von Karl Barth*. Neukirchen.

Reventlow, H.G. (ed.). 1997. *Eschatology in the Bible and in Jewish and Christian Tradition*. Sheffield.

Ricoeur, P. 1984. *Time and Narrative*, vol. 1. Chicago and London.

Ricoeur, P. 1985. *Time and Narrative*, vol. 2. Chicago and London.

Ricoeur, P. 1988. *Time and Narrative*, vol. 3. Chicago and London.

Rüsen, J. 2000. *Das Andere denken: Herausforderungen der modernen Kulturwissenschaft*. Ulm.

Rüsen, J. 2002. *Geschichte im Kulturprozess*. Cologne.

Rüsen, J. 2003. *Kann gestern besser werden? Zum Bedenken der Geschichte*. Berlin.

Sauter, G. 1973. *Zukunft und Verheissung: Das Problem der Zukunft in der gegenwärtigen theologischen und philosophischen Diskussion*. Zürich.

Steinberg, J. 2002. *Midlands*. Johannesburg.

Thoma, C. (ed.). 1976. Zukunft in der Gegenwart: Wegweisungen in Judentum und Christen-tum. Bern.

Part II

FROM AN INTERCULTURAL PERSPECTIVE

CHAPTER 9

Holocaust Experience and Historical Sense Generation from a German Perspective

JÖRN RÜSEN

Hätte ich doch unbekannte Worte, fremde Sprüche, in neuer Sprache, die noch nicht entstanden ist, ohne Wiederholung – keine Sprüche der Vergangenheit, die schon die Vorfahren gesagt haben.
—Doctrine of Chacheperresenub, 2nd millennium BC[1]

Statt des Schlafes tropft vor das Herz schwer die Erinnerung und ihre Qual, und ob der Sinn sich auch sträubt, es kommt die Erkenntnis.
—Aeschylus[2]

Denn da wir nun einmal die Resultate früherer Geschlechter sind, sind wir auch die Resultate ihrer Verirrungen, Leidenschaften und Irrtümer, ja Verbrechen; es ist nicht möglich, sich ganz von dieser Kette zu lösen.
—Friedrich Nietzsche[3]

Holocaust as Borderline Experience

The Holocaust is one of the most radical experiences of crisis in history. It stands out in its genocidal character and its radical negation and destruction of the basic values of modern civilization. As such it negates and destroys even the principles of its historical interpretation.

It has often been characterized as a 'black hole' of meaning that dissolves every concept of historical interpretation. It occludes the construction of a meaningful narrative connection between the time before and after it. It is a 'border-line experience' of history, which does not allow its integration into a coherent narrative. Every attempt to apply comprehensive concepts of historical development fails here.

Nevertheless, it is necessary to recognize the Holocaust as a historical event and to give it a place in the historiographical pattern of modern history, within which we understand ourselves, express our hopes and fears for the future, and develop our strategies of communication with others. If we placed the Holocaust beyond history by giving it a 'mythical' significance (Friedländer and Broszat 1990: 102–134; see Rüsen 2005: 163), it would lose the character of a factual event with empirical evidence. At the same time, the realm of historical thinking's approach to the experience of the past would be limited by the loss of this very remarkable event. This contradicts the logic of history. Thus the Holocaust represents a 'borderline event', the importance of which consists in its transgression of the level of the subject matter of historical thinking and reaches into the core of the mental procedures of historical thinking itself.

I would like to analyze this 'borderline' character of the Holocaust in respect to the role historical thinking plays in the process of building collective identity. I will mainly deal with problems of German (especially West German) identity after the end of the Second World War, though that these problems include elements of identity formation that can be found in many other societies as well.

Identity

The interpretative work of historical consciousness is a procedure of identity building (Rüsen 2004a; Assmann 1995; Megill 1998; Berger 1997; Giesen 2000; Maier 1988). This is true for individuals as well as for groups. Identity is a concept of the coherence of oneself in relationship to others and to oneself as well. This coherence has a synchronic and a diachronic dimension. Synchronically, identity integrates the different relationships of an individual or collective 'self' to others into a unit in which the self is aware of itself. It 'reflects'[4] the relationship to others back to the self, thus furnishing an internal unity in the variety of its manifold relations to others. Diachronically, this self-reflectedness is related to the change of the self and its relationships to others in the course of time. In this respect identity is a concept of continuity of the sameness of oneself in the changes that every person and group must undergo in the course of existence.

In my further considerations I will neglect the relationship between the synchronic and diachronic dimension of identity and deal with the diachronic dimension only. Here I will focus on two issues: the intergenerational extension of identity, and its grounding in events of the past that are kept present by causal consequences and by memory.

The temporal coherence of the human self is not limited by the lifespan of individuals. Social units of individuals that form a collective identity tend to extend their temporal self-awareness and self-relationship into an intergenerational duration and continuity. Belonging to such a self furnishes the individual members with an awareness of an eternity-like duration; they transform the biological chain of generations within which they live into a cultural unit of time that comprehends past, present and future beyond their individual lifespan. It is this temporal unit – which they feel and think of as being their collective self, beyond the limits of their births and deaths – that defines the cultural nature of their social relationship. Brought about by historical consciousness, this temporal unit of a collective self consists in a synthesis of experiences of the past and expectations of the future. In this synthesis the past is present as a mentally moving force loaded with the entirety of powers that direct the human mind towards the future. It is the force of memory that shapes the features of identity and makes the past a projection of the future.

Thus memory and historical consciousness are closely interrelated, but they are not the same. Historical consciousness is grounded in the mental forces of memory, but it transgresses memory in a decisive step: it keeps, or makes, the past alive where it lies beyond the memory of the social unit concerned. It even influences and shapes the memory of the people with conceptualized experiences they themselves have not had. Historical consciousness enlarges the temporal extension of memory into an intergenerational continuity and duration of the collective self. The idea of this continuity, which meets the desire of transgressing birth and death, moves the cultural procedures and practices in which a society thematizes and confirms its togetherness and its difference from others.

Depending Upon and Working On the Past

Collective identity is rooted in the presentation of events, which function as roots in the form of 'historical events'. 'Historical' means that the events have a specific meaning and significance in the life orientation of the people who rely on them when they consider who they are, and when they characterize the otherness of the others. A 'historical' event is therefore a synthesis of factuality based on experience on the one hand and intentionality (traditionally called 'spirituality' and today mainly called 'fictionality') based on the creative forces of the human mind on the other. These two elements should be carefully distinguished when analyzing the process of identity building by historical consciousness. To distinguish them is an artificial act, but it is necessary, as the dynamics of identity building are constituted in a mental process in which an event becomes historical, and in which the experience of the past is moulded into a meaningful history by interpretation and representation.

Dependence upon the past means that historical consciousness takes place in a context where the past has brought about conditioning presuppositions for the mental activities of remembering it. These presuppositions are not freely disposable but must be recognized in order to pursue their mental procedures and to fulfill the orienting function of historical consciousness. They are the result of developments in the past, which determine the lives of the people in the present and are looked upon by them as being fateful. This dependence concerned can be characterized as 'causality by fate'. 'Causality' can be concretized as a place in a chain of generations, aside from and independent of the awareness and the deliberate relationship to the past of those who have to live their lives in this given time. They are bound into this specific link of the chain of generations. Here the past has grown into the external and internal circumstances of present-day life, without, and sometimes even against, the will of those who have to come to terms with their situation. In this perspective historical consciousness depends upon the past, which it has to transform into sense – and meaningful history.

This 'causal' or 'fateful' relationship is not limited to external conditions of human life but includes its internal conditions as well, the mental pre-formations and possibilities in culturally dealing with the past when making history out of it. The fateful generational chain has a mental dimension effective in traditions, prejudices, resentments, threats, hopes, value systems, basic convictions and – not to forget – the forces of subconscious attitudes and instincts guided by suppressive forgetfulness.

In the other perspective, the past becoming history depends upon the mode of those for whom it has the meaning and relevance of history. Now the events are, so to speak, raw material, which has to be formed into a concept of temporal change with which topical human activity and suffering can be oriented towards the future. The burden of the past, pressing human identity into the responsibility for things and events that happened without their participation, has now changed into the creativity of the human mind. It shapes the past into a perspective of development, which ends in the projection of the future-bearing identity of the people along the lines of their self-esteem. Fateful causality is replaced by value-guided commitment, deliberately related to the events of the past. They are treated as if they had to be redeemed in the future course of temporal change of the human world.

In the frame of this tension between fateful causality and value-guided commitment, historical consciousness pursues its operations of identity building.

A Catastrophic Root of German Identity

In most perspectives of historical consciousness, the Holocaust constitutes German identity by a catastrophe. As a pre-given event to be dealt with, the Holocaust belongs to those events of the past that have determined the life situation of Germany today. It is a part of a history that led to a complete defeat of the nation, to a destruction of large parts of the country, to the political division of Germany, to a loss of land and the expulsion of its people, and to a mental burden of guilt, responsibility, shame, horror, suppression and trauma.

The pre-given temporal chain of generations is the channel through which this event is related to the external and internal circumstances under which the Germans have to live. It would be misleading to look at this channel as one single string combining the Nazi past with the Germany of today. In fact, it is a very complex texture of threads knitting together through different knots and strains, the different parts of the German people. The historical perspective that comprehends this texture is a complex mixture of sub-perspectives in which different groups of Germans today are related to different groups of Germans and non-Germans in the past. Concerning the people whose activities and sufferings constituted decisive elements of the fateful relationship to Nazi society, one can distinguish different groups: the contemporaries, bystanders, profiteers, perpetrators, victims and opponents. There is no clear and evident historical relationship between these groups of Germans in the Nazi period and specific groups of the German people of today. The majority may be objectively related to bystanders and perpetrators, but one should not overlook that a notable part of the victims and opponents were Germans as well. This is even true for those among the Jewish victims who regarded themselves as Germans.

Through this network of generational relationship, the specific German fateful tie to the Holocaust can be typologically differentiated into four classes of determinations. First are the consequences of the Nazi period that are in-built in the life conditions of the German people of today. I have already mentioned some of the consequences (e.g. division of the nation), but here I add two more: the rupture in the genealogical chain caused by the high death rate of soldiers and civilians due to the events of the war, and the disappearance of influential Jewish elements in German culture.

Second, on the mental level there can be observed a 'silent continuity' of attitudes, including a change in at least some parts of these attitudes (e.g. authoritarian personality, a certain kind of work ethic, power-protected inwardness (*machtgeschützte Innerlichkeit*), anti-Western resentment). It is not so much a single attitude that combines the generations, but rather a certain mode of realization and its relationship to others that characterizes German identity and its alteration. The historical character of its relationship between past, present and future is a synthesis of continuity and change, caused by the change in the life circumstances of the people.

Third, a specific element of these continuous attitudes, mentioned separately, consists of different kinds of traumatic transference, the heritage of the victims as well as that of the perpetrators, handed down to their children and grandchildren (or at least to a part of them).

Finally, the memory of those who participated in the Holocaust is a deter-mining factor of historical consciousness. This memory changed in the course of time according to new experiences, such as the Cold War, and new interpre-tations that changed the content and the patterns of significance of the memory of the Holocaust. But this memory (including a suppressive forgetfulness) re-mains the most important representation of the Holocaust as an event of central importance for German identity.

All the factors together form the 'starting point' of historical conscious-ness in Germany. It is initiated by these pre-given circumstances, so far as future-directed intentions and pre-given reality differ structurally and have to be bridged. Historical consciousness must work through these circumstances in presenting them as an end of historical development, which started in, or at least passed, the Nazi period and will lead into a different future. Bridging the gap between the conditioning past and the intended future, historical con-sciousness changes the fateful dependence into a value-guided acceptance or legitimacy of identity. The experience of catastrophe remains a decisive point in this transformation. On the intentional level it works as a normative factor that decides on the interpretation by which the past becomes history for the present. Catastrophe here works as a negative evaluation structuring the deci-sive events in the narrative flow of historical arguments that shape German self-awareness, their idea of collective identity and their distinction of otherness.

The Holocaust has not always been the decisive Nazi-era event in respect to which the Germans related themselves to the Nazi period. On the contrary: the postwar development of German historical consciousness is characterized by an increasing importance of the Holocaust with growing temporal distance from it. Since this distance brings about the already mentioned difference between memory and historical consciousness, one can say that the Holocaust gained its historical significance in the transforming process by which the memory of the Nazi period developed the features of historical consciousness.

I would like to characterize the very complex development of postwar German identity in an ideal typological way, distinguishing three main stages. It would be misleading to understand this distinction of three stages as if they replaced each other. In fact, they coexist and form different constellations and mixtures. But logically, and even in respect to temporal sequences, they can clearly be distinguished.

Concealment

In the first stage (from 1945 to the late 1960s), the crimes of the Nazi era remained in the minds of the perpetrators and victims who still lived in Ger-many, and of those who knew about them. As such they bore the importance of events against which identity was shaped, or at least the importance of events that changed the collective identity substantially. The Germans entered the post-war era with a feeling of a collective catastrophe, a complete defeat. This catastrophe was also seen as a rupture of identity, which radically weakened the hitherto strong nationalism. The self-esteem that belongs to traditional nationalism had become impossible vis-à-vis its role in the Nazi period. Only a certain manifestation of it could survive: the self-esteem of being industrious and effective in work (Trommler 1985: 220–229).

For the purpose of mental survival the Germans had to bridge the rupture within their historical identity and to overcome its fundamental crisis. The answer to the challenge of rupture was – at least on the level of intellectual debate and educational system – a recollection of national traditions that could be interpreted as opposed to Nazi ideology. Friedrich Meinecke (1946), for example, recommended Goethe as a renovating historical element of German identity. No wonder that many, in search of something for collective identity to positively refer to, looked for long-gone positive events or good historical elements of German history that bypassed the Nazi era and the Holocaust. The Holocaust was not a historical element that fitted into the realm of 'our' history. If it had an identity-building role at all (on the level of deliberate mental activity and not in the unconscious) it indicated and manifested 'otherness'.

The crisis of collective identity was overcome by leaving aside, if not suppressing, the memory of the Holocaust and related crimes in the realm of public discussion and political activity. The new West German democracy became very successful, and one condition for this success was the integration of the greater part of the elite of the Nazi system into the new republic. This integration had a mental dimension: there was an unspoken agreement not to deal with the far-reaching entanglement in the Nazi system.[5] In the mental strategy of identity building, the threatening features of the Nazi period were projected into the otherness of the perpetrators, beyond the limits of one's own self. The Nazis were demonized and exterritorialized into a realm beyond the main lines of German history. Nazism and Nazi dictatorship shrank into an invasion by a relatively small group of political gangsters who came out of nowhere to occupy Germany.[6] The 'ordinary' Germans – meaning those who had to come to terms with their own past – were characterized as victims of a diabolical Nazi seduction.[7] The psychological strategy of this kind of moulding collective memory in order to get rid of the burden of one's own entanglement is described in psychoanalysis as the procedure of 'reversing'. It can even be observed in the subtlety of academic discourse (cf. Nolte 1987: 13–35).

The concept of totalitarianism later confirmed this exterritorialization: during the Cold War period 'the others' could be identified beyond the Iron Curtain, and the burdening experience of Nazism could be inscribed into the face of a common enemy, the Communists. Thus a collective conviction could be brought about: not we, but the others were guilty.[8]

Still later, this strategy of public silence and exterritorialization was criticized as a mental failure, a structural deformation of the German mind. This criticism was the consequence of a new, moralistic approach to the Nazi period, which constitutes the second period discussed here. This criticism, most prominently documented in Alexander and Margarete Mitscherlich's *Die Un-fähigkeit zu trauern* 1967 (*The Inability to Mourn* 1975), overlooked the limited possibilities of mental survival and the function of forgetfulness in overcoming a deep identity crisis owed to a rupture of historical continuity.

The only line of continuity that crossed the Nazi period to the current and real German history, and therefore what was publicly commemorated, was the German opposition to Hitler (except for its Communist branch).

Moralization

The second stage (from the late 1960s to the late 1980s) arrived with the coming of age of the next generation of Germans, who had to develop their own concept of collective identity by struggling with their parents. Their concept's relationship to the Holocaust was characterized by two tensional intentions. The first was to remember the Holocaust and give it historical relevance and importance for German collective memory. For the first time it was placed in a historical perspective that ended in the mental field of historical German self-understanding. It was not especially the Holocaust, but the Nazi period in general that played a new role in building collective identity. Now it was used as a counter-event, constituting German identity in a negative way. In this negative way the Nazi period became an integral part of German history.

The new generation grounded its self-esteem in a strictly moralistic criticism of this period, using universal standards of political culture that had become valid in their political socialization. In its most elaborate form, this negative constitutive role was confirmed and realized by an identificatory step into the period of Nazism: selfness acquired its moralistic power through identification with the victims. The others were the perpetrators and bystanders. Otherness now lost its transhistorical status and became a part of German history itself, against which the new Germany was contrasted.

What were the consequences of this integration of the Holocaust into German history for the concept of collective identity? In respect to its peculiarity it lost the features of an obligatory tradition. Tradition was replaced by universalistic values and norms. This universalism now became a constitutive factor in reshaping German identity. It got its mental power and the strength of its conviction from the negative historical experience of Nazi history. Brought onto the horizon of German self-awareness, it pushed the new generation into the mental attitude of standing for its contrary, and of placing itself strictly beyond any historical relationship reaching into the centre of oneself. By this approach otherness became a part of one's own history: now it was manifest in the past of one's own people, but in such a way that it was excluded from the realm of oneself.

This relationship of German identity to the Nazi period shows a fragile mixture of a metahistorical universality of norms and values, and historical experience, mediated by contradiction. It still prevails among many Germans. The next step is dedicated to the task of overcoming the fragility of this mixture to move into a full historicization of the Nazi past, including the Holocaust.

Historicization

The third stage has just started. It is an open question whether it will lead to a particular new form of collective identity; but there are clear indications that it will do so. The decisive new element reshaping German identity is an opening of Germans' minds to the genealogical relationship to the perpetrators. The moralistic criticism of the Holocaust, accompanied by identification with the victims, has kept this relationship outside the constitutive historical elements of the Germans' self. The growing distance of the generational change enables the Germans to bridge the mental gap that separated them from their fathers and grandfathers in the historical perspective of their self-awareness. Those who perpetrated the Holocaust were 'the others'. But these 'others' were, at the same time Germans, like those who morally distance themselves from them. In the period of moralization it was not possible to share the same line of German history with them. This has changed: prominent historians start to say 'we' to the perpetrators (Meier 1990; cf. Koselleck 1997).

This indicates a challenging need to reconceptualize German identity. The objectively pre-given genealogical chain of generations has become a structural element of the historical perspective within which German identity is shaped. The Germans have begun to define themselves as a result of a historical trans-formation in which the perpetrators and bystanders become integral parts of the historical experience, moulding the feature of German peculiarity as a mirror of self-reflection. The atemporal moral distance of the second stage is trans-formed into a specifically 'historical' distance. The Holocaust is about to obtain a place in the chain of events that constitute the shape of German identity. To be sure, in this 'historical' place the Holocaust has not lost its character as the contrary of any valid system of values that the Germans feel collectively com-mitted to. The point is that this otherness is now a part of a person's own self.

It is not yet clear what this means in respect to the symbolic order of his-torical experience as a feature of the collective self of the Germans. Such a fea-ture always requires a certain coherence in the arrangement of past events into a concept of temporal order that can function as a pattern of self-understanding and of cultural orientation. Coherence gives constitutive values a legitimating role. For the Germans, the Holocaust can never serve to legitimize their pe-culiarity as a nation. The reason is complex. Certainly there is a genealogical line between the Germans of today and the perpetrators, but this line does not exclusively combine them with the perpetrators, since a number of the victims and of the opponents were Germans as well. On the other hand, this line is so strong that any legitimating approach to the Holocaust would put today's Ger-mans into the role of the successors of the perpetrators, which strictly contradicts the universalistic values that are deeply rooted in today's German political culture and form a constitutive element of their collective identity. As long as the perpetrators are integrated into a common 'Germanhood', that is, as long as they are recognized as Germans, German collective identity is featured by a negative constituting event as an inclusive part of their own history.

This inclusion of the otherness of the Holocaust requires a new logic of historically shaping collective identity: the strict exclusion of negative elements in the horizon of historical experience related to one's own people has become impossible. The temporal chain of events constituting historically collective identity includes the Holocaust with its negative meaning and significance. This significance prevents any form of coherence in the historical feature of oneself, which is brought about by an entire positive identification with the past. The historical feature of oneself has been fragmented and is loaded with tensions and even contradictions. But as long as this fragmentary character and negativity are conceptualized by a principle of historical sense, they may serve as a reliable cultural frame of orientation and identity building. 'Sense' in this respect means an essential openness to the temporal dimension of historical identity (Rüsen 2001), a counterfactual validity of fundamental regulative ideas, placing the collective self just on the borderline between past and present, where the transformation of pre-given circumstances takes place. Here an essential insufficiency of historical origin ends in the projective force of the human mind; this discloses creative chances for change. Identity – whether personal or collective – is always a synthesis of what one has been and what one would like to become. In respect to this tensional synthesis, the constitutive force of the Holocaust in the historical perspective of German identity evokes its complement. It asks for a projection of a future that is committed to the categorical consequence of the Holocaust that Adorno has stated (1969: 85) as a general principle of human thinking: that it should never happen again.

Within this new feature of collective identity, the relationship of crisis and identity has essentially changed. In traditional cultural procedures of commemoration, identity overcomes the crisis: the discontinuity and rupture caused by contingency are transformed by historical consciousness into a new meaningful coherence in the temporal connection of past, present and future. Now crisis has become an element of identity itself. This means that the people cannot rely on a deep conviction that their form of life is fundamentally legitimated. Nor can they depend on the permanence of their life form, at least not in its essential elements. Yet an inbuilt 'critical' element in this feature furnishes this permanence and legitimacy with projective elements and regulative ideas of practical reason. They are permanently generated and pushed forward by the sting of memory that keeps the Holocaust present. The memory of the Holocaust has been transformed into a historical consciousness that relativates one's self-esteem with a character of imperfectability, and this imperfectability can be realized as a chance for practical activities.

Concerning this third stage, one can only observe indications and starting points. It is an open question whether and how this new logic of identity building through the memory of the Holocaust will bring about a new relationship between German national identity and the Holocaust. We may expect a new structure in the concept of collective identity, where otherness and selfness will have a new mediation beyond the cultural logic and practice of identity building by the exclusion of otherness.

Is this German case an exemption of, or does it indicate, a general issue of historical sense generation? I think that the sequence of the three types of approach (concealment, moralization and historicization) can be applied to other cases of coming to terms with burdening pasts as well. This is a matter for further research and international and intercultural comparison.

Be that as it may, there remains a general problem of how to do history today: Integrating negative, even traumatic events of the past into a concept of historical identity requires new efforts of the human mind and new modes of collective memory in historical culture. In the last part of this chapter I want to discuss two possible answers to this challenge, which may become important for historical thinking wherever it has to come to terms with catastrophic experiences of the past: mourning and forgiving.

Mourning

At first glance history has nothing to do with mourning. Mourning is emotional and related to losses that have recently occurred, whereas history is cognitive and related to a remote past. But this impression is misleading, since history and mourning have something essential in common: both are procedures of memory and are committed to its logic of sense generation.

Mourning is a mental procedure of commemorating somebody or something lost. The loss has the specific character of a loss of oneself with the passing away of a person or something of a high personal value. This mode of commemoration aims at gaining back oneself by 'working through' the loss (in the words of Sigmund Freud). Gaining back oneself means coming back to life by the death of the beloved person or object. In a certain way, even the lost (subject or object) comes back. This return takes the form of the presence of absence, which enlarges the mental horizon of the mourning person by elements of transcendence.

The archaic paradigm for this mental procedure, which of course is a procedure of social communication, is the ritual that transforms the dead person into an ancestor. As ancestors, the dead are given a new form of life, in which they are invisible but very powerful. This mental individual and social practice can easily be applied to history (though, suprisingly, this has not been done yet).

I do not think that history today is ancestor worship, but at least it has some logical similarity to it. In its very logic, historical thinking follows the logic of mourning at least partly in a formal way: it transforms the absent past, which is a part of one's own identity, into a part of present-day life. In fact, only the past that is important for the people of the present can become history. This importance of the past can be characterized by its relevance to what is essential for people in their present-day life. Identity is an issue of historical consciousness. If we realize this, the past in the mental procedures of historical consciousness is essentially related to the feeling of belonging together in a group and of being different from others. With respect to the identity of a person or a group, the past is not part of the outside world – not external, but an issue related to the internal life of the human subject. The relationship to the past can be compared to the relationship to deceased persons or objects in the mourning process.

There is an astonishing similarity between historical consciousness and mourning. History mainly refers to the very past that is relevant to human identity. The absent past is present in the depth of human subjectivity. And this is exactly what mourning is all about. So in a simple logical argumentation one can say that mourning is constitutive for historical thinking in general and in principle. If those who have died contribute positively to the self-esteem of the people of today (which is the rule in the context of historical consciousness all over the world), the remembrance of them keeps or makes them alive beyond their death. In other words, in historical consciousness the dead are still alive. And what makes them alive beyond their death? What else but mourning? I think that metahistory has completely overlooked this constitutive role of mourning in the procedures of historical memory.

The difference between history and mourning lies in the character of the act of regaining oneself by revitalizing the past. In the case of mourning, the process is full of bitterness and pain. The experienced loss opens a wound in one's mind. History, on the contrary, seems to be a procedure of remembrance that does not have this hurting element; rather, it is conceived of as a gain, as taking over a heritage, as bringing about self-esteem. But if the past of which history speaks has this very relevance for identity, can we even think of its passing away as something that does not hurt? Does it not leave a gap open to be filled by mental activity? It is worthwhile to consider whether the procedures of historical consciousness are grounded in a mourning-like process. So far, history writing has been seen not in comparison to the process of mourning but as having a totally different kind of quality: that of recovering independent facts as if they were things that can be picked up and integrated into the properties of oneself.

I would like to illustrate this with the issue of humankind as a constitutive factor of historical identity. A historical experience that negates the universal validity of the category of humankind by depriving others of their status as human beings goes to the very heart of all identity concepts based on the category of humankind. If this negation is executed physically, it effectively destroys one's own self in its universalistic historical dimension. Under these conditions, the persuading power of the criterion of humankind as a basic value is fundamentally weakened, to say the least. Such a historical experience results in the loss of the self in its specifically human quality. It deprives civilized modern societies of their historical foundations and cannot possibly be integrated into the course of time in which past and future are seen as being held together by the unbroken validity of humaneness as a normative value. It destroys the continuity of a history in which civil subjectivity has inscribed its own universal norms.

What does it mean to face traumatic historical experiences? First and above all, it means to realize that the criteria of sense generation that to date were culturally dominant have lost their validity for the historical discourse (Diner 1988). But a loss is not a sell-out. (Selling out the criteria of sense generation in historical discourse on the grounds of deconstructing ideology would mean the cultural suicide of modern subjectivity – a subjectivity that relies on the category of equality as the basis of mutual esteem in human relations.) Acknowledging a loss without recognizing what is lost leads back to the topic of mourning by history in a compelling way. At this point we are talking about historical mourning in the sense of humankind confronted with the historical experience of drastic inhumanity. In this case mourning could lead to the recovery of one's self as fundamental human. Mourning would have to consist of *acknowledging the loss*. This implies two aspects: first to admit that humankind as a normative concept is lost or absent in historical experience, and second to accept that whatever has been lost remains one's own (or better still: remains one's own in a new and different way).

What does this mean for the humanity criterion of historical identity? Humanity in the sense of the widest extension of modern subjectivity is deprived of its historical significance, which had so far been regarded as part and parcel of one's own culture (or civilization). It dies as a consequence of the historical experience of crimes against humanity, which are in effect crimes against the self (or better: its mental disposition). The self as defined in relation to humanity dies in historical experience. Postmodernity has drawn a melancholic conclusion from this: it is no longer interested in the humanity orientation of modern subjectivity.[9] Thus, it leaves the subject of modern societies disoriented, and incapable of acting, exactly at the point where its real-life context – in terms of political, social, economic and ecological issues – is characterized by its objective universality: in its demand for human rights, for equality as a regulating category of social conditions in the globalizing process of capitalism and in the global endangering of natural resources of human life.

In contrast to this melancholy, mourning would be a cultural achievement. The subject could recover its own human dimension by moving beyond the deadly experience of a rupture of civilization. This way of mourning would not simply incorporate this experience into culture, but would regard it as an effective stimulus to accentuate the validity of an orientation towards humanity in a passionate, yet disciplined and patient manner.

What do we mean by humanity reappropriated by mourning? What do we mean by humanity that is present in its absence? Mankind is no longer a naturally justified fundamental value of human activity per se. In a historical discourse based on mourning, humanity has literally become utopian because it has lost its fixed and steadfast position in people's everyday world ('*Lebenswelt*'). As a consequence of its dislocation, it no longer can be taken as a plan for a world to be created (for that would correspond to death invocation, and the designed world would be a phantom or ghost). As utopia it would have an effusive, literally metaphysical status, beyond the reality of a civilized world. It would have to be taken as the yardstick for its criticism, a disturbing factor of insufficiency with respect to the achievements of civilization.

But what do we mean by *presence* in its absence? Is it more than a shape, a phantom of what could be but unfortunately (because humans are disposed as they are) is not? In its absence, the notion of humanity could be no more than a conditional 'as if' of the human understanding of the world and oneself. It could but take the effect of a mental driving force for human action, a regulative concept for something that cannot be obtained but can only be put into practice. It would be not transcendently (as in empirically based metaphysics) but transcendingly effective as a value-loaded medium of sense definitions that stimulates action by serving as a guiding principle in the process of defining an aim. One could speak of fiction in the sense of a real conditional 'as if'. As lost, humanity is reappropriated in the form of a standard pointing in the direction of an improving civilization, and the fact that this has not yet been achieved urges man into action. The lost reliable and valid norms are retrieved as disturbance, criticism, utopia and the motivation to keep one's own world moving in a direction indebted to these norms.

Forgiving

Mourning is a mental activity to overcome a loss. It contributes to making sense of a self-destructing experience. In the case of history it is the matter of a loss of oneself. Historical mourning refers to those historical experiences that are embedded in one's own historical identity and threaten this identity. As identity always implies the relationship to others, these threatening events of a loss disturb this relationship as well. This is inevitably and especially the case when the disturbing events are brought about by a person or a group that can clearly be defined as 'the others'.

Even beyond this destructive element of a loss within the historical perspective of identity, the relationship between self and others in general is a fundamental problem, since identity is shaped by a positive esteem of self and a less positive, or even a negative, image of the others. In historical culture this asymmetrical evaluation is effective as the power of ethnocentrism (Rüsen 2004a). This power increases when historical memory includes events in which one's own people have been harmed by others. If this event can be judged by universally valid standards of morality, this morality will deeply influence the process of forming historical identity and of constituting specific problems in the relationship between self and others.

Evaluation of past events always plays an important role in historical identity, but when it follows moral standards that have to be accepted by the others who were morally devaluated, a special interrelationship emerges – namely, that between victims and perpetrators. In recent decades the status of being a victim has become a very effective factor for the forming of collective identity. Its convincing power lies in a set of generally accepted universal values: a group of people (e.g. a nation) has to accept that in the past they themselves or their forefathers have done something that is morally damnable. This agreement on the moral quality of what has happened in the past confirms the positive moral status of the victims and their offspring. The perpetrators and their offspring, in turn, are put into the dark shadows of history. Their otherness is constituted by a negative moral evaluation, which they have to accept since they share the same universal moral standards as the victims.

In a general historical perspective this moralistic mechanism is rather new. Traditionally people tend to ascribe the highest standards of civilization to themselves (Müller 2000: 317–343). Identity is a matter of pride in having achieved these standards and their historical realization. A victory, therefore, usually is a common event to brush up one's own historical self-esteem. Take for example the Second German Empire, whose victory over the French Empire was transferred into its collective memory. The day of the Battle of Sedan (in which the army of the German Alliance, or Deutscher Bund, defeated the French army and took Napoleon III prisoner) became an official day of commemoration. This traditional one-sidedness is typical and confirmed by the way morality is treated. It is claimed only for one's own culture; otherness is defined by a lack or a negative deviation from it. Thus traditional ethnocentrism is embedded in a double morality: the moral standards within one's own culture are not valid for and applicable to others, who are treated according to a different value system that principally attributes lower moral standards to others.

But in the modernization process, this double morality has vanished in favour of universalistic moral standards. These standards are based on a general and fundamental value of humaneness, which has to be applied not just to oneself but to others as well. In the pattern of this morality, crimes against humanity are historical events that serve as very effective means to evaluate moral qualities of people according to the comprehensive value system of humaneness. It has become a worldwide accepted strategy of historical culture to use universal standards to shape the difference between oneself and others. The historical features of the division between oneself and the otherness of the others have been drawn on the canvas of a universalistic morality. Historical identity has become a unique feature in the face of humanity.

This moralistic impact has a problematic consequence: it leads to a new, modern form of ethnocentrism. The Germans, the Japanese and other people of today are held responsible for what their forefathers did. Indeed, this responsibility plays a role in international relations: representatives of nations officially apologize for what their people have done to others (Lübbe 2001). What this 'historical' responsibility really means is a philosophically unsolved problem (cf. Rüsen 2004b: 195–213), since the established modern morality holds responsible only the direct authors of the misdeed – their offspring cannot be held morally responsible. Nevertheless, on the level of everyday life and of symbolic politics, this responsibility seems to have been accepted as a specifically historical responsibility.

Morality furnishes historical identity with the mental powers of innocence on the one hand and of guilt or shame on the other. The attractiveness of victimization has its roots in the superiority of innocence and the ability to put the blame on the otherness of the others.[10] But it is the underlying morality that causes problems in this kind of forming identity. Those others who are ridden by guilt and shame can only get their historical self-esteem (which is necessary for a life-serving identity) through self-condemnation – which is a contradiction in itself. When the offspring of the perpetrators identify with the victims (in order to get moral quality into their self-esteem), they ignore the historically objective intergenerational relationship with the perpetrators. This identification obscures the lack of this interrelationship in the historical perspective of one's own self awareness. This astute and rigid morality cuts the historical ties that objectively constitute historical identity.

The issue of intergenerational victimization is problematic as well. It burdens self-esteem with the experience of suffering and paralyses the historical dimension of action. In this case the future perspective can be brought about only by a shift from passive suffering to action – but even this action lacks a positive quality, as for example the slogan 'never again' reveals: here the suffering in the past shall lead to a future of nothing but never again. (The natural reaction – the turn from suffering to the activity of revenge – runs against the morality of victimhood.)

Through these tensions and contradictions morality tends to transcend itself within the cultural processes of identity formation. Victimization furnishes the people with the self-esteem of being innocent and morally superior to the perpetrators, but at the same time it saddles people with the heavy burden of suffering. Suffering tends to push people to end and reverse it, and their activities in doing so are guided by a vision of happiness. Being a victim is a challenge to liberate oneself from victimhood and to become able to be the master of one's own life. Does this imply that the innocence of victimhood has to be given up? Can the pain of victimhood be ended only by losing one's moral superiority?

The same tendency to reshape one's own self is effective in the minds of those who are weighed down by the heavy burden of immorality, or crime – in the worst cases, of crimes against humanity. Such perpetrators face the fact that they put their inner self into the dark realm of having lost their own humanness. Without a light in this darkness, how can history furnish their self-esteem with a future that stands for the contrary of what happened in the past?

This push beyond morality stems from the relationship between the victims and the perpetrators and their offspring as well. Morality separates them. Shared and mutually confirmed moral principles of humanness constitute an abyss of mutual exclusion. It is the shared universality of values that sets them apart. They mutually confirm the burden of a disturbing legacy in their historical identity. They live like Siamese twins whose inescapable bond prevents both from leading an independent and self-determined life in which each can pursue shared moral values according to their different life conditions. Separating the twins is a difficult task with no guarantee of success.

The easiest and most frequently practiced way of overcoming this dilemma of morality in identity formation is to forget the events that have to be morally condemned. Should we praise the wisdom of ancient Greek peace treaties, which included an obligation to forget the facts that caused the war and the events that happened in it (cf. Flaig 1991: 129–149)? The permanent waging of wars in Greece despite this commanded oblivion indicates that hurtful historical experiences cannot simply be forgotten, even if political reason demands it. This is all the more the case when the events have become engraved in the features of one's own mind and that of the former enemy. At least on the level of the unconscious, there is a tradition and memory where the forgotten remains alive.

Thus there is no alternative to the bitter task of working through the burdening experiences in such a way that one can escape the exclusiveness of morally constituted identity. The first step to this future perspective has to be a move away from the immediate (if not supertemporal) connection with the past. This distance can be brought about by mourning. The loss of humaneness the victims and their offspring have experienced becomes mentally realized, and at the same time their lost elements of identity (e.g. their dignity as human beings) become apparent by their absence, thus providing the damaged identity with a new dimension and quality of memory. A similar transformation can be realized by the perpetrators and their offspring. They can become aware of the loss of humaneness that the immoral and criminal acts caused within themselves. Thus they may discover it, take it back in its (historical) absence and reclaim it. And by pursuing this they may enlarge the realm of their identity with a constitutive awareness of their (historically) absent humaneness.

How does the act of mourning affect the fact that the loss of human identity occurred? The lost humaneness cannot be revitalized. But through the act of mourning, the haunting quality in the broken identity will disappear. Those who suffer from the deed done to them (while aware of their innocence and their [historical] responsibility) may find a place for it within their identity. Then it has changed its character – from sheer destructiveness to a challenge to pursue a meaningful life.

With a successful mourning process, mourners have achieved a new quality of their memory and historical consciousness. They have transcended the exclusive character of morality, where good and evil define themselves and the others. (In the case of the perpetrators and their offspring, they themselves have become the others in themselves.) The dark side of their history is no longer exterritorialized for the sake of rescuing a remainder of self-esteem, be it the moral quality of innocence or self-condemnation by taking over (historical) responsibility. Now their crimes have become a part of their own history – 'own' in the sense of being appropriated as a part of themselves into their memory and historical consciousness.

This appropriation is a chance to overcome the burden of an innocent victim and a responsible perpetrator and their moralistic mutual exclusiveness. It is a chance for forgiving. By forgiving, the realm of morality as a mental power of identity formation is transgressed. Those who forgive and those who are forgiven are given back themselves and each other on a level of identity beyond the strict validity of universalistic values.[11] It is the level of pre- and postmoral self-affirmation, where the human subject is able to recognize the humaneness of those who have radically lost or violated it.[12] It is the constitutive level of human intersubjectivity, in which recognition of others is a primary condition of human life (Tomasello 2002).

There is no established culture of historical forgiving in modern societies. But there is a growing awareness that bridges have to be built over the abyss of good and evil. This culture has started with official apologies for historical injustice and immorality. And there have already been motions for forgiving as well.[13] It is an open question whether this indicates a change in memory and history towards a new recognition of humaneness vis-à-vis, and in full presence of, inhumanity in the past.

Notes

1. 'That I had unknown words, strange sayings in a new language, not yet born and unprecedented, no sayings from the past which the forefathers have already used' (Helck 1987).

2. 'Instead of sleep memories and their pain heavily drip to the heart and with the sense resisting cometh cognition' (Agamemnon 177f.).

3. 'Since we are the results of former generations we also are the results of their aberrations, passions and errors, even their crimes; it is impossible to completely sever from this chain' (Nietzsche 1988: 270)

4. Latin *reflectere,* 'to bend back'.

5. This is the famous thesis of Hermann Lübbe (1983) that originally caused much emotional contradiction but since then has gained widespread acceptance.

6. An example of this exterritorialization is the inaugural speech of Leopold von Wiese (1948: 29) at the first postwar meeting of German sociologists: 'Die Pest kam über die Menschen von außen, unvorbereitet, als ein heimtückischer Überfall. Das ist ein metaphysisches Geheimnis, an das der Soziologe nicht zu rühren vermag' ('The plague came upon the unprepared people from the outside. This is a metaphysical secret, not to be touched by a sociologist').

7. A rather late example of this presentation of the Nazi period is the film *Hitler – eine Karriere,* directed in 1976 by Christian B. Herrendörfer and Joachim Fest.

8. This again can be exemplified by Nolte's thesis (1987) that Nazi dictatorship was only a reaction to Bolshevism and the Holocaust only an answer to a 'more original' event, namely the October Revolution and the crimes of the Bolsheviks.

9. Karlheinz Bohrer brilliantly characterizes the 'attraction' of 'melancholic rhetoric' in human sciences as 'a popular resting place where due to the discourse on modernity that failed to move beyond the early stages, a frightened scientific community in the meantime gathers strength for new quasi-teleological design/ideas' (1996: 40). He holds 'no future' (*Zukunftslosigkeit*) against the hopes for the future by a radical (and fortunately only) poetic farewell. The question is how far his interpreting repetition and affirmation against all historical thinking can be read as a desperate attempt to delay this farewell real-historically. It corresponds with the title of his book, in which mourning categorically takes precedence over melancholy (without being justified by objective reasons in his explanations).

10. A recent example known worldwide is Goldhagen 1996.

11. A very impressive example of forgiving is the chapter of Eva Mozes Kor in this book.

12. This issue of rehumanizing the inhuman perpetrators is impressively presented by Pumla Gobodo-Madikizela in her chapter in this book. See also Gobodo-Madikizela 2003.

13. See the example of Johannes Rau, the President of the Federal Republic of Germany, with his speech in the Knesset (the Israeli parliament), cited in Lübbe (2001: 15).

Bibliography

Adorno, T.W. 1969. 'Erziehung nach Auschwitz', in T.W. Adorno, *Stichworte: Kritische Modelle 2.* Frankfurt: 85-101

Assmann, J. 1995. 'Collective Memory and Cultural Identity', *New German Critique* 65: 125–133.

Berger, S. 1997. *The Search for Normality: National Identity and Historical Consciousness in Germany since 1800.* Providence.

Bohrer, K. 1996. *Der Abschied: Theorie der Trauer: Baudelaire, Goethe, Nietzsche, Benjamin.* Frankfurt.

Diner, D. 1988. *Zivilisationsbruch: Denken nach Auschwitz.* Frankfurt.

Flaig, E. 1991. 'Amnestie und Amnesie in der griechischen Kultur: Das vergessene Selbstopfer für den Sieg im athenischen Bürgerkrieg 403 v.Chr.', *Saeculum* 42(2): 129–149.

Friedländer, S. and M. Broszat. 1990. 'A Controversy about the Historization of National Socialism', in P. Baldwin (ed.), *Reworking the Past: Hitler, the Holocaust, and the Historians' Debate.* Boston. 102–134.

Giesen, B. 2000. 'National Identity as Trauma: The German Case', in B. Strath (ed.), *Myth and Memory in the Construction of Community: Historical Patterns in Europe and Beyond.* Brussels: 227–247.

Gobodo-Madikizela, P. 2003. *A Human Being Died That Night: A Story of Forgiveness.* Claremont.

Goldhagen, D.J. 1996. *Hitler's Willing Executioners: Ordinary Germans and the Holocaust.* New York.

Helck, W. 1987. 'Ägypten im frühen Neuen Reich: Grundzüge einer Entwicklung', in A. Eggebrecht (ed.), *Ägyptens Aufstieg zur Weltmacht:* Mainz. 11–28.

Koselleck, R. 1997. 'Vier Minuten für die Ewigkeit', *Frankfurter Allgemeine Zeitung*, 9 January, 27.

Lübbe, H. 1983. 'Der Nationalsozialismus im deutschen Nachkriegsbewußtsein', *Historische Zeitschrift* 236: 579–599.

Lübbe, H. 2001. *'Ich entschuldige mich': Das neue politische Bußritual*. Berlin.

Maier, C.S. 1988. *The Unmasterable Past: History, Holocaust, and German National Identity*. Cambridge.

Megill, A. 1998. 'History, Memory, Identity', *History of the Human Sciences* 11(3): 37–62.

Meier, C. 1990. *Vierzig Jahre nach Auschwitz: Deutsche Geschichtserinnerung heute*. Munich.

Meinecke, F. 1946. *Die deutsche Katastrophe*. Wiesbaden.

Mitscherlich, A. and M. Mitscherlich. 1967. *Die Unfähigkeit zu trauern: Grundlagen kollektiven Verhaltens*. Munich

Mitscherlich, A and M. Mitscherlich. 1975. *The Inability to Mourn: Principles of Collective Behavior*. New York.

Müller, K.E. 2000. 'Ethnicity, Ethnozentrismus und Essentialismus', in W. Eßbach (ed.), *Wir – Ihr – Sie: Identität und Alterität in Theorie und Methode*. Würzburg: 317–343.

Nietzsche, F. 1988. 'Vom Nutzen und Nachteil der Historie für das Leben', in F. Nietzsche, *Sämtliche Werke*, vol. 1. Munich: 243–334.

Nolte, E. 1987. 'Zwischen Geschichtslegende und Revisionismus?' in *'Historikerstreit': Die Dokumentation der Kontroverse um die Einzigartigkeit der nationalsozialistischen Judenvernichtung*. Munich: 13–37.

Rüsen, J. 2001. *Zerbrechende Zeit: über den Sinn der Geschichte*. Cologne.

Rüsen, J. 2004a. 'How to Overcome Ethnocentrism: Approaches to a Culture of Recognition by History in the 21st Century', *Taiwan Journal of East Asian Studies* 1(1): 59–74.

Rüsen, J. 2004b. 'Responsibility and Irresponsibility in Historical Studies: A Critical Consideration of the Ethical Dimension in the Historian's Work', in D. Carr, T. Flynn and R.A. Makkreel (eds), *The Ethics of History*. Evanston: 195–213.

Rüsen, J. 2005. *History: Narration – Interpretation – Orientation*. New York.

Tomasello, M. 2002. *Die kulturelle Entwicklung des menschlichen Denkens: Zur Evolution der Kognition*. Frankfurt.

Trommler, F. 1985. 'Arbeitsnation statt Kulturnation? Ein vernachlässigter Faktor deutscher Identität', in F. N. Mennemeier and C. Wiedemann (eds): Deutsche Literatur in der Weltliteratur. Kulturnation statt politischer Nation? (*Akten des VII. Internationalen Germanistenkongreß*, vol. 9). Göttingen: 220–229.

von Wiese, L. 1948. 'Die gegenwärtige Situation, soziologisch betrachtet', in *Verhandlungen des Achten Deutschen Soziologentages vom 19. bis 21. September 1946 in Frankfurt am Main*. Tübingen: 1–6.

CHAPTER 10

Ayodhya, Memory, Myth

Futurizing the Past from an Indian Perspective

RANJAN GHOSH

Introduction

'While the emanation of individual memory', writes Nancy Wood,

> is primarily subject to the laws of the unconscious, public memory – whatever its unconscious vicissitudes – testifies to a will or desire on the part of some social group or disposition of power to select and organize representations of the past so that these will be embraced by individuals as their own. If particular representations of the past have permeated the public domain, it is because they embody an intentionality – social, political, institutional and so on – that promotes or authorizes their entry. (1999: 2)

Indian history, with its mythical underpinnings and unavoidable blending of fact with fancy, provides 'fragments' and discontinuous stretches of historical past that render it vulnerable to misappropriations. With the emphasis, somewhat self-indulgent at times, on tradition, religious essence and cultural heritage, the idea of the past can be seen to congeal around a 'few bits of the past' that go beyond the threshold of strict historical representation. On several occasions it becomes captive of mythic exegeses that make the past intelligible through selection, whereby it acquires 'permanence, relevance' and 'universal significance' (Finley 1965: 283). To what extent does a myth help re-present the past meaningfully? Who should judge the meaningfulness of such representation? How can memory be configured through the *ab*use of myth or a certain constellation of historical knowledge born out of strategic selection? What implications will it have when narratives of varying ideological-epistemic cut and thrust vie at their crossroads for legitimacy and authenticity? Within the space of such issues as the myth of Ayodhya (the birthplace of the Hindu cultural icon Lord Rama), the momentous demolition of the Babri Masjid in 1992 and the ceaseless nationalist sociocultural mobilization to build a temple to Ram at the site of the destruction, this chapter briefly tries to develop a critique of collective memory and historical consciousness that have been religiously and politically generated through the 'selective mediation' of historical facts and the imbibing of certain notions and attitudes embedded within a distinct Indian approach to history and historiography.

Dwelling on the 'distinctness' of Indian historiography, Nikam writes:

> What is history but a 'regressive' perspective of time; and, every culture has a sense of history; every culture has its 'golden age' and a memory of the deeds of its heroes, and has its tradition. But as a regress into the past is always possible so there is 'history' behind history, and so the paradox of history is that in human culture the beginnings of history are not in history but in 'pre-history', and pre-history merges into the myth. Indian culture, Hinduism in particular, is the forgotten memory of the beginninglessness of an undated tradition *sanatana dharma* alive to look back upon its own past in order to live in a changing time. (1967: 10–11)

Given the character of the 'Indian mind' (cf. de Reincourt 1986: 102–130), it has always been easy to cultivate an allegiance to *sanatana dharma,* as the Hindu ethos would deem it sacrosanct and muster unstinted communal fealty. At one level 'progress' for the Hindus would mean a movement towards 'achieving the heights of the glorious past' (mythicized, for instance, in the notion of the *Ramrajya*), and 'there is always an attempt in modern India to interpret the present in terms of past and the past in terms of present' (Despande 1979: 11). History is a lived-in reality for the Hindus. Prakash Desai notes that 'the survival of major treatises for centuries, written down perhaps only after the development of the Brahmi script (considered to have been finished in about 300 BCE) attests to the emphasis placed on memory – remembering the past and interpreting it to serve the present. This gives to the Hindu culture both a paleocentric and mythopoetic character' (Desai 1989: 10). So more than the hard crust of facts, what become niched are the emotion and ideas orbiting round the myths, the crystallization of concepts springing from the Hindu way of life, which knows less history and more philosophy and literature, and the unique cultural formations that dominate the nation's socioreligious consciousness.

The Ayodhya issue has fleshed itself up within a consciousness (bolstered by a formidable oral tradition as well[1]) woven around the myth of Ram and his birthplace Ayodhya and the production and proliferation of a memory of injustice perpetrated by Emperor Babur, who ordered his nobleman Mir Baqi to destroy the temple at Ayodhya and build a mosque instead in 1528–1529.

Presumably the order for building the mosque was given during Babur's stay in Aud (Ayodhya) in AH 934. At this time he would have been impressed by the dignity and sanctity of the ancient Hindu shrine it (at least in part) displaced. But as an obedient follower of Muhammad he was intolerant of any other faith and would regard the substitution of a temple by a mosque as dutiful and worthy. The mosque was finished in AH 935, but there is no mention of its completion in the Babar Nama (the memoir written by the Mughal emperor Barbar in the sixteenth century). The diary for AH 935 has many minor lacunae, and much of that of the year AH 934 has not survived; it breaks off before the time when the account of Aud might be looked for.

In the *District Gazetteer* of Faizabad, Nevill (as quoted by Nama 2003: 26) also says:

> In AD 1528 Babar came to Ayodhya (Aud) and halted a week. He destroyed the ancient temple (marking the birthplace of Rama) and on its site built a mosque, still known as Babar's Mosque. ... It has two inscriptions, one on the outside, one on the pulpit; both are in Persian; and bear the date AH 935.

Thus Hindu communalists, feeling disfavoured by a particular slice of history – though largely inappropriately, given that the historicity of such records has come under persistent fire – churn out their own 'ideology-inflected' narrative, which consensually agrees that some seventy-six battles had to be fought in the defence of the Janmabhumi (birthplace). The first aggressor was the notorious king of Lanka, Ravana, who destroyed Ayodhya during the time of the ancestors of Shri Ram. The second attack came from the Greek king Milind or Menander; the third assault was waged by Salar Masud, a nephew of the much maligned Muslim plunderer Mahmud Ghaznavi. All this preceded the arrival of Babur:

> This ungrateful plunderer [ungrateful in that he had been given refuge, food and shelter by people in different parts of India] responded to India's native tolerance and hospitality by ordering his Commander-in-Chief, Mir Baqi, to destroy the huge, palatial Shri Ram Janmabhoomi temple that had stood in Ayodhya since Vikramaditya's time, in order simply to please two evil Muslim 'faqirs'. But ... the people [the country] rose in fierce opposition to this vile attack on their national honour. The historian Cunningham writes: 'At the time of the destruction of the Janmabhoomi temple the Hindus sacrificed everything and it was only after 1 lakh, 74 thousand Hindu lives had been lost that Mir Baqi succeeded in bringing down the temple with his cannons. (Pandey 1994: 1524)

Playing on this consciousness is a proliferating body of literature[2] whipped up to drive home the validity of a collective memorialization of Ayodhya converging on issues of depredation and desecration by the Muslim 'other', the religio-cultural rights of the Hindus in the making of a Hindu nation, and the romanticization of the past, informed by essentialism and ethnicity, to rediscover the Hindu identity. *Organiser,* the organ of Rashtriya Swayamsevak Sangh, abetted the surge of historical writing in favour of such a notion and ensured that public memory is largely governed by communal discrimination and prejudice, which it claim originated with the advent of Islam on the Indian subcontinent. The valorized representations of the Hindu past have sunk their teeth deep by riding the political encouragement that is part of a deft well ministered homework.[3] Also, Valmiki's *Ramayana* and Tulsidas's *Ramcharitmanas* are proclaimed to be the authentic versions of the Rama myth, regardless of other narratives that 'form part of the broader cultural idiom of the country' (Thapar 1990) on this subject. This authentication legitimizes Ayodhya as the birthplace of Rama; meanwhile, very few people know that Valmiki borrowed the story from *Dasharatha Jataka,* a work of Buddhist literature. This calculated move sacralizes Valmiki's *Ramayana* and makes Ayodhya throb at the centre of the Hindu revivalist surge.

Ayodhya is built up as a specific 'act of remembering' where the past is the remembered present – shallow in terms of chronology but emphatically topocentric. Ayodhya then becomes a strategic campaign to create a common memory, a feeling of *participation mystique,* and thereby a 'heritage' that seeks a communal consolidation around issues: Hindus have been wronged by the construction of the Babri Masjid at the 'sacred spot' where Lord Rama was born; the temple that stood at this holy site was pulled down to construct the Babri Masjid; such desacralization should unite the Hindus to embark upon a temple rebuilding mission. This promotes a degree of 'creative freedom' in the use and interpretation of contents (Funkenstein 1989: 10–11). It promotes certain images of the past that render some facts of history 'intelligible', without caring and daring to expose itself to challenges that new findings can spring on it. Such a crystallization of consciousness and reprocessing the past, thus, cannot evade cultural-political fallout.

Alon Confino writes: 'the crucial issue in the history of memory is not how a past is represented but why it was received or rejected. For every society sets up images of the past. Yet to make a difference in a society, it is not enough for a certain past to be selected: It must steer emotions, motivate people to act, be received' (1997: 1390). The Ayodhya phenomenon is worked up to channel emotions, thereby carving out a certain 'scheme of acceptability' and inspiring the desired strata of motivation. But the generation of historical meaning through a carefully engineered collective consciousness also demands identity formation; as John R. Gillis observes, 'the notion of identity depends on the idea of memory, and vice versa' (1994: 3). The discourse of Hindu identity, polarized by the Ayodhya issue, is embedded in a moral valence within an enduring set of beliefs and ideals. The historical consciousness justifies collective actions in which the 'other' is strongly identified and 'memorialized' as phobic and apathetic given its engagements with the past.

Perhaps the strategy of creating 'memory' that demands a collective allegiance derives its sustenance from a manipulative working on the 'historical distance'. This is a strategy to create an 'inheritance' of an event that lies far back in the past and is large enough to have accumulated a body of historical evidence supporting it. Developing a collective memorialization that would validate a political-religious agenda and help build a community of unflinching believers requires a shortening of historical distance. Such a foreshortening excites the affective and ideological consciousness required to accept history with a mythic construct. It is a way to position the community to rally around an event of the past.

Ayodhya is one such potential instance. As part of the adroit 'past-retrieval' game, the political historians and religious enthusiasts have successfully familiarized the distance separating the birth of Rama, the supposed demolition of the temple in the sixteenth century and the almost existential need to rebuild it. The mechanism of artificial reconstruction can thus 'project the present back, the past forward'. It 'produces' heritage, an act of religio-political contrivance, and in such constructedness the past is clarified so as to 'infuse them with present purposes' (Lowenthal 1996: xi). This crowns the historical consciousness with a shared ideological bind that is impervious to multiple perspectives and fosters an 'affect' that denies 'historicity of events', clamouring against any pretence to objectivity or rigorous ways of doing history.

Creating what I call a 'consolidated memory' around Ayodhya has been difficult. Engagements with the past are undergirded with religious passion, which generates the abiding discourse with mythic archetypes. Making it less of an intellectual problem that would have relinquished pretensions to objectivity and taken heed of divided opinions, the memory building programme interpreted history simplistically and fomented zones of private sympathies, making history a stooge of well-carpentered ideological-impositional modes of representation. It helped nurture a 'communal' connection with the past that is strong and well-narrated enough to look out for its continuing presence in the present. Consolidated memory generation worked on the dimensions of fusing distances – what the past means and the present wants it to mean – engaging the distant with a desire and affirming the singularity of emotional colour, so that despite the distance, the past collapses into the present through emotional homogenization. Thus the historical distance separating the 'target' event from the present is made good by a scaffolding that takes liberty with objectivity and rational-critical discourse and works on exclusionist fundamentalist assumptions.

Memory also calls for the character and viability of 'distances'. The memory around Ayodhya is not a disengaged or disinterested historical position but a commitment to a discourse of religious emancipation, a contrived historical necessity, a form of historical reasoning that resurrects a particular race against the venal wrongs of an imperial and historically sanctioned oppressive 'other'. The incremental discourse constructed around Ayodhya is not just a way for the communities to establish a common memory that speaks in the unimpeachable language of deprivation and discrimination, thus legitimizing redress. It is also a means of developing the inspiration to essentialize one's cultural existence, which eventually serves the ends of powerful partisan sentiments (see Phillips 2003, 2004).

The relation between remembrance and forgetfulness is strategic and exploitative. The usability and knowability of the past can be fed upon to allow memory to grow on us, and it is here that the objective recording of the past is conflictually counterpoised. When history and memory need not necessarily go hand in hand, claims of their persistent cohabitation can spell danger: memory memorialized, inheritance grown and acknowledged through texts, and primordial moments kept alive through certain historical forces keep feeding our understanding of the past. Forgetting, forgetfulness, remembering and remembrances form a complex matrix where the usability of the past holds promises of alteration, redefinition, selectivization and constructivism.

Besides 'Ayodhya' this reconstruction of memory brings us similarly to see the build-up of historical consciousness around the Somnath temple in Gujarat, a state in the western part of India, which is described as having been attacked seventeen times by Mahmud Ghaznavi (1026), inaugurating the seemingly irreconcilable schism between Hindus and Muslims. Despite recent challenges to such narratives by Romila Thapar (2004), the myth, memory and history around Somnath has been carefully built. K.M. Munshi's novel *Jaya Somanatha* (1927) and his book *Somanatha, the Shrine Eternal* set the tone of a consciousness that is difficult to dislodge and easy to perpetuate.[4] The linking of the two – Ayodhya and Somnath – in the construction of memory supporting the agenda of a Hindurashtra is clearly evident in the Bharatiya Janata Party's white paper on Ayodhya and the Rama Temple Movement (April 1993), which emphatically affirms that 'the evolution from Somanath was suspended after the death of Sardar Patel and … Ayodhya is the recommencement from the point where the spirit of Somnath stood suspended' (Noorani 2003: 12). Van der Veer (1996: 160–161) argues pertinently that 'what nationalism does, though, is to reinterpret the nature of the contest in the past to serve its purposes in the present. Hindu nationalism provides the link between Somnath and Ayodhya.'

The myths of Ayodhya and Somnath, and whatever history has to say on them, are part of a tradition that holds an ineluctable sway over the Hindu mind at different levels of its unfolding. Its transmission does not require much in the way of conscious efforts at identification and promulgation because society perpetuates it through narration and a certain unconscious absorption; here, reliability and precision are often casualties. However, within the Hindu cultural fabric inaccuracies and affect do not rip the society apart as long as religious maximalists and their astute political counterparts refrain from upsetting this fine-tuned balance. Ayodhya came down silently and sacrally as part of a tradition. However, once the deliberate construction of 'programmed' memory opens up irrevocable cleavages, political and religious differences start explaining the origination and unspooling of memory. 'Memory thus', writes Confino (1997: 1395), 'becomes a prisoner of political reductionism and functionalism.'

The 'politics of commemoration' thus raises the power of projecting a master narrative that negates the contesting claims to revise this particular issue of Hindu history. The project of representing the past is carried over to the act of controlling the reception, which in turn creates the uncontested zone of collective memory. From the symbolic and mythic networks emerges the consciousness that turns a 'community memory' into a national memory that takes advantage of repressed consciousness and a historical legacy of recorded and mythicized animosity, and engineers unwritten narratives into the discourse that manages to inspire 'collective belief'. It is construction of a social reality where a reception born of promulgation and dominant establishment of an agenda does not seem to cohabit with claims purporting to thwart it.

Ayodhya is projected as a wholesome memory. Other narratives contesting and disclaiming it do not gain ground, for the specific 'transmission strategy' seemingly leaves no room for ambiguity and contradiction. The mind of the common Hindu feels itself to be a part of the imagined community that cultivates a 'shared destiny' and easily succumbs to the art of representation that manipulates contexts. This tries to produce a national memory that 'succeeds to represent, for a broad section of the population, a common destiny that overcomes symbolically real social and political conflicts in order to give the illusion of a community to people who in fact have very different interests' (Confino 1997: 1400).

Ayodhya promotes an authenticity that in the words of Allan Megill

> amounts to a species of validity, overriding any problems of accuracy arising from an original misperception or from distortions introduced in the lapse of time. But the authenticity in question is clearly not the kind of authenticity that one attributes to a document from the past whose provenance one has verified. Rather, it is authenticity in the existential sense, deriving its force from the alleged fact that it emerges directly and immediately from the subject's encounter with the world. (1998: 46).

So Ayodhya lies at the intersection of official and vernacular memory, and within the philosophy of the right-wing government the latter determines the former (cf. Bodnar 1992: 13–14). This vernacular memory became the progeny of elite manipulation. Megill (1998: 56) points out that 'far from being history's "raw material" memory is an "Other" that continually haunts history. Memory is an image of the past constructed by a subject in the present. It is thus itself subjective; it may also be irrational, inconsistent, deceptive and self-serving.' The unavoidable open spaces formed out of the intermeshing claims of historical objectivity, intrusive mythic formations, archaeological truth-claims and ideological slant, which quite easily conquer popular imagination, make 'community-designations' and 'identity' constructions easier and manipulative.

For a country where religion is deeply informed by superstition and rituals that form a significant portion of the existential pith, history and memory cannot function without the transformative pressures of religion. Religion creates identity, influences our understanding of history, constructs a historical bias and excites community consciousness. The understanding of Ayodhya thus straddles both communicative and cultural memory to plough up what has always been difficult to produce – the construction of 'popular consciousness' (Assmann 1995: 132).

Notes

1. See the important contribution on oral memory in this volume by Annekie Joubert: 'History by Word of Mouth: Linking Past and Present through Oral Memory'.

2. For instance, Pratap Narain Misra's *Kya Kahati Hai Sarayu Dhara* (1985) triggered the surge in such essentialist writings; see also *Sri Ramjanmabhumi ke Bare me Tathya* (The Truth about Ramjanmabhumi, New Delhi, 1989), and Ram Gopal Pandey, *Sri Ram janmabhumi ka romanckari itihas* (The Exciting History of Sri Ramjanmabhumi; Ayodhya, 1976).

3. The Sanskrit text Skanda Purana is cited by the Visva Hindu Parishad (VHP) to validate their claim. But research shows that Ayodhya-mahatma, a part of the Purana that recounts the benign advantages of a pilgrimage to Ayodhya, is an eighteenth-century insertion. Perhaps the inauthenticity of the VHP claim is most evident in the face of the finding that the core of the Purana was compiled no earlier than the second half of the fourteenth century. Thus the declaration that Ayodhya occupies the pith of Hindu imagination and has come to reign in the Hindu psyche for ages does not hold its ground. The groundswell of the 'Ayodhya myth' can be noticed after the sixteenth century, when Muslim domination brought the communal schism to prominence and the common Hindu minds played into the hands of the religious and self-serving community leaders.

4. Munshi writes: 'I can assure you that the "collective subconscious" of India today is happier with the scheme of reconstruction of Somnath sponsored by Government of India than with many other things that we have done and are doing' (quoted in Noorani 2003: 15).

Bibliography

Assmann, J. 1995. 'Collective Memory and Cultural Identity', *New German Critique* 65: 125–133.

Bodnar, J. 1992. *Remaking America: Public Memory, Commemoration, and Patriotism in the Twentieth Century*. Princeton.

Confino, A. 1997. 'Collective Memory and Cultural History: Problems of Method', *American Historical Review* 102(5): 1386–1403.

De Riencourt, A. 1986. *The Soul of India*. Honeyglen.

Desai, P.N. 1989. *Health and Science in the Hindu Tradition: Continuity and Cohesion*. New York.

Despande, M. 1979. 'History, Change and Permanence: A Classical Indian Perspective', in G. Krishna (ed.), *Contributions to South Asian Studies*. Delhi.

Finley, M.I. 1965. 'Myth, Memory, and History', *History and Theory* 4(3): 281–302.

Funkenstein, A. 1989. 'Collective Memory and Historical Consciousness', *History and Memory* 1(1): 5–26.

Gillis, J.R. 1994. 'Memory and Identity: The History of a Relationship', in J.R. Gillis (ed.), *Commemorations: The Politics of National Identity*. Princeton.

Lowenthal, D. 1996. *Possessed by Past: The Heritage Crusade and the Spoils of History*. New York.

Megill, A. 1998. 'History, Memory, Identity', *History of the Human Sciences* 11(3): 37–62.

Nikam, N.A. 1967. *Some Concepts of Indian Culture: A Philosophical Interpretation*. Shimla.

Noorani, A.G. (ed.). 2003. *The Babri Masjid Question 1528-2003: A Matter of National Honour*. New Delhi.

Pandey, G. 1994. 'Modes of History Writing: New Hindu History of Ayodhya', *Economic and Political Weekly* (June): 1523–8.

Phillips, M.S. 2003. 'Relocating Inwardness: Historical Distance and the Transition from Enlightenment to Romantic Historiography', *PMLA (Journal of the Modern Language Association)* 118(3): 436–449.

Phillips, M.S. 2004. 'Distance and Historical Representation,' *History Workshop Journal* 57(1): 123–141.

Thapar, R. 1990. 'Misuse of the Ramayana', *The Telegraph*, 19 April.

Thapar, R. 2004. *Somnatha: The Many Voices of a History*. New Delhi.

Van der Veer, P. 1996. *Religious Nationalism, Hindus and Muslims in India*. Delhi.

Wood, N. 1999. *Vectors of Memory: Legacies of Trauma in Postwar Europe*. Oxford.

CHAPTER 11

Human Suffering and Forgiveness

A Dialogue with Kim Dae-jung from an East Asian Perspective

HAN SANG-JIN

Historical Context and Rationale

What will follow this short introductory essay is a dialogue between a student of Seoul National University and Kim Dae-jung, former president of the Republic of Korea (1998–2003), that took place in a classroom at Seoul National University (SNU), Seoul, Korea on 26 September 1997. As an invited speaker, Dae-jung first delivered a forty-minute lecture on the topic of 'Asian Values and Democracy' and then had a question-and-answer type of debate for one hour with students and faculty members in a fully packed auditorium. The following dialogue is only a small part of this debate, whose topics were diverse. The central theme of this part of the debate is forgiveness and its relationship with reconciliation. As the text shows, the student challenged the very conditions and truthfulness of the forgiveness expressed by Dae-jung towards the two military-originated former presidents, Chun Doo-Whan and Roh Tae-Woo, who ruled the country from 1980 to 1993.

Dae-jung came to the university on my invitation to meet undergraduate students in my class entitled 'Contemporary Society and Human Rights'. He had spoken at SNU on various previous occasions, invited by professional schools such as the Graduate School of Public Administration, but this was his first time meeting undergraduate students in a regular class. Because of this his lecture attracted wide attention from not only students but also faculty members.

When I was asked to write a short introductory note to this dialogue, I gladly accepted the invitation. I thought it might be useful to clarify the immediate context of this dialogue as well as the historical background of democratization from which the issue of forgiveness emerged as a public issue, deeply entrenched in many ambiguities and misrecognitions. Furthermore, I wanted to make use of the opportunity to seek an answer to a problem that intrigues me. Simply put, my problem is as follows. When we try to come to terms with history and deal with a systematic transgression in the past, all the problems can be quite reasonably solved if the perpetrators accept that they have committed a crime and beg for pardon. Even if this condition is satisfied, of course, there may still be legal and political issues to be adequately addressed, but the overall framework and possibility of coming to terms with history is much more favourable than in cases where this condition is lacking.

Problems emerge, however, if and in so far as the offenders do not admit their wrongdoings and instead attempt to justify their actions by recourse to some kind of convention or ideology such as national security. We are then blocked from moving further. We find ourselves in a dilemma, so to speak. We can neither forgive them nor simply punish all who were involved in committing the wrongdoings. The latter course may create more problems than it solves. What can we do in this situation? Can the victims still forgive the offenders in a meaningful and justifiable way? If so, under which conditions can this come about? This is the question that has preoccupied me for some time (Han 1995). And, to my surprise, I heard one of my students raising exactly the same question that I had in my mind – to which Dae-jung responded straightforwardly, rather than answering in a diplomatic way. In a tense mood, I was deeply moved. I felt my nerves trembling. When I heard his reply I thought I understood him well. But I find it difficult to explain it in a reasonably rational manner. So – and this is the motivation behind the present essay – I would like to reflect on the issue again and share my thoughts with readers in the intercultural context of this publication.

Let me first say something about the immediate political context of the debate. When Dae-jung came to the campus in 1997, he was running as the presidential candidate of the major opposition party in the country. Since the election was less than three months away, people interpreted his words and actions from a political standpoint. This was also the case with Dae-jung's idea of forgiveness. People regarded it as a politically motivated move towards a regional rapprochement. Politically, South Korea is divided into an eastern and a western bloc. For three decades since the 1960s, the political power and socioeconomic mainstream had been controlled by the leaders representing *Kyung-sang* province, the core of the eastern bloc, whereas the western bloc, particularly *Chon-la* province, continued to be suppressed, marginalized or discriminated against. The Kwangju democratic uprising in 1980 can be seen as a consequence of this systematic injustice and discrimination. As a national opposition leader as well as a symbol of such regional suppression, Kim Dae-jung thus found it an urgent matter for his own political interest to overcome this regional division, since the eastern bloc had far greater power than the western in terms of the number of voters and socioeconomic resources. Consequently, he pursued as much regional rapprochement domestically as he did towards North Korea with his sunshine policy. The public understood his idea of forgiveness as part of this strategy. However, there were many critics from the radical groups. On the day of his lecture at SNU, for instance, two dozen radical students protested against Dae-jung in front of the auditorium with placards proclaiming 'No Forgiveness to Military Dictators'.

His lecture could not have been better prepared. He was well versed in the topic, having written an article criticizing Lee Kwan-Yew's concept of Asian values in the journal *Foreign Affairs*. The students enjoyed and welcomed the intellectual side of Dae-jung as a national leader. As he was leaving after the lecture and debate, he was surrounded by a throng of students wanting to shake hands with him or get his autograph. However, the question-and-answer feedback session was full of tension because students raised sharp and penetrating questions. One of the burning issues was the matter of forgiveness. As the text clearly demonstrates, the student was suspicious of the political motive behind Dae-jung's approach to forgiveness. Dae-jung's answer was quite reflexive and sobering, in that he did not altogether exclude the possibility of such a motive. However, he stated that his idea of forgiveness was not merely strategic, but involved a political principle. He added that it was based on his political philosophy. This was an important assertion, in my view, but he merely declared it without properly explaining it. Neither his lecture nor answer provided an adequate explanation. We therefore need to examine it in more depth.

In the discussion Dae-jung mentioned that Chun Doo-Whan had apologized and gone to the Baekdam Buddhist temple in 1989. Nevertheless, Kim Dae-jung appears to have asked again for an apology. The historical context of this request needs to be clarified. In Korea, after twenty-six years of military rule, the first direct presidential election was held in 1987. Roh Tae-Woo (the successor of Chun Doo-Whan) won, largely owing to the split of democratic forces into two camps led by Kim Young-Sam and Kim Dae-jung. Still, in the civil society and among opposition parties there were strong pressures towards democratization. Faced with mounting difficulties, the ruling group somehow reached an agreement that Chun Do-Whan, as the primary target of criticism, should apologize and leave Seoul to mobilize sympathy for his penitential life in a Buddhist temple. This was a typical case of a calculated political gesture with no concrete reference to any wrongdoing he committed. Consequently, the victims of the human rights suppression during the past military regimes, particularly those of the Kwangju massacre in 1980, had no reason to accept it as sincere remorse.

Furthermore, in December of 1995 the incumbent President Kim Young-Sam, who had succeeded Roh Tae-Woo by way of his party's merger with the then ruling party in 1989, made an abrupt decision to arrest Chun Doo-Whan on the charge of military treason. The military actions under his influence, from December 1979 up to the ruthless crackdown of the Kwangju democratic uprising in May 1980, were interpreted as unlawful actions destroying the constitutional order. Thus, both Chun Doo-Whan and Roh Tae-Woo were prosecuted on the charge of a crime against the safety of the state and served time in prison, though they were later pardoned and released.

Here, too, the situation was highly ambiguous. It appeared to be a great victory of democratization to put two generals and former presidents in prison. This rarely happens in Asian culture. In reality, however, all actions were visibly political. Kim Young-Sam's decision was not well thought through. Chun Doo-Whan made a strong protest by reading a statement before being arrested. There was not the slightest sign of repentance. The general public saw the event as a power struggle between two competing personalities rather than internally related to the issues of establishing truth and justice in historical transition. Note the following observation by Douglass Cassel:

> Now facing national assembly elections in April [1966], [the President] has chosen this moment to arrest Generals Chun and Roh for Korea's most infamous atrocity since the war – the Kwangju massacre. Not surprisingly, many Koreans suspect that the arrests have more to do with the President's sagging popularity than with his commitment to justice. ... A less cynical interpretation may also be defended. ... He may simply feel that now, with the discrediting of General Roh for corruption, and the growing consolidation of Korean democracy, it is finally safe to prosecute those responsible for the massacre, without serious risk of provoking another coup. (Cited in Offe 2005:20)

An important point to remember is that the most salient issue discussed at that time was of a legal nature, not about truth and justice. This was because a special law was promulgated which made the prosecution of the two generals possible. The alleged crime of unlawful military actions could not be properly prosecuted since the period allowed for it had already expired. Only a special law could offer a new interpretation, according to which the legal clause of the effective time for prosecution remained suspended during the years when the perpetrators assumed office. As can easily be understood, the recourse to a special law brought about many doubts and objections, since it is often held that retroactive lawmaking contradicts the classical idea of the rule of law.

The point I am making is that the dominant trend and debates at the time were far removed from any serious consideration of how to achieve truth, justice and reconciliation. For this reason, the coming to terms with history was seen by many as incomplete. In this respect, Kim Dae-jung proposed four conditions for reconciliation during the discussion: truth, restoring the honour of the victims, compensation and memorial activities. He also emphasized that the perpetrators should express sincere repentance so that it can begin to heal the wounds of the victims. In the context of 1997, however, there were not many viable options available. Some progress had already been achieved with regard to these four conditions, albeit not satisfactorily. Since Chun Doo-Whan and Roh Tae-Woo had already served prison sentences, it would not have made much political sense to demand retributive justice again. What remained to be done, according to my interpretation of Kim Dae-jung's intentions, was sincere repentance by Chun Doo-Whan, which would enable the victims and the nation as well to accept it by way of forgiving them, thereby achieving a new national community going beyond threatening divisions of many kinds.

From the side of Chun Doo-Whan, however, after the painful experience of a life of banishment to a temple in the mountains and penal servitude, there was probably no clear reason why he should express remorse. In this situation, Kim Dae-jung made an impressive move towards the idea of 'unilateral' or 'unconditional' forgiveness. Unilateral means 'a form of forgiveness that does not require an apology' (Kaposy 2005: 217). This may be possible when 'the victim has community support, or she has the strength of her convictions'. In contrast, Derrida (2001) suggests an unconditional ideal of forgiveness as pure forgiveness or, to use his terms, as 'forgiving the unforgivable'. It seems rather difficult, however, to draw a clear boundary between these two types of forgiveness, which differ from the position that requires apology and remorse as a condition of forgiveness. When Kim Dae-jung said, 'even if the offenders do not apologize, the victim can still forgive', he implied a categorical difference between the offender and the victim in terms of the moral power to initiate changes though forgiveness rather than taking the 'hard line' of retributive justice. But his explanation is rather brief, inviting creative interpretation.

Such an interpretation may proceed in two directions. The first is to focus on the negative consequences brought about by unilateral and unconditional forgiveness. To forgive the offenders unconditionally is hardly justifiable if it serves to legitimate the offender's wrongdoings or weaken public vigilance, thereby inviting the recurrence of the same mistake. To forgive without first holding the wrongdoers to account is arguably to concede too much too soon. On the contrary, one may claim that retribution should be applied before forgiving offenders in order to affirm a commitment to shared norms. Because the defence of unconditional forgiveness runs counter to this forceful legal argument, it is important to investigate whether such negative consequences can be avoided. In other words, we can ask whether a wide consensus already exists in civil society and in political circles as well as about the wrongdoings committed during the past authoritarian regimes. As Kaposy (2005: 217) observes, 'the community may recognize the wrongness of an act even though the offender is unrepentant, and thus provide enough support to forgive the victim.' Under these circumstances, one may forgive offenders who do not offer an apology. Even though the process of coming to terms with history may still be incomplete with respect to truth and justice, the offenders are forgiven in order to create a new space of political community.

I would interpret Kim Dae-jung's idea of unilateral or unconditional forgiveness along this line of thinking. This makes sense to me since I believe that the majority of the Korean people have learned something crucial through the processes of democratic transformation. No matter whether Chun Doo-Whan apologizes or not, society recognizes the crimes against humanity in which he was involved. I would say that the deterrent force is strong enough not to tolerate the recurrence of such genocides as we experienced in the Kwangju massacre and other terrible incidents.

According to Kim Dae-jung as a politician, the best option is always characterized by a win-win, positive-sum situation, beginning from establishing truth, moving to repentance, then to forgiveness and finally to historical reconciliation. When a sincere repentance is missing, however, he suggests the second-best option of unilateral forgiveness, which is possible only when the political conditions for it are met, as is explained above. Seen in this way, Kim Dae-jung's idea of forgiveness is grounded in his estimation of the strength of democracy in Korea.

The second move is to focus on the positive consequences that unilateral or unconditional forgiveness may initiate. In this regard, I find Schaap's (2003) argument quite persuasive: against the 'art of compromise' and the 'hard line' of retributive justice, he attempts to create a political reasoning in line with Arendt, an approach that is characterized by unconditional forgiveness. The key question is here whether and how one can be true to the past 'without making forgiveness conditional on the wrongdoer's repudiation of her acts' (Schaap 2003: 80). Unconditional forgiveness is meaningful because it enables us to understand the other as 'more encompassing than her singular relation to us as our transgressor' (Schaap 2003: 79). To forgive is to release the other from the consequences of the original wrongdoing. As Schaap (2003: 81) notes, 'as long as an actor remains bound to the consequences of an original act, her capacity to act anew is reduced.' In contrast, forgiveness affirms our shared potentiality to act anew. In other words, forgiveness is predicated on the assumption that even our offenders have potential to begin anew. 'Trust may be ventured for the sake of establishing a new relation based on mutual recognition of each other as co-builders of a common world' (Schaap 2003: 82).

We cannot be sure, however, whether and when these retrospective and prospective aspects of unconditional forgiveness can be realized in this world. This question can be answered not by theory but by concrete politics. One may argue on good grounds that these have been realized in South Africa, for instance, where 'it was not the acknowledgment of wrongdoing by perpetrators, which opened the way to forgiveness. Rather, it was the disposition to forgive, a willingness on the part of those wronged to defer the right to just retribution, that cleared the way for perpetrators to publicly disclose the wrongdoing they were involved in' (Schaap 2003: 84).

Though Korea differs from South Africa in many respects, I would interpret Kim Dae-jung's views as also aiming at this possibility when he upheld his idea of unconditional forgiveness during the dialogue at SNU in 1997. This interpretation is based on a previous discussion I had with him, in which he remained consistent in acknowledging the human potential to act anew and the need to break away from the vicious cycle of past wrongdoings.

Furthermore, I would suggest that Kim Dae-jung's idea of unconditional forgiveness entails an awareness of 'virtual reciprocity' in historical wrongdoings. 'We forgive because we may also need to be forgiven', as Schaap (2003: 83) puts it. To forgive fosters a reciprocal humane understanding between the perpetrators and the victims in terms of biographical stories:

> Such a story is not intended to show the other as one worthy of forgiveness by separating the sin from the sinner. Rather, it situates the wrongs done against us in the biographical context within which the other makes sense of her own actions. This leads to a kind of understanding that confirms our perception of the past and the injury perpetrated against us. However, it does not demand that the one who wronged us be different from what she is. We find grounds for overcoming resentment by making our transgressors' actions intelligible "by forgivingly understanding how they have made sense of their lives" (Calhoun 1992: 96). Importantly, in the context of a reconciliatory politics, this means engaging with the collective meanings and narratives by which our former enemy might have made sense of his life as, for instance, a freedom fighter rather than a terrorist (Schaap 2003: 80).

In conclusion, I would like to make some comments on religion. Kim Dae-jung is a faithful Catholic with deep knowledge of the Bible and of religious tenets. He has often explained how he sees the difference between the New and the Old Testament: the former is deeply touching with its stories of unconditional love and forgiveness, whereas the latter relies more on the traditional idea of retributive justice and revenge. I find that Kim Dae-jung's view comes close to Solomon's (2002) interpretation of the difference between rabbinic Judaism and Christianity. What I am implying here is that a religious motive underlies Kim Dae-jung's idea of unilateral or unconditional forgiveness. As a politician, Kim Dae-jung has been deeply engaged in improving the real conditions of life and rights of the ordinary people. At the same time, he appears deeply engaged philosophically and psychologically in pursuing a universal perspective through the Christian norms of love and forgiveness. This is why he has never been satisfied with a mere contractual norm of exchange nor a legal conception of retributive justice. On the contrary, Kim Dae-jung has consistently upheld a universal paradigm of human understanding, reciprocal care and love, and global leadership. In a crucial sense, I believe that Dae-jung's idea of unilateral or unconditional forgiveness has something to do with his religious predisposition and worldview.

The Dialogue*

Question

My father is one of your enthusiastic supporters. I have heard him saying many times that 'Kim Dae-jung really must become President this time.' Fortuitously, having heard that Kim Dae-jung would be visiting the campus of Seoul National University, I had a talk with my father last night. I had this to say to my father, as an ardent supporter of Kim Dae-jung: 'Even if Kim Dae-jung becomes president, nothing will change.'

With a suspicious look, my father asked me why I thought in the way that I did. I replied: 'Being acquainted with Kim Dae-jung's opinions, here is a man who says that he will pardon former dictators such as Chun Doo-Hwan and Roh Tae-Woo with no conditions. If such a man becomes president, how would he differ at all from our notorious former presidents?'

I continued: 'There is no problem with the principle of forgiveness in its own right. However, I believe that a pardon is something that we should only give when the person about to be punished solemnly declares that he/she will not commit the offence again. If a pardon is given to those who continue to maintain that they did nothing wrong, or if a pardon is made with the consciousness of votes and popularity to be gained from such a move, then I believe that such a pardon must be a burden on the conscience of you who fought so hard against the military dictatorship in times past.

Answer

You have posed a very good question. I will attempt to elaborate on this issue for all those present. Although I fear that you will misunderstand me, due to you all being young students, nevertheless I will try to answer your question truthfully and frankly.

In my life so far, I have survived five close encounters with death. One attempt was made on my life by communists, three attempts by those allied with President Park Chung-Hee, and another attempt on my life was made during the era of President Chun Doo-Hwan. On top of that, I experienced life in prison for a period of six years, and spent ten years either in exile or under house arrest. Therefore, my life has been interrupted for a total of sixteen years.

Some people look at me and say that I look young, but I reply to them by noting that this is something that should be obvious. 'Other people have lived normal lives, so they should have grown old in a normal time-frame, but as my life has been interrupted for sixteen years, isn't it obvious that the process of me growing old should have been interrupted too?' In any case, for sixteen years I experienced a period of incredible difficulty and suffering. Thinking through this period of suffering, the time when I experienced the worst privation was during the period of President Chun Doo-Hwan's rule during the 1980s. The reason why I tell you about these things is because I feel that such words might be of some aid to you as you live your own lives.

This is not the first time that I have told this story in public. In 1980, when I was sentenced to death by the court, I had this to say when I was asked to make my final statement. 'Before the 1980s are finished, this country will gain democracy. Although I will be gone from the world by then (I absolutely expected my impending death at the time) nevertheless I will now give you all my last words. Whatever happens, please uphold democracy. Please reveal the fallacies that cover us to be the falsehoods that they are, and please restore our honour. Please always side with victims and those who have suffered privations. But at the same time always be lenient towards those who have done us wrong and those who have oppressed us.'

Furthermore, I noted that upon those who had committed theft or robbery (and other economic violations), heavy fines and levies should be imposed. For those who have killed others, strict corporal punishment should be imposed. However, for those who have inflicted political dictatorship upon others, the deprivation of their dictatorial power and their honour and name should be the greatest punishment that is inflicted upon them. This is the crux of what I had to say at that time.

At the time, I was also thinking of Abraham Lincoln. Lincoln had said these words around the time of the conclusion of the civil war, 'Victorious I may be, but I will not punish the South.' Whereupon a fiery opposition opened up within Lincoln's own camp that labelled Lincoln a liar, dishonest, a murderer and worse. And yet, it was the strength of Lincoln's spirit that prevented the fragmentation of America into North and South at the time.

After this, I was luckily saved from the jaws of death by help from heaven. In 1987, when I was campaigning nationwide as a presidential candidate, I declared that there would be four undertakings that we would push for should we be elected. Firstly, we would reveal the truth about the Kwangju massacre; secondly, we would restore the honour of those who had false charges laid against them (in fact, to this day I still hold a criminal record for this reason). Thirdly, because the regime unjustly wronged them, we declared that we would give rightful compensation to the victims, and finally we pledged that we would construct a memorial to the Kwangju democratization movement. As these assertions received wide attention and support among citizens, Chun Doo-Hwan had to make an apology [with no substantive content: translator] in front of the people and went to Baekdam Buddhist temple in 1989.

I have held a consistent belief with regard to this issue. This also happens to encompass my political philosophy and my personal convictions. Recently, I told Chun Doo-Hwan again to apologize for the Kwangju massacre. If one apologizes, then it is possible to move beyond forgiveness and towards reconciliation. In a recent interview with a weekly magazine, I said the following words. 'To be able to reconcile is the most desirable situation. However, even if the offenders do not apologize, the victim can still forgive.' Thus, I think it is desirable to forgive during the term in office of current President Kim Young-Sam.

I am not motivated by the thought of gaining votes in the upcoming election. Of course, I thought about votes too, no sane politician would not do so, but in terms of this issue, my position is one that I have maintained consistently since the time I was sentenced to death in 1980.

What I want to tell all of you here today is that there is a difference between forgiveness and reconciliation. Although reconciliation is the most ideal outcome, nevertheless forgiveness is still important. I am frankly telling you this, but there was a time when those who tried to kill me were talking to me about reconciliation by offering the possibility that I might become Vice-President. That is to say, they told me that they would waive the death penalty and let me live, if I cooperated. However, I refused.

You probably do not realize what a frightening thing death is because you have most likely not had the experience of death moving rapidly towards you. Just imagine a rope being tied around your neck ready to drop. Of course one's heart is sinking. However, I honestly could not betray the people. Therefore, I refused their offer. Even so, because I really wanted to live, I sincerely wished that I would only be given life imprisonment. I was looking up towards the presiding judge at my trial just willing him to open his mouth.

I was just willing the judge to open his mouth and pronounce the words 'life imprisonment.' Ladies and gentlemen, try saying the words 'life' (in Korean 'mu-gee'). When one says the 'mu' of 'mu-gee' (life imprisonment) in Korean, doesn't one's mouth move towards the front? Contrariwise, when one pronounces the words 'sa-hyung' (death sentence) in Korean, doesn't the word 'sa' cut and split open the mouth? Therefore, I was sinking inside myself just thinking to myself, 'if the mouth moves out then life, and if it splits then death.' Even though I earnestly wished to live, it was because I believed at the time that to cooperate with them would be betraying the people that I did not give in.

In 1989, when President Roh Tae-Woo was planning the three-party merger that took place, a message was sent to me. The message communicated to me that I should merge with the incumbent party. Roh Tae-Woo told me that should I accept his offer, he would turn down the three-party merger with Kim Young-Sam and Kim Jong-Pil and merge only with my party, promising to leave to me the make-up of the next administration. To the messengers who were whispering to me the possibility of such deals, I said that they were throwing dirt in my ears and told them to stop their entreaties.

What is the fundamental basis for democracy? I reply boldly that it is the maintenance of fundamental values such as justice, human rights and the rights of workers. I am someone who has pursued politics as his life's work. I will guarantee and protect the rights to free political expression for workers. I have already said that if we gain office, we will enshrine the level of freedom advocated by the International Labour Organization. It was only yesterday that I talked on television and radio about the need to release all prisoners of conscience. I have also asserted the need to revise or replace the National Security Law, establish the self-rule of the local governments and bring into being a unified national scheme of medical insurance policy. I have also stressed the importance of independence and autonomy of the Bank of Korea. Regarding such important principles, there is not an inch of ground that I will concede when pursuing them.

While pursuing such fundamental principles, I also will push for reconciliation wherever possible, and forgiveness when reconciliation is beyond reach. I have well understood the forthright criticism and concern of all of you gathered here today. However, never will there be a time when I either fail to meet your expectations, or betray you and the people at large.

Notes

* Originally published in Han 1998: 54–58.

Bibliography

Calhoun, C. 1992. 'Changing One's Heart', *Ethics* 103 (Oct): 76–96.
Derrida, J. 2001. 'To Forgive the Unforgivable and the Imprescriptible', in Caputo, M. Dooley and M. Scanlon (eds), *Questioning God*. Bloomington: 21–51.
Han, S.-J. 1995. *Nunca Mas: Never Again*. Seoul.
Han, S.-J. (ed.). 1998. *Looking out from the East towards the World: Kim Dae Jung's Lecture at Seoul National University and Debate on Human Rights*. Seoul.
Kaposy, C. 2005. 'Analytic Reading, Continental Text: The Case of Derrida's "On Forgiveness"', *International Journal of Philosophical Studies* 13 (2): 203–226.
Offe, C. 2005. 'Transition Justice after Democratization: Options, Patterns, Objectives, Dilemmas, and the Role of International Politics'. Paper presented on the occasion of the Centenary of Korea University, Seoul, Korea.
Schaap, A. 2003. 'Political Grounds for Forgiveness', *Contemporary Political Theory* 2 (1): 77–87.
Solomon, S. 2002. *Wounds Not Healed by Time: The Power of Repentance and Forgiveness*. Oxford.

Part III

TEXTS FROM THE PRAXIS OF MEMORY, TRAUMA, FORGIVENESS AND HEALING

CHAPTER 12

Remorse, Forgiveness and Rehumanization

Stories from South Africa's Truth and Reconciliation Commission*

PUMLA GOBODO-MADIKIZELA

Introduction

South Africa's Truth and Reconciliation Commission (TRC) has been acclaimed for bringing the awful facts of apartheid to light, for creating a context for those who suffered to tell their stories and for managing this difficult process in an even-handed way that avoided acrimony. But over and above the TRC's role in documenting the past, and even the opportunity it provided to those who for years have suffered in silence to put their stories on record, there is a more inward dimension of the commission's work that has received relatively little coverage from either social scientists or the media. In offering an account of their deeds, some of the perpetrators were able to move beyond mere description and to reflect on the ethical component of their actions – to begin to feel sorry for what they had done. Not many of them in fact ever apologized, and not all of the apologies that were delivered seemed sincere. But the rendering of apologetic remarks, offered directly to families who had lost loved ones, laid the groundwork for the TRC hearings to engender something even more important than reams of testimony: it opened the door to the possibility of forgiveness.

In this chapter I explore the phenomenon of forgiveness, drawing examples from encounters between victims and perpetrators from different settings. I focus on examples from South Africa's TRC, especially the encounter

---

between Eugene de Kock, perhaps the most feared and certainly the most notorious of apartheid's henchmen, and the widows of two men in whose deaths
de Kock has been implicated.

Amnesty, Justice and the TRC

The TRC was promulgated by an act of parliament, the *National Healing and
Reconciliation Act of 1995,* with a mandate to focus mainly on three issues, namely
to (a) establish as complete a picture as possible of past human rights violations
committed all along the political spectrum, (b) give victims of human rights
abuses a chance to speak publicly about the abuses they suffered in the past,
and (c) grant amnesty to perpetrators of human rights abuses on the condition
that they give full disclosure of acts that they committed and prove that these
acts can be characterized as having a political motive. The conditions attached
to amnesty distinguish the South African process from other amnesty processes,
such as those in Brazil and some South American countries, where outgoing
military and civilian leaders granted themselves amnesty and blanket amnesty
to their foot soldiers.

    A central dilemma facing many countries that are making a transition from
an oppressive authoritarian state to democracy is what to do about the human
rights abuses of the past regime. The issue becomes particularly wrenching when
there has been a record of torture, murders and other crimes against humanity.
Should government figures and leaders of opposition groups be held responsible for crimes that they usually did not commit themselves or did not always
explicitly authorize? And if responsible, should they be prosecuted or granted
immunity from prosecution in exchange for a confession? A crucial part of the
negotiations process in South Africa concerned the question of amnesty and
whether perpetrators of gross human rights violations from both sides of the
political conflict would be granted political pardon. Some proposed that there
should be no amnesty, while others, in particular former President F.W. de
Klerk and his colleagues, who were eager to protect their men in the army and
police – and themselves – urged that there should be general amnesty without
any declaration of atrocities committed and without any public hearings.

    The idea of 'blanket amnesty' has been a hotly contested issue in many
countries going through democratic transition (Hayner 1994; Skaar 1999). Skaar
argued that the option of blanket amnesty depends on the relative strength of
the outgoing government's demand for impunity and the public's demand for
truth and justice. In Chile, for example, it could be argued that the strength of
the outgoing dictatorship of Augusto Pinochet enabled the military to demand
blanket amnesty, which they hoped would prevent any future prosecutions
of its members. However, this amnesty law was 'put to shame' (Skaar 1999:
1123) with the trial of some former generals in 1995. Following the arrest and

detention of Pinochet in Britain and the debate over whether he should stand trial for the murder of Spanish citizens during his regime, the tables turned dramatically against Pinochet with the withdrawal of the immunity he enjoyed as a former head of state in Chile.

The conditional amnesty granted to perpetrators in South Africa had less to do with power dynamics in the relationship between the former apartheid government and the ANC than with South Africa's attempt to build social cohesion and to restore peace instead of revenge.

Mass Atrocity and the 'Duty to Prosecute'

Perhaps the best discussion yet on the complexity of the question of amnesty comes from Minow (1998). She concluded that following the example of the Nuremberg trials and the international covenants that emerged as a result of the process, some researchers see the 'duty to prosecute' after mass atrocities as the only viable option. She observed, however, that decisions on whether to follow the amnesty route (conditional or blanket amnesty), truth commissions or prosecutions 'represent different considerations, some principled, some practical, that depart from the 'duty to prosecute'' (1998: 28).

Some consider the duty to prosecute to be the only option if justice is to be done. The problem with this view is that it frames justice only in terms of legal procedures. There are other, equally effective models; restorative justice (Little 1999; Tutu 1999) is a particularly promising one. For almost all victims who appeared on the TRC stage, the majority of whom were black, the very notion of justice was a misnomer. What was legally acceptable under apartheid – the use of violence by state police and the army to silence the opposition – was defended during apartheid by its crafters right up to the halls of justice, in which many judges failed to stand at a critical distance from the oppressive laws of apartheid (Bizos 1999; Gobodo-Madikizela 2003). Thus, victims of gross human rights abuses appealing the law in South Africa had a different experience of the justice that many take for granted. For these victims, being given a voice for the first time – being able to speak before an official body – gave them the sense of affirmation and validation that is so important for victims of trauma. Unlike in a court of law, where victims are brought into the picture only in relation to the perpetrator's deed, the TRC put victims at the centre of the process, allowing them to tell their stories in the way that they chose before a listening audience, validating experiences that were denied by the apartheid state for many years.

Felman and Laub have highlighted the critical role that listening plays in witnessing about trauma. They argue that when victims testify about their traumatic experiences, the listener 'takes on the responsibility for bearing witness that previously the (victim) felt he bore alone' (1992: 85). There is something transformative and cathartic about the moment of public testimony (Minow 1998). Many victims who appeared before the TRC spoke about their witnessing as an experience that gave them a degree of control over their trauma. Brison argued that in the case of human-inflicted trauma, the act of bearing witness moves the victim from being the object of the perpetrator's speech or behaviour 'to being the subject of one's own' (1999: 39). It is about making peace with the past – not *forgetting* the past – in the presence of an attentive, sympathetic audience.

When dealing with mass atrocity, punitive justice alone may not be enough. The legal model followed in international tribunals needs to be at the very least broadened to include a process that will affirm victims, giving them some control over their narratives of trauma and thus significantly contributing to the victim's recovery process. Of course, this is not an argument against pursuing prosecution, but only an argument for expanding the model beyond prosecution. The prosecution model frames justice in legal terms alone and does not make room for the importance of the psychological healing that victims may experience when they are given full freedom to tell their stories in the presence of a supportive audience. In a world rife with state-sanctioned violence, debates aimed at promoting justice and reconciliation should consider the idea of redefining justice. I think this is important to make the transition from vengeful citizens to caring citizens, particularly if victims and perpetrators are ever to be able to live together again.

What Is Forgiveness?

The subject of forgiveness arouses a lot of scepticism among people who find it hard to imagine how perpetrators can apologize genuinely and meaningfully other than in self-interest, and how victims can forgive in the face of tragedy.

Simon Wiesenthal's book *The Sunflower* (1976), that discusses a plea for forgiveness by a dying SS soldier, and Sister Helen Prejean's (1993) account of a gesture of forgiveness by the parent of a victim to the victim's murderer, address us on the question of forgiveness and provide an illuminating contrast between two different responses to perpetrators' apologies. Simon Wiesenthal (1976) pondered the dilemma he faced in a Nazi concentration camp: a dying SS soldier, who was haunted by his role in the slaughter of Jews in Nazi Germany, was desperate to find a Jew from whom to beg forgiveness. From his deathbed he asked a nurse to find a Jew from among the prisoners in the camp, and the nurse found Wiesenthal. With Wiesenthal at the bedside, the soldier confessed his atrocity, pleading for forgiveness. Simon Wiesenthal writes that he found himself unable to extend forgiveness to the soldier. Prejean (1993) describes a man who asks and is granted forgiveness by the father of one of the victims he had murdered. Offered a chance to say his last words before execution, the prisoner faced the father of one of the dead victims, addressed him directly and asked for his forgiveness. Prejean informs us that the murdered victim's father tearfully nodded his head, signalling forgiveness.

These stories raise two issues with particular poignancy. One of these is that when people who have committed heinous acts ask for forgiveness, they are in a sense asking to be admitted to the world of moral humanity. One may be inclined to think that an apology by someone who has committed a deliberate act of violence is futile or unworthy of a victim's forgiveness. But as Prejean (1993) has shown, and as I will also demonstrate in this chapter, this is not a black and white issue; the capacity to forgive may extend to those deeds that are usually considered unforgivable. Some may think that vengeance is the only thing that victims have in mind when they encounter those responsible for their anguish. But the relationship between those who have committed evil deeds and their victims is not as predictable as this may suggest. In my work with victims and perpetrators who came to the TRC, I was struck by how some victims, in their encounter with perpetrators, seemed to be looking for reasons to forgive. Similarly striking was how desperate some perpetrators were for forgiveness. Even after they had been granted amnesty – political pardon – some perpetrators seemed anxious to hear words of forgiveness from their victims. It was as if they wanted something more – the cleansing power of the victim's forgiveness – to 'free' them, even if symbolically, from the burden of their dark past.

Another issue raised by these stories of forgiveness concerns the question of moral contradiction. How can what is morally depraved be forgiven? How can perpetrators even apologize for such deeds? Is forgiveness in these cases an embrace of evil?

Unlike beneficiaries of privilege who support an oppressive system, perpetrators are the ones who are visible and who commit the evil deeds enshrined in policies created at the highest level of the oppressive system. I think that the act of forgiveness resists separating perpetrators from this network of human others, and instead recognizes that perpetrators are part of the same fabric. Thus forgiveness opens up relationship possibilities not just with perpetrators, but also with the society of bystanders who kept silent.

Forgiveness: A Humane Connection with Another Human Being

The two accounts in Prejean (1993) and Wiesenthal (1976) also highlight two important factors in forgiveness. These are a remorseful apology, which is a key element in forgiveness (Bies and Tripp 1996), and acknowledgement of wrongdoing. These factors are present in Prejean's story of the prisoner's encounter with his victim's father. However, this story stands in marked contrast with

Simon Wiesenthal's encounter with a dying SS soldier. It seems that Wiesenthal is faceless, nameless, and simply a Jew when he appears before the SS soldier. The behaviour of the SS soldier suggests a person who is absorbed in his guilt with little or no concern about Wiesenthal's pain and suffering. In asking forgiveness without an attempt to appreciate Wiesenthal's pain – without making a *human* connection with him – the SS soldier's plea has an empty ring to it. It is tantamount to adding insult to injury.

Victims need much more than the signs of humaneness suggested by a remorseful state of mind. They need to reclaim their dignity and respect and to feel that they are in control. Intentionally inflicted trauma shatters one's sense of self and destroys the sense of continuity between self and others (Apfel and Tellingator 2000; Brison 1999). It means that 'one *can be oneself* in relation to others' (Herman 1992, cited in Brison 1999: 41). Apfel and Tellingator (2000) describe the social conditions that are necessary to restore the continuity destroyed by a traumatic event. They suggest that connections to cultural roots and supports (such as church, neighbourhood and family) are an essential part of healing for people who have suffered irreparable loss. Without a sense of continuity with a community of others, regaining one's sense of self may itself be a traumatic process. The importance of continuity in the process of healing trauma and the effects that its absence may have on the individual may help explain why Simon Wiesenthal (1976) was unable to forgive the apologetic and dying SS soldier. As a prisoner in a Nazi camp, and in addition to his anonymity before the soldier, Simon Wiesenthal was living with trauma as a result of the uncertainty of his own life and the lives of loved ones. He had control over neither his life nor his future. This frame of mind was hardly conducive to forgiveness.

Forgiveness Offered Instead of Revenge

Durham aptly describes forgiveness as 'mourning the passage of revenge' (2000: 70). It is offering forgiveness *instead* of revenge (Minow 1998). The idea of 'mourning' the passage of one's vengeful emotion implies a 'letting go' of something that was valued. Anger, resentment and revenge – all of which are 'negative' emotions – are an important part of working through one's traumatic loss. However, after a long period of resentment and vengeful feelings, the victim may experience these emotions as a burden. Forgiveness can help relieve victims of these burdensome emotions.

Forgiveness, according to a participant in a reconciliation workshop at Stanford University, is not necessarily about forgiving other people 'but forgiving yourself and the situation and setting it aside so you can go on with your life' (Hamilton 2001: 78). However, forgiveness does not mean letting go of the pain, nor does it mean that the victim's anger will necessarily go away. Victims face daily the *lived memory* of their trauma (Gobodo-Madikizela 2001, 2003). Their trauma is the touchstone of reality (Friedman 1998), so a return of some of the emotions associated with the loss, maybe including anger and resentment, is not unexpected. Forgiveness is a kind of a turning point, the embrace of a new way of dealing with one's trauma and the emotions it evokes. Anger sometimes dominates a victim's life. Forgiveness, however, creates a possibility for reflection on one's life of anger and resentment towards the person responsible for the pain and suffering.

The search for a turning point does not always culminate in forgiveness. Statements made by some family members of victims killed in the Timothy McVeigh bombing of the federal building in Oklahoma City illustrate this point. Although McVeigh refused to apologize for his actions, as his execution drew closer some family members of victims dissociated themselves from the collective anger and hate expressed by the majority who either lost loved ones or were injured in the bombing. They were concerned that the anger and hatred was slowly destroying their lives. For instance, one family member reported that he was 'disturbed by the blood lust he saw' in many of the survivors and family members of the victims of the bombing (O'Brien 2001: 43). He admitted that he had been extremely angry with McVeigh and that he still felt angry with him, but that anger was no longer central in his emotions. The following statement from another family member of victims killed in the McVeigh bombing shows that letting go of anger is sometimes a conscious decision taken regardless of what a perpetrator does or says: 'McVeigh and Nichols were full of revenge and hate ... and now we're full of revenge and hate for McVeigh and Nichols, and the cycle of violence just goes on and on. I just decided this has to stop' (O'Brien 2001: 43).

Some victims may choose not to let go of their anger and hatred. These feelings may take on a life of their own, exacting considerable power over the victim, making it increasingly harder to let go. Sometimes victims cannot let go in part because perpetrators have not given them 'good reason' to forgive (Minow 1998). If victims do not feel that perpetrators have told the truth about what happened to their loved ones, their doubts about perpetrators' truthfulness may give them good reason *not* to forgive. One of the widows of the Cradock Four, who were abducted and killed in a notorious incident in South Africa, expressed disappointment at the lack of truth in the testimony of the men responsible for her husband's killing. 'I can't forgive and forget', said Nyameka Goniwe, 'or go on with my life until I know the actual killers' (Bizos 1999: 219–220).

Knowing the truth does not imply any promise of forgiveness on the part of the victim. Rather, it frames one's trauma in language that can be understood. Knowing the truth allows conversations with oneself that were previously inaccessible. Forgiveness may simply be one of the things that happen after the 'air' has been cleared.

Acknowledgement of responsibility by the perpetrator not only clarifies questions of fact for the victim: it also clarifies what the perpetrator wants to be forgiven for. This enables the victim to make the choice whether to grant or deny forgiveness. It also helps to reestablish the victim's self-respect (Haber 1991) by giving the victim control over something that the perpetrator needs. Minow has argued that 'the ability to dispense, but also to withhold, forgiveness is an ennobling capacity and part of the dignity to be reclaimed' by victims (1998: 17).

The Apology and the Offer of Forgiveness

Apologies are not always expressed with sincerity (Moore 1988). An insincere apology lacks the sense of guilt and remorse that are necessary to transform an apology into a 'speech act' (Tavuchis 1991: 119–120). The significance of an apology lies in its ability to perform and to transcend the apologetic words. In other words, to validate the victim's pain and suffering, an apology must communicate the appropriate emotion.

The following example illustrates an apology that performs as a 'speech act'. Two widows whose husbands were killed in an explosion that was masterminded by Eugene de Kock, the apartheid government's chief assassin, met with de Kock in an encounter that led to forgiveness. Their husbands were part of a group of three black policemen in the Eastern Cape who were killed to prevent them from exposing the identity of white policemen who were involved in the murder of four black activists, the Cradock Four.

Eugene de Kock, as the head of the apartheid government's covert operations, commanded an army of death squads on a secret farm near Pretoria. De Kock, the most decorated police officer of the apartheid regime, is now serving 212 years and two life sentences for his crimes. Like all perpetrators of politically motivated crimes, he applied for amnesty from the TRC. Although de Kock was granted amnesty for most of his crimes, he was denied amnesty for this incident for which he received a life sentence.

At a TRC amnesty hearing, de Kock explained that he had received instructions from his superiors to 'make a plan' for the 'elimination' of three policemen who had threatened to reveal the identity of the policemen responsible for the murder of the Cradock Four. A dramatic moment came at the hearing during de Kock's testimony when he requested a private meeting with the widows who were present at the public hearing. They agreed to meet with him. A private room was then arranged by the TRC for the widows, Pearl Faku and Doreen Mgoduka, and their lawyer to meet with de Kock and his lawyer.

I met Pearl and Doreen for debriefing sessions over a weekend following their meeting with de Kock. They described the meeting as a moving experience, firstly because it gave them an opportunity to speak directly to the man responsible for the death of their husbands, and secondly because de Kock was the only person who had broken the secrecy and silence maintained by other white policemen. They also described de Kock's impassioned plea for forgiveness and explained why they forgave him. Here Pearl Faku explains:

> I was profoundly touched by him, especially when he said he wished he could bring our husbands back. I didn't even look at him when he was speaking to us. I don't think I looked at him, at least I don't remember looking at him in that room. Yet, I felt the genuineness in his apology. I couldn't control my tears. I could hear him, but I was overwhelmed by emotion, and I was just nodding, as a way of saying yes, I forgive you. I hope that when he sees our tears, he knows that they are not only tears for our husbands, but tears for him as well … I would like to hold him by the hand, and show him that there is a future, and that he can still change.

The image of the widow reaching out to her husband's murderer is an extraordinary expression – and *act* – of empathy, shedding tears not only for her loss, but also, it seems, for the loss of de Kock's moral soul – wishing to hold his hand to lead him into a future where 'he can still change' and rejoin the world of moral humanity. Extraordinary as it is, such a profound act of forgiveness raises many questions, not least the question of whether de Kock was deserving of the forgiveness shown to him. Some might say Eugene de Kock is too evil – *Prime Evil,* as the nickname he has been given by the South African media suggests – and unworthy of forgiveness. But perhaps there is another question to be asked, that is, whether evil was intrinsic to de Kock, or whether, in a society sustained by a violent political system, evil became part of his life as he forged his way deeper into his role as head of apartheid's covert operations unit.

One of the problems with labelling de Kock as evil is that it closes any further discussion on the subject, a point that Lifton (1983) makes about such labelling of perpetrators. If de Kock is prime evil, then we need not look any further; the matter has been explained. He is evil, and we 'who interview and write and judge, we are clear-eyed' (Rosenberg 1996: 86) about who is good and who is evil. Without suggesting that there is a de Kock, or a silent bystander, lurking behind each of us, very few of us know with absolute certainty how we would have behaved had we been part of privileged white society in apartheid South Africa. I think that to pride oneself on one's moral values is an act of little relevance until one is tested, that is, until one is asked to choose between good and evil, between speaking out and silence. Rosenberg has argued that '[i]t is … [our] extreme good fortune that we will never face this test' (1996: 86).

'Radical Evil' and Forgiveness

In this section, I want to deal briefly with the question of whether people who perpetrated evil deeds sanctioned by their governments are forgivable. One of the most important texts on the study of evil is Hannah Arendt's book *Eichmann in Jerusalem: A Report on the Banality of Evil* (1994). Arendt's task is a formidable one because she was trying to reach deep conclusions about Eichmann's inner motivations on the basis of only written testimony and his oral testimony during his trial. Nevertheless, her phrase 'the banality of evil' has come to embody all that should be understood about the complexity of factors that lead human beings to commit unspeakable acts under totalitarian governments.

Amèry (1980), in his account of his experiences in Auschwitz, criticized Arendt for developing a theory based on looking at a perpetrator 'only through the glass cage' (Amèry 1980: 25). Another criticism of the idea of labelling atrocities simply as evil comes from Lifton (1983). Lifton argued that using the religious injunction and simply labelling atrocities as evil helps us only to label something that we struggle with by removing it from the human realm. It does not help us to understand the 'psychological currents that contribute to this evil' (1983: 46).

In an earlier study, Arendt pointed out that 'radically evil' acts 'transcend the realm of human affairs' and are therefore neither punishable nor forgivable (1958: 241). On the scale of horrible things that happen to people, there may be some for which the language of apology and forgiveness is inappropriate. However, to simply say that evil deeds are unforgivable does not capture the complexity of the social context within which gross human rights abuses are committed. For example, in South Africa, where the language of 'reconciliation' defined the way that society dealt with its traumatic past, many stories of forgiveness emerged. And in Rwanda, although 'the "r" word' (reconciliation) was taboo for a few years after the 1994 genocide of Tutsis (E. Staub, personal communication, 19 June 1999), that country has now established a National Reconciliation Commission (A. Inyumba, personal communication, 7 February 2001). Therefore, I think it is more instructive to talk about the conditions that may or may not foster forgiveness than to suggest that certain categories of acts are unforgivable. As I show in this chapter, when perpetrators express regret, guilt and remorse, what lies 'beyond the purview of apology' (Tavuchis 1991: 21) may be transformed from an unforgivable deed into one that can be forgiven.

It is important to note that not all victims who came to the TRC were willing or able to forgive perpetrators. Still, observations from the TRC can help us chart the path along which forgiveness takes place, as well as the conditions that may discourage apologies and forgiveness. The example of de Kock's encounter with the widows of his victims is a particularly interesting one because of the public perception of de Kock as the embodiment of apartheid's evil. In the more than forty-three hours of interviews I spent with de Kock, I found that for all the horrific singularity of his acts, he sought to affirm to himself that he was still part of the human universe (Gobodo-Madikizela 2003) and not simply the monster that his nickname, Prime Evil, portrays him to be.

This does not make his deeds any less evil than they were. But it 'humanized' him and made it possible for family members of his victims to reach out to him with forgiveness.

What happened on the TRC may not be generalizable to other situations. What the examples presented in this article suggest, however, is that there are other alternatives to revenge. An important goal of democratization after totalitarian rule is to forge a vocabulary of peace and reconciliation in the aftermath of mass tragedy. One of the challenges of this phase of transition is creating the conditions that will make old enemies regard one another as fellow human beings.

Seeing the other as a human being – feeling and responding to the other's pain with remorse – is probably the most crucial starting point in the encounter between victims and perpetrators of evil. Laub (1991) illustrated the importance of the human connection between former enemies in his account of a Holocaust survivor who witnessed some of the worst atrocities of the Second World War and lost many members of her family. At the end of the war, she participated in the hunting down and killing of Nazi collaborators. When a German youth was captured and brought to her for her to take revenge, however, she ended up caring for him, cleaning and re-bandaging his wounds before handing him over to the POW group. When asked why she had responded sympathetically to the POW, she replied: 'How could I kill him – he looked into my face and I looked into his' (Laub 1991: 85).

Empathy is what enables us to recognize another person's pain, even in the midst of tragedy, because pain cannot be evil. Empathy deepens our humanity. Its absence, whether at a collective level or in interpersonal relationships, signals the separation of human beings from one another and is an assault on the essence of what it is to be human. When perpetrators apologize and experience the pain of remorse, showing contrition, they are *acting as human beings*.

What Is Remorse?

There is a conceptual similarity between remorse and guilt. Although guilt is central in remorse, there is a subtle but important distinction between the two concepts. Remorse is a more mature type of guilt and can be a vehicle for motivating change (Shaw 1988).

Remorse stems from a potential for empathy, which is borne out of early positive affective human relationships (Gould 1972). This suggests that remorse is more likely to be concerned with the other, whereas guilt seems more focused on the self. Furthermore, unlike guilt, in which there might be attempts to justify acts carried out or to deny responsibility, remorse is preceded by acknowledgement of wrongdoing and clarification of the deed committed by the perpetrator. Naming the deed, owning up to responsibility without any rationalization, clarifying what was involved and showing regret allow victims to process their emotions about trauma.

In some circumstances, guilt may be experienced without remorse, which tends to result in denial, rationalization or justification. When people are *stuck* at the level of guilt, they have a painful awareness of responsibility for an act without necessarily openly and consciously acknowledging this responsibility. In contrast, remorse reminds the offender of the moral code that was broken and signals his or her heartfelt regret. Remorse is particularly painful when horrible acts have been committed, because of the level of shame that is commensurate with the deeds.

Forgiveness and the Paradox of Remorse

Remorse does not always evoke forgiveness; however, when remorse does bring about forgiveness, the dialogue between the victim and perpetrator may lead to what I call 'the paradox of remorse'. The feelings of regret for the horrible deed of murder, the desperate and impossible wish to restore the loss suffered by the victim, and other self-reflective thoughts and emotions associated with remorse all become incorporated into the perpetrator's self and produce the paradoxical experience of the perpetrator as a wounded self. This, I think, is where the gravity of the moment lies. The tipping point is when the victim perceives this 'woundedness' in a perpetrator, that is, the 'pain' of remorse.

One of the interviews I had with de Kock exemplifies this 'woundedness'. When de Kock described the details of the meeting with the two widows of his victims, his face immediately dropped. Sitting directly across from me in the small prison consulting room where I saw him, he shifted his eyes uncomfortably. His feet shuffled, and I could hear the clatter of the chains that bound him to the chair, which was bolted to the floor. His mouth quivered and there were tears in his eyes. As he started to speak, his hand trembled and he became visibly distressed. With a breaking voice he said: 'I wish I could do much more than "I'm sorry". I wish there was a way of bringing their bodies back alive. I wish I could say, here are your husbands', he said, gesturing with shaking outstretched arms and bending them in a holding position. 'But unfortunately … I have to live with it.' At that moment de Kock invited my empathy, and over several other interviews I had with him it was clear that he was full of remorse for what he had done. My encounter with de Kock is explored more fully in my book (Gobodo-Madikizela 2003).

A victim's empathic connection with a perpetrator in response to his or her remorseful apology could perhaps be compared with what moves us in strange situations with which we are not consciously connected. We are 'touched' by something in the other person, 'moved' to tears, and we 'identify' with someone who is in pain. Segal's (1973) conception of projective identification as a form of empathy offers a helpful guide for understanding how we become drawn in another's pain. In projective identification and introjective identification, there is something in the other that is felt to be part of the self and something in the self that is felt to belong to the other. Empathy is about feeling *with* (identifying with) and responding *to* the pain of the other. There is a reciprocal emotional process that occurs between two people, one asking for empathy and another offering it. This shared emotional process, I think, is what evolves between a perpetrator who pleads for forgiveness and a victim who offers it.

Another example that shows how remorse evokes empathy comes from an article on Jewish–German dialogue. Rothschild (2000) articulated the experience of empathy and making a humane connection with the descendants of Nazi mass murderers from the point of view of a daughter of a Holocaust survivor. 'I felt compassion with the pain these people carried', Rothschild explained, 'not just for their families but also for the majority of Germans' (2000: 49).

Remorse is a special language that can only come from a deep feeling of pain about what one has done. Similarly, forgiveness that reaches out with empathy to the offender can only come from humane motives. Forgiveness is a response that is evoked by a truly 'human moment' when two people recognize each other's pain: the perpetrator as author of the pain suffered by the victim, and the victim acknowledging the perpetrator's 'suffering' as a result of remorse. This is not a statement about whether it 'makes sense' for victims to respond to evildoers with empathy. Rather, it is an observation of the process involved when victims connect with perpetrators in a way that many may find unimaginable. Forgiveness seems to be reaching out to the other person and saying: I can feel the pain you feel for having caused me pain.

Two outcomes from this process can be identified. The first is the humanization of the victim, whether a survivor or a victim who died, that is, to see the victim as a human being instead of a dehumanized 'other'. The second is the rehumanization of the perpetrator and the opening of the door for his readmission into the realm of moral humanity.

The Humanization of the Victim

There is a general consensus that when perpetrators commit their horrible acts, they exclude victims from moral obligations (Bauman 1989; Lifton 1986; Staub 1989). Moral exclusion of victims results in the effacement of victims' pain: their experience of pain becomes invisible. No matter how screamingly present the victim's pain is, dehumanization makes it 'invisible, inaudible' (Scarry 1985: 44). When perpetrators feel remorse, they are validating the victim's pain and seeing what they could not see because of the depersonalized images they had constructed of the victim at the time they inflicted the trauma. Some may

argue that perpetrators *chose* not to see the victim's pain. In totalitarian societies, however, the issue of choice is not as straightforward as it is in societies
that encourage debate and welcome diversity of opinion. Besides, if, from a
very early developmental stage, an individual's moral obligations are divided in
terms of 'us and them', and the images of 'them' are such that *they* exist only
as objectified, dehumanized others, then the idea of 'choosing the right thing'
has a totally different meaning from the one desirable for building respectful
intergroup relationships and tolerant societies.

When perpetrators feel remorse, they are recognizing something they
failed to see when they violated the victim, which is that victims feel and bleed
just as do others with whom they, the perpetrators, identify. Remorse, therefore, transforms the image of victims as objects of violation to victims as human
other. Through the perpetrator's public acknowledgement and expression of
remorse, a murdered victim is symbolically 'resurrected' through the affirmation of his or her humanness. At the same time, remorse recognizes the pain
of the surviving family member. Doreen Mgoduka, one of the widows who
forgave Eugene de Kock, illustrates this point about the humanization of the
victim:

> De Kock is the only one who helped us to retrace the steps of what really hap-
> pened. You have no idea how much of a relief knowing the truth about my hus-
> band was. De Kock brought us the truth so that we can be with our husbands;
> understand what happened to them and then release them again. Now I can
> mourn properly because this has helped me to retrace his steps in life in order to
> let him go in death.

Another example that illustrates this idea of the humanization of the victim
is the testimony of a man whose wife was killed in a 1993 grenade attack at
a mainly white church, the St. James Church Massacre, in Cape Town. When
John Ackerman came face to face with the members of APLA (the Azanian
People's Liberation Army - the armed wing of the Pan African Congress) who
were applying for amnesty at a TRC public hearing, he acknowledged the
apologies that they had made through their written submissions to the TRC.
Ackerman, however, was more interested in *seeing* the men's faces. Sitting on
a higher floor level behind the men, he asked them to turn around and face
him and to apologize in their own language so that he could see for himself if
they meant their apologies. After each of the men had expressed their apologies, Ackerman addressed them as follows: 'My wife was sitting next to me
in the front pew. She was wearing a long blue coat.' As he said this his voice
started to break. Speaking through uncontrollable sobs, he continued: 'I want
you to tell me if you saw her. Do you remember firing at my wife? If you don't
remember I'll accept it, but I want to know if you saw her, if you remember
firing at her.'

This is an example of a surviving family member expressing a deeply felt
need for the humanization of his loved one. APLA's war cry was 'one settler

one bullet.' It seems Ackerman wanted the perpetrators to resurrect the dignity of his wife and identify her as a *person* whose life they shattered, a human being 'in a long blue coat' who was his wife and his children's mother, and not just a 'settler', as the killers saw her. Perpetrators cannot undo the deed, but their acknowledgement, contrition and recognition of the victim's pain can go a long way in contributing to the victim's journey towards mastery of the traumatic memory.

Rehumanization of the Perpetrator

Studzinski (1988) pointed out that it is a dramatic turn of events that forces a review of one's life. A long prison term can provide the push for a perpetrator to confront some unpleasant truths about him or herself. Eugene de Kock's fall from power, for instance, was quite a dramatic turn of events for someone who masterminded systematic violations of human rights and received the highest honours from his government for his role. Abandoned by his masters, his isolation in prison probably contributed to the feelings of remorse that seemed evident in my interviews with him (cf. Gobodo-Madikizela 2003).

I agree with Solomon (1978) that remorse is a form of self-inflicted punishment. Remorseful perpetrators look back and confront the reality that what they defined as 'moral' duty towards their country was murder. Part of the issue is that when crimes are committed in the name of a highly ideologically driven cause such as apartheid, Aryan supremacy or continued Serbian control, the belief system that accompanies the crimes is so strong and so totalistic that those at or near the centre of its whirlwind probably believe in what they are doing. Some of these people continue to *not see* what emotional destruction they caused. P.W. Botha, former president of apartheid South Africa, who refused to appear before the TRC, waged murderous havoc with his policies but refused to acknowledge any wrongdoing.

It is not clear what the state of mind of people like Botha is. It is possible that on one level, a person in Botha's position really believed that he was not guilty of any crimes and that he was a benevolent benefactor of white South Africans, and perhaps even black South Africans. Is that madness, blissful ignorance, a cunning display of the ability to lie or simply 'the banality of evil' (Arendt 1994)? Peter Malkin, who captured Eichmann, discovered this state of mind in a perpetrator of genocide who seemed to have believed that he committed no crime. In the book *Eichmann in my Hands,* Malkin and Stein (1990) describe a conversation that Malkin had with Eichmann in which Eichmann showed a total lack of remorseful reflection. When Malkin asked Eichmann to explain the brutal killing of Malkin's two cousins in Auschwitz, Eichmann seemed to express surprise that the question was asked at all. 'They were Jews, weren't they?' he responded (Malkin and Stein 1990: 110).

I think that when perpetrators express remorse, it is a sign that they are part of the human universe and that they are emerging from a world where they were able to silence their conscience and kill without emotion. Solomon (1978) has suggested that remorse is a kind of self-punishment that emerges when perpetrators confront their past deeds and reflect on the consequences of their actions.

Of course, expressions of remorse cannot be used to predict the direction a perpetrator's life will follow. Forgiveness, however, *does* offer a perpetrator an opportunity to change. Whether a perpetrator rises to the call or not may depend on a range of circumstances, including whether the perpetrator has real opportunities to pursue a different lifestyle. An example that illustrates change after an act of forgiveness is the story of two young men who were members of the military wing of the Pan African Congress. Ntobeko Peni and Easy Nofemela were involved in the stabbing death of Amy Biehl, a Stanford University student who was killed in a Cape Town township. During their amnesty application, Peni and Nofemela apologized to Peter and Linda Biehl. In his response, Peter Biehl opened his statement at the TRC hearing with the following words: 'We come to South Africa as Amy came, in a spirit of committed friendship and to extend a hand of friendship in a society which has been systematically polarized for decades.' They visited the men's families, offered their forgiveness and returned to Cape Town to establish the Amy Biehl Foundation in memory of their daughter. The Biehls offered Peni and Nofemela an opportunity to train as mechanics in a skills training project run by the foundation. After they completed the course Peni and Nofemela were offered employment, and they have been working at the Amy Biehl Foundation for at least the past ten years.

Peter and Linda Biehl, it would seem, committed their lives to creating an opportunity for their daughter's killers to move forward in life and pursue a different future for themselves and for their children. They travelled between the United States and South Africa several times a year. During one of their trips to South Africa I interviewed them about their relationship with Peni and Nofemela. 'I have no hatred in my heart,' said Linda, 'all I am concerned about is how these young men can reenter their community and rebuild their lives' (L. Biehl, personal communication, 5 July 2000). Since Peter Biehl's death, Linda Biehl has continued to run the Amy Biehl Foundation, and the two men are still part of the staff at the foundation.

Some people believe that when perpetrators express remorse it can only be 'stage' remorse, a performance in order to get sympathy. This point of view implies that perpetrators are irredeemable and therefore unforgivable. Although we may take comfort in the view that perpetrators are cut from different fabric than is the rest of humanity, such a perspective is not supported by evidence. Studies (Conroy 2000; Gibson 1991; Glover 1999: Haritos-Fatouros 1988) clearly show how men and women who perpetrate terrible deeds have histories rooted in the same moral humanity that guides the rest of us.

Perpetrators whose past deeds were supported by voters who turned a blind eye to the gross human rights abuses against other groups and kept oppressive regimes in power, are usually ostracized by that same society of voters, who distance themselves from perpetrators' actions when oppressive regimes lose power. It is important not only to focus on the evil nature of perpetrators' actions, but also to shift the gaze to the conditions that encourage such evil. What is the structure of incentives and fear produced in a violent political culture and a police state that has a moralistic ideology? How does that context encourage silence and obedience? How does it facilitate psychological splitting – in individuals and in society – so that people can go on with their lives while their neighbours are being murdered, 'disappeared', or tortured? How does that context enable people to rationalize terrible conduct – because they are rewarded for it, because they are punished for not doing it, because they have a stirring story to justify it? I raise these questions here to highlight the extraordinarily complex factors that may influence the behaviour of perpetrators in the context of a society and political structure in which systemic abuses are legitimized.

Remorse and the Cry to Rejoin the Ranks of Moral Human Beings

The significance of remorse lies in its ability to repair, even if only in part, the relationship with the wounded victim and potentially to transform aspects of the perpetrator's inner life. Shabad (1988) points out that remorse is the manifestation of the 'bite' of conscience, and has to do with one's ethics of conscience.

Conscience is a critical aspect of an individual's identity as a human being. When people experience the 'bite' of conscience, it is a sign of their connection to moral humanity. It was interesting to observe how at critical moments in my interviews with Eugene de Kock, especially when I probed into his violent past, de Kock brought up the story of his meeting with the widows who offered him forgiveness. It seemed as if this was a special vignette for him to keep returning to, as if to convince me of the humane side lurking behind the side of him for which he was known as 'Prime Evil'. He probably also needed the story to convince *himself* of his human side. It was as if his feelings of remorse – breaking down with emotion when he recalled his meeting with the two women – and being forgiven by the two widows were all he had to prove to himself that he was not a monster after all. I concluded that this was less to deny his past than an attempt to make his 'human' side more visible, and thus to be recognized as a human being capable of humane emotions.

Conclusion

South Africans faced the challenge of how to embrace the past without being swallowed by the tide of vengeful thinking. The TRC was a strategy to break the cycles of politically motivated violence. There are important lessons to learn from the TRC, not least the question of how the human spirit can prevail in spite of the cruelty visited upon a society's victims in the past. If memory is kept alive to kindle and cultivate old hatreds and resentments, memory is likely to culminate in hateful vengeance and in a repetition of cycles of violence. But if memory is kept alive to transcend hateful emotions, to free individuals or the groups to which they belong from the burden of hatred, then remembering, through public acknowledgement of the pain and suffering that victims suffered, can be healing. Much more still needs to be done in South Africa, and social transformation and the healing of victims will only come about if the issues of economic justice and the myriad problems in post-apartheid South Africa are addressed.

Gross human rights violations almost always 'hide' their true natures. Perpetrators of human rights violations redefine morality and start believing that they can commit systematic murder and other atrocities 'for the greater good'. Thus, in addition to the evil component of these crimes, there is also the perspective component. The evil component of crimes against humanity is the moral failing. The perspective component is the distortion in mental processing that both precedes the evil and is intensified by it. The foot soldiers who are swept up by the ideology of the evil regimes like apartheid South Africa should be held morally responsible for the evil deeds they committed, but some of them may need compassionate understanding because of the power and influence of corrupt leadership, which is often strengthened by increasing support from voters who keep a corrupt and repressive government in power.

Eugene de Kock, for instance, languishes in prison, ostracized by his own people for whom he believed he was fighting. The experience is probably like believing in something you are doing, when all of a sudden the ideological or political climate changes, power shifts and you find yourself in a new environment where everyone is saying that what you were doing was wrong, and you yourself are beginning to see their point of view, which you could not see before. The TRC denied de Kock amnesty for the crimes for which he was sentenced to life, so it is likely that he will spend the rest of his life in prison. I spent many hours interviewing him and found him remorseful and carrying a heavy burden of shame. I think that de Kock, and many beneficiaries of apartheid privilege who now regret their silence, should have our sympathy, even forgiveness. At the same time, their willingness to exercise their 'free' will to choose against the deepest parts of their conscience should invite our condemnation. The end point of condemnation in this model is to be able to move beyond condemnation and take both the perpetrator and society towards corrective and restorative measures, whereas in the conventional model of justice based on retribution, the condemnation is the end point.

Many people find it difficult to embrace the idea of forgiveness, and it is easy to see why. To maintain some sort of moral compass, to hold on to some sort of clear distinction between what is humanly depraved but conceivable and what is simply off the scale of human acceptability, there is a desire – an inward emotional and mental pressure – *not* to forgive, as if forgiveness somehow signals acceptability, and acceptability signals some amount, however small, of condoning. Yet how do you forgive, unless you can find claims of remorse credible? And how do you find them credible, unless you first attempt to understand why the perpetrators did their crimes? Yet how do you understand, when the actions that are being retold are so abhorrent? There is a desire to draw a line in the sand and say: 'Where you have been, I cannot follow. Your actions can never be regarded as part of what it means to be human.' Yet not to forgive means closing the door to the possibility of transformation. Some might say it also means usurping the role of divine judgement.

Notes

* This is a revised version of the article originally published in the *Journal of Humanistic Psychology* 42: 1, 7–32 (2002). It is included in this volume with the permission of the author.

Bibliography

Améry, J. 1980. *At the Mind's Limits: Contemplation by a Survivor on Auschwitz and Its Realities,* trans. S. Rosenfeld and S.P. Rosenfeld. Bloomington.

Apfel, J.R. and C.J. Tellingator. 2000. 'What can we learn from children of war?' in S. Geballe, J. Gruendel and W. Andiman (eds), *Forgotten Children of the AIDS Epidemic.* New Haven: 107–121.

Arendt, H. 1958. *The Human Condition.* Chicago.

Arendt, H. 1994. *Eichmann in Jerusalem: A Report on the Banality of Evil.* New York.

Bauman, Z. 1989. *Modernity and the Holocaust.* Ithaca.

Bies, R.J. and T.M. Tripp. 1996. 'Beyond Distrust: "Getting Even" and the Need for Revenge', in R.M. Kramer and T.R. Tyler (eds), *Trust in Organizations: Frontiers of Theory and Research.* Thousand Oaks: 246–260.

Bizos, G. 1999. *No One to Blame? In Pursuit of Justice in South Africa.* Claremont.

Brison, S.J. 1999. 'Trauma Narrative and the Remaking of the Self', in M. Bal, J. Crewe and L. Spitzer (eds), *Acts of Memory: Cultural Recall in the Present.* Hanover: 39–54.

Conroy, J. 2000. *Unspeakable Acts, Ordinary People: The Dynamics of Torture.* New York.

Durham, M.S. 2000. *The Therapist's Encounter with Revenge and Forgiveness.* London.

Felman, S. and D. Laub. 1992. *Testimony: Crisis of Witnessing in Literature, Psychoanalysis, and History.* New York.

Friedman, M. 1998. 'Why Joseph Campbell's Psychologizing of Myth Precludes the Holocaust as Touchstone of Reality', *Journal of the American Academy of Religion* 66 no 2: 385–401.

Gibson, J. 1991. 'Training People to Inflict Pain: State Terror and Social Learning', *Journal of Humanistic Psychology* 31: 72–87.

Glover, J. 1999. *Humanity: A Moral History of the Twentieth Century.* New Haven.

Gobodo-Madikizela, P. 2001. 'Traumatic Memory', in J. Edelstein (ed.), *Truth and Lies: Stories from the Truth and Reconciliation Commission in South Africa.* New York.

Gobodo-Madikizela, P. 2003. *A Human Being Died that Night: A South African Story of Forgiveness.* New York.

Gould, R. 1972. *Child Studies through Fantasy: Cognitive Affective Patterns in Development.* New York.

Haber, J.G. 1991. *Forgiveness: A Philosophical Study.* Lanham.

Hamilton, J.O. 2001. 'How Much Can You Forgive?' *Standford Magazine* (special issue on reconciliation): 74–81.

Haritos-Fatouros, M. 1988. 'The Official Torturer: A Learning Model for Obedience to an Authority of Violence', *Journal of Applied Social Psychology* 18: 1107–1120.

Hayner, P.B. 1994. 'Fifteen Truth Commissions – 1974 to 1995: A Comparative Study', *Human Rights Quarterly* 16 no 4: 597–655.

Laub, D. 1991. 'Truth and Testimony', *American Imago* 48 no 1: 75–91.

Lifton, R. 1983. 'The Doctors of Auschwitz: The Biomedical Vision', *Psychohistory Review* 11 no 2–3: 36–46.

Lifton, R.J. 1986. *The Nazi Doctors: Medical Killing and the Psychology of Genocide.* New York.

Little, D. 1999. 'A Different Kind of Justice: Dealing with Human Rights Violations in Transitional Societies', *Ethics and International Affairs* 13: 65–80.

Malkin, P.Z., and H. Stein. 1990. *Eichmann in my Hands.* New York.

Minow, M. 1998. *Between Vengeance and Forgiveness: Facing History after Genocide and Mass Violence.* Boston.

Moore, T. 1988. 'Remorse: An Initiatory Disturbance of the Soul', *Psychotherapy Patient* 5: 83–94.

O'Brien, M. 2001. 'Letting Go of McVeigh', *The New York Times Magazine,* 13 May, 40–44.

Prejean, J. 1993. *Dead Man Walking: An Eyewitness Account of the Death Penalty in the United States.* New York.

Rosenberg, T. 1996. *The Haunted Land: Facing Europe's Ghosts after Communism.* New York.

Rothschild, M.H. 2000. 'Transforming Our Legacies: Heroic Journeys for Children of Holocaust Survivors and Nazi Perpetrators', *Journal of Humanistic Psychology* 40: 43–55.

Scarry, E. 1985. *The Body in Pain: The Making and Unmaking of the World.* Oxford.

Segal, H. 1973. *Introduction to the Work of Melanie Klein.* London.

Shabad, P. (1988). Remorse: The echo of inner truth. *Psychotherapy Patient, 5,* 113–133.

Shaw, J. 1988. 'The Usefulness of Remorse', *Psychotherapy Patient* 5: 77–82.

Skaar, E. 1999. 'Truth Commissions, Trials – or Nothing? Policy Options in Democratic Transitions. *Third World Quarterly* 20: 1109–1128.

Solomon, R.C. 1978. *The Passions.* New York.

Staub, E. 1989. *The Roots of Evil: The Origins of Genocide and Other Group Violence.* New York.

Studzinski, R. 1988. 'Transcending a Past: From Remorse to Reconciliation in the Aging Process', *Psychotherapy Patient* 5: 207–218.

Tavuchis, N. 1991. *Mea culpa: A Sociology of Apology and Reconciliation.* Stanford.

Tutu, D. 1999. *No Future with Forgiveness.* New York.

Wiesenthal, S. 1976. *The Sunflower.* New York.

CHAPTER 13

Healing from Auschwitz and Mengele's Experiments

EVA MOZES KOR

Dear Fellow survivors, Dr Markl, Dr Sachse, Doctors, Scientists, Researchers and Guests.[1]

Fifty-seven years ago I was a human guinea pig in Auschwitz. Much progress has been made in order for us to be here at the KWI/MPS, the institute that was in charge of our experiments. I thank you for holding this symposium. I hope we can all learn from the past and begin to heal our pain.

Twenty years ago, I began thinking about the other Mengele Twins and started actively searching for them. From the time I began to the time that we made our historic trip to Auschwitz and held the Mock Trial in Jerusalem in 1985, I mailed out nearly 12,000 letters looking for my fellow survivors. With the help of my late twin sister, Miriam Mozes Zeiger, by 1984 we had succeeded in locating 122 individuals/survivors of the twins' experiments.

I care deeply for the Mengele Twins. Even though I am the founder and the president of C.A.N.D.L.E.S[2]., I am not a spokesperson for all the twins. I am speaking today only for myself. I know that some of my fellow survivors do not share my ideas. But we are all here to be honest, learn the truth and learn from this most tragic chapter of human history.

My speech is divided into two parts: firstly, how I survived Auschwitz and how it felt to be a child guinea pig in Mengele's lab and secondly, the lessons that I have learned from this tragedy.

How I Survived Auschwitz

It was the dawn of an early spring day in 1944 when I arrived in Auschwitz. Our cattle car train came to a sudden stop. I could hear lots of German voices yelling orders outside. We were packed like sardines in the cattle car, and above the press of bodies I could see nothing but a small patch of grey sky through the barbed wires on the window. Our family consisted of my father, age 44; my mother, age 38; my oldest sister, Edit, age 14; my middle sister Aliz, age 12; and Miriam and I, who were only ten years old.

As soon as we stepped down onto the cement platform, my mother grabbed my twin sister and me by the hand, hoping somehow to protect us. Everything was moving very fast; as I looked around I suddenly realized that my father and two older sisters were gone – I never saw any of them ever again. As Miriam and I clutched my mother's hand, an SS hurried by, shouting: 'Zwillinge! Zwillinge! Twins – Twins!' He stopped to look at my twin sister and me because we were dressed alike and looked very much alike.

'Are they twins?' he asked.

'Is it good?' asked my mother.

'Yes', nodded the SS.

'Yes, they are twins', said my mother.

Without any warning or explanation, he grabbed Miriam and me away from Mother. Our screaming and pleading fell on deaf ears. I remember looking back and seeing my mother's arms stretched out in despair as she was pulled in the opposite direction by an SS soldier. I never got to say goodbye to her because that was the last time we saw her. All that took thirty minutes. Miriam and I no longer had a family. We were all alone. We did not know what would happen to us. All that was done to us because we were born Jewish. We did not understand why this was a crime.

We joined a group of about eight sets of twins and waited at the edge of the railway tracks under SS supervision. Eight more sets of twins and one mother joined our group. We were taken to a huge building and ordered to sit on bleachers naked while our clothes were taken away. It was late in the afternoon when our clothes were returned with a big red cross painted on the back. Then our processing began. When my turn came, I decided that I would not allow them to do whatever they wanted to me and fought back. When they grabbed my arm to tattoo it, I began to scream, kick and struggle. Four people – two SS and two women prisoners – restrained me with all their strength while they heated a pen-like gadget to red hot, then dipped it in ink and burned into my flesh, dot by dot, the number capital letter A-7063.

We were taken to a barracks filled with girls, all twins, ages 1 to 13 years old. Shortly after our arrival everybody rushed to the front of the barracks, where the evening meal was being distributed. The food consisted of a very dark, 2½ inch slice of bread and a brownish liquid they called coffee. Miriam and I looked at each other, and although we had not had anything to eat or drink for four days, there was no doubt in our minds that we could not eat that bread because it wasn't kosher.

Then we offered our portions to the two girls who were showing us around. They grabbed it before we changed our minds and, laughing at our innocence, said: 'Miriam and Eva, you can not be fussy here. You have to learn to eat everything if you want to survive.' After the evening meal, the two girls briefed us about everything in the camp. It was then that we learned about the huge, smoking chimneys and the glowing flames rising high above them. We learned about the two groups of people we had seen on the selection platform and what had happened to them. We learned we were alive only because Dr Mengele wanted to use us in his experiments.

It was late in the evening when Miriam and I lay down on a bottom bunk to sleep. I could not sleep even though I was physically tired and mentally drained. As I tossed and turned, I noticed something big and dark moving on the floor. I began counting – one, two, three – four ... five : I jumped up from my bunk, screaming: 'Mice! Mice!' I was always scared of mice when I encountered them on our farm in Transylvania.

'Those are not mice, they are rats. You will have to get used to them because they are everywhere,' yelled a voice from the top bunk.

Before trying to sleep again, Miriam and I went to the latrine at the end of the barracks. There on that filthy floor were the scattered corpses of three children. Their bodies were naked and shrivelled, and their wide-open eyes were looking at me. Then and there, I realized that could happen to Miriam and me unless I did something to prevent it. So I made a silent pledge:

> 'I will do whatever is within my power to make sure that Miriam and I shall not end up on that filthy latrine floor.'

From that moment on, I concentrated all my efforts, all my talents and all my being on one thing:

Survival.

In our barracks we, the children, huddled in filthy beds crawling with lice and rats. We were starved for food, starved for human kindness and starved for the love of the mothers we once had. We had no rights, but we had a fierce determination to live one more day – to survive one more experiment. No one explained anything to us, nor did anyone try to minimize the risks to our lives. On the contrary, we knew we were there to be subjects of experiments and were totally at the mercy of the Nazi doctors. Our lives depended entirely on the doctors' whims.

Nothing on the face of the earth can prepare a person for a place like Auschwitz. At age ten, I became part of a special group of children who were used as human guinea pigs by Dr Josef Mengele. Some 1,500 sets of multiples were used by Mengele in his deadly experiments. It is estimated that fewer than 200 individuals survived.

In Auschwitz, we lived an emotionally isolated existence. During the whole time I was in Auschwitz, Miriam and I talked very little. All we could say to one another was 'Make sure you don't get sick' and 'Do you have another piece of bread?' It took every ounce of my energy to survive one more day, to live through one more experiment. We did not cry because we knew there was no help. We had learned that within the first few days.

I remember being hungry all the time. I had a big decision to make every night when we received our daily ration of bread, approximately 2½ inches. It was an agonizing decision each night when I would ask myself: 'Should I eat the bread tonight? If I do, then I will have a whole day tomorrow without any food.' The days seemed to be very long, and without any food they were even longer. While I was awake, I could feel the hunger – a pang in my stomach that sent pain through my skinny body. It was logical that I should save the bread for the next day. But if I put it under my head, by the next morning it was gone – stolen or eaten by the rats.

I became very ill after an injection in Mengele's lab. I tried to hide the fact that I was ill because the rumour was that anyone taken to the hospital never came back. On my next visit to the lab they measured my fever, and I was taken to the hospital. The next day a team of Dr Mengele and four other doctors looked at my fever chart and then declared: 'Too bad, she is so young. She has only two weeks to live.' I was all alone. The doctors I had did not want to heal me. They wanted me dead. Miriam was not with me. I missed her so very much. She was the only kind and loving person I could cuddle up with when I was hungry, cold and scared.

I refused to accept their verdict. I refused to die!

I made a second silent pledge:

'I will do anything in my power to get well and be reunited with my sister, Miriam.'

In the hospital barracks we received no food and no medication. People were brought to this barracks to die or to wait for a place in the gas chamber. I was very ill, burning up with fever, between life and death. I remember waking up on the barracks floor. I was crawling because I could no longer walk. I wanted to reach a faucet at the other end of the barracks. As I crawled, I faded in and out of consciousness. I kept telling myself: 'I must survive. I must survive.'

After two weeks, my fever broke and I began to feel stronger. I decided to devise a plan that would show a gradual improvement in my condition. So when the so-called nurse would come in and place the thermometer under my arm and leave the room, I would take it out and read it, and if it was too high I would shake it down a little. Then I would stick it back under my arm with the end sticking out. After three weeks my temperature showed normal and I was reunited with Miriam. What a happy day that was!

Had I died, Mengele would have killed Miriam with an injection to the heart and would have done comparative autopsies on our bodies. This is the way most of the twins died. Three times a week we walked to the main Auschwitz camp for experiments. These lasted six to eight hours. We had to sit naked in a room. Every part of our body was measured, poked, compared to charts and photographed. Every movement was noted. I felt like an animal in a cage. Three times a week we went to the blood lab. There we were injected with germs and chemicals, and they took a lot of blood from us. I saw some twins faint from the great amount of blood that they lost. I believe the Nazis wanted to know how much blood a person can lose before it causes death.

The experiments were in various stages, and Mengele had an unlimited supply of guinea pigs in the camp. If a twin died as a result of the experiments, the other twin was given a phenol injection into the heart and comparative autopsies were done on both. When one pair of twins was lost to the experiments, another pair of twins would come in on the next transport to replace the pair who had been killed.

On a white snowy day, 27 January 1945, four days before my eleventh birthday, Auschwitz was liberated by the Soviets and we were free. We were alive. We had survived. We had triumphed over unbelievable evil.

The Lesson I Have Learnt

I have told you my story because there are some important lessons to learn from it.

I, Eva Mozes Kor, a survivor of Mengele's medical experiments, have learned that human rights in medical experimentation is an issue that needs to be addressed. Those of you who are physicians and scientists are to be congratulated. You have chosen a wonderful and difficult profession: wonderful because you can save human lives and alleviate human suffering, but difficult because you are walking a very narrow line. You have been trained to use good judgement, to be calm, cool and collected, but you cannot forget that you are dealing with human beings. So, make a moral commitment that you will never, ever violate anyone's human rights or take away anyone's human dignity. I appeal to you to treat your subjects and patients with the same respect you would want if you were in their places. Remember that if you are doing your research solely for the sake of science and not for the benefit of mankind, you have crossed that very narrow line and are heading in the direction of the Nazi doctors and the Dr Mengeles of the world. Medical science can benefit mankind, but medical science can also be abused in the name of research.

We are meeting here as former adversaries. I hope we can part as friends. My people, the Jewish people, are hardworking, intelligent and caring. My people are good people. We did not deserve the treatment we received. No one deserves such treatment. Your people, the German people, are hardworking, intelligent and caring. Your people are good people, but you should never have permitted a Hitler to rise to power. There is a lot of pain that we, the Jewish people, and you, the German people carry around. It does not help anyone to carry the burden of the past. We must learn to heal ourselves from the tragedies of the Holocaust and help our people to heal their aching souls.

I would like to share with you my ultimate act of healing from the horrors of fifty-six years ago. I do realize that many of my fellow survivors will not share, support or understand my way of healing. There might be some people on both sides who will be angry with me. I understand that. I believe we should not go on suffering forever. This is the way I healed myself. I dare hope that it might work for other people.

I have forgiven the Nazis. I have forgiven everybody. At the fiftieth anniversary observance of the liberation of Auschwitz, in a ceremony attended by my children, Alex and Rina, and by friends, I met with a Nazi doctor, Dr Hans Münch, a former SS doctor at Auschwitz, and with his children and granddaughter.

In July 1993 I had received a telephone call from Dr Mihalchick of Boston College, who asked me to lecture at a conference on Nazi medicine. Then he added: 'Eva, it would be nice if you could bring a Nazi doctor with you.' I said: 'Dr Mihalchick, where am I going to find a Nazi doctor? The last time I looked they were not advertising in the yellow pages.' 'Think about it', he said.

In 1992 Miriam and I had been co-consultants on a documentary on the Mengele Twins done by ZDF, a German television company. In that documentary they had interviewed a Nazi doctor by the name of Dr Hans Münch. I contacted ZDF to ask them if they would get me Dr Münch's address and phone number, in the memory of my sister who had died the month before. An hour later I had his address and phone number. A friend of mine, Tony Van Renterghem, a Dutch Resistance fighter, contacted Dr Münch. Tony called him and then called me to tell me that 'Yes, he's alive, willing to give you a videotape interview.' That was July 1993. By August I was on my way to meet Dr Münch.

In August of 1993 I arrived at Dr Münch's house. I was very nervous. I kept asking myself, 'How would I feel if he treated me like nothing – the way I was treated in Auschwitz?' Dr Münch treated me with the utmost respect. As we sat down to talk, I said to him: 'Here you are – a Nazi doctor from Auschwitz – and here I am – survivor of Auschwitz – and I like you, and that sounds strange to me.' We talked about many things. I asked him if, by any chance, he knew anything about the operation of the gas chambers. And he said, 'This is the nightmare I live with.' Then he proceeded to tell me about the operation of the gas chambers and that when the bodies were dead, he had signed the death certificates.

I thought about it for a moment, and then I said: 'Dr Münch, I have a big request to make of you. Would you please come with me to Auschwitz in January 1995, when we will observe fifty years since the liberation of Auschwitz and sign a document at the ruins of the gas chambers and in the presence of witnesses about what you have told me?' He said yes. I went home delighted that I was going to have a document about the gas chambers at Auschwitz – a document that would help me combat the revisionists who say that there were no gas chambers.

I tried to think of a way to thank Dr Münch. Then one day, I thought, 'How about a letter of forgiveness?' I immediately realized that he would like it. I also realized that I had the power to forgive. *No one* could give me this power and *no one* could take it away. I began writing my letter to Dr Münch, and friends who spell better than I do met with me to correct the letter. One of them threw a question at me: 'Would you be willing to forgive Dr Mengele?' It was an interesting question, and I thought about it and decided that I could. Well, if I forgave Mengele, I might as well forgive everybody. I had no idea what I was doing. I only knew that it made me feel good inside that I had that power. In January 1995, my children, Alex and Rina, my friends and I, and Dr Münch with his children and granddaughter arrived in Auschwitz.

On 27 January 1995, we were standing by the ruins of one of the gas chambers. Dr Münch's document was read and he signed it. I read my Declaration of Amnesty and then signed it. I felt that a burden of pain was lifted from shoulders. I was no longer a victim of Auschwitz. I was no longer a prisoner of my tragic past. I was finally free. So I say to everybody:

Forgive your worst enemy. It will heal your soul and set you free.

The day I forgave the Nazis I forgave my parents because they failed to save me from a destiny in Auschwitz, and I also forgave myself for hating my parents.

My latest thoughts on how to heal the pains of the past are different from most victims'. As I understand it, most governments and world leaders bear a heavy burden in trying to keep the world at peace. In my opinion, they have failed miserably by not advocating, encouraging and helping survivors of tragedies such as the Holocaust to forgive their enemies, which is an act of self-healing.

Most governments and world leaders advocate and support one thing only – *justice*. Justice does not exist, and by demanding justice they condemn the victims to lifelong suffering. Let us explore a possible scenario that could have changed things for both victims and victimizers. Imagine that all the Nazi criminals had been encouraged to come forward to testify to the crimes they had committed, in return for their freedom. The perpetrators or victimizers would also have paid financial retribution for 5–10 years, and those funds would have gone into a special reconciliation fund to assist the victims in rebuilding their lives. The victims could testify if they so choose. The victimizers' testimonies would validate the victims' suffering.

As it is today, I still don't know what was done to us. But Mengele could have solved this problem by testifying. Both the victims and the victimizers – by verbalizing their painful memories – could have started the healing at once. As it really happened, the victims were silent and hurting. The victimizers were silent, hurting and hiding. The victims languished in pain. The victimizers languished in pain, shame and fear of being caught. The added tragedy of all this is that the victims have passed on to their children a legacy of pain, fear and anger. The victimizers have passed on to their children a legacy of pain, shame and fear. How can we build a healthy, peaceful world while all these painful legacies are festering underneath the surface? I see a world where leaders will advocate and support with legislation the act of forgiveness: amnesty and reconciliation rather than justice and vindictiveness. We have seen in Bosnia, Kosovo and Rwanda that victims have become victimizers and victimizers have become victims.

Let's try something new to end this vicious cycle.

I would like to end my lecture by saying that I hope this courageous gesture of Dr Markl and the Max Planck Society becomes an example to the world of how we might learn to cope with the past. As a German friend of mine has said, 'Why can't your people and my people be friends?'

I would also like to thank Dr Benno Müller Hill for his years of friendship and his role in pioneering this symbolic apology.

I would also like to quote from my Declaration of Amnesty:

I hope, in some small way, to send the world a message of forgiveness; a message of peace, a message of hope, a message of healing.

Let there be no more wars,
no more experiments without informed consent,
no more gas chambers,
no more bombs,
no more hatred,
no more killing,
no more Auschwitzes.

Notes

1. Address at the opening of the symposium on 'Biomedical Sciences and Human Experimentation at Kaiser Wilhelm Institutes: The Auschwitz Connection', Berlin, 7 June 2001.
2. Children of Auschwitz Nazi Deadly Lab Experiments Survivors.

Notes on Contributors

Justin Bisanswa hails from the Democratic Republic of the Congo and is a specialist in African literature. He holds a doctorate from the Université de Liège, where he also taught. He has been visiting professor at various prominent universities. Currently he holds the Canada Research Chair in African Literature and Francophony at the University of Laval in Québec, Canada. He is author of *Conflit de mémoires* (2000) and editor of *Francophonie en Amérique* (2005).

Mamadou Diawara is Professor of Anthropology in Frankfurt. He has lectured in Paris, Bayreuth, Birmingham, Yale, Leiden and Georgia (USA). He was a fellow at the Institute for Advanced Study in Berlin and the founding director of Point Sud, The Center for Research on Local Knowledge, Bamako, Mali. He is author of *La graine de la parole* (1990); *L'interface entre les savoirs paysans et le savoir universel* (2003); *L'empire du verbe - L'éloquence du silence: Vers une anthropologie du discours dans les groupes dits dominés au Sahel* [The Power of Speech – The Eloquence of Silence: Studies Toward an Anthropology of Speech among the Lower Classes in the Sahel] (2003); and 'Mobilizing Local Knowledge', *Comparative Labor Law and Policy Journal* 27(2): 225–236.

Ranjan Ghosh teaches in the Department of English at the University of North Bengal. He was an Alexander von Humboldt Fellow in Germany and European Research Fellow in London. He is published in journals such as *The Oxford Literary Review, History and Theory, Nineteenth Century Prose, Rethinking History, Storia della Storiographia, Angelaki, Studies in the Humanities* and others. His many books include *(In)fusion Approach: Theory, Contestation, Limits* (2006); *Edward Said and the Literary, Social and Political World* (2009); *Globalizing Dissent: Essays on Arundhati Roy* (2008).

Pumla Gobodo-Madikizela is Associate Professor of Psychology at the University of Cape Town. She served on the Human Rights Violations Committee on South Africa's Truth and Reconciliation Commission and coordinated victims' public hearings in the Western Cape. Gobodo-Madikizela is the author of the critically acclaimed book *A Human Being Died That Night: A Story of Forgiveness,* which won the 2004 Alan Paton Award in South Africa and the 2004 Christopher Award in the United States. Her current research interests include conscious and unconscious dynamics of working through trauma, the intrapsychic dimensions of forgiveness, and the relationship between forgiveness and mourning after traumatic loss.

Albert Grundlingh is Professor and Chair of the History Department at the University of Stellenbosch. He works in the field of war and society and is the author of *The Dynamics of Treason: Boer Collaborators during the South African War of 1899–1902* (2006) and *Fighting Their Own War: South African Black People and the First World War* (1987). He also co-authored a book on the social history of rugby in South Africa and has published numerous articles in the area of sociocultural history as well as South African historiography.

Han Sang-Jin is Professor Emeritus at Seoul National University and currently teaches at Tsinghua University in China. He specializes in critical social theory, comparative study of democratic transformations, the middle class politics and civil society, and Third Way development. He has lectured at Columbia University in New York, École des Hautes Études en Sciences Sociales in Paris and Beijing University in China. He served as Chairman of the Presidential Committee on Policy Planning of the Republic of Korea and President of the Academy of Korean Studies, among other posts. He is the author of *Habermas and the Korean Debate, Contemporary Society and Human Rights, Theory of the Middling Grassroots, Korea's Third Way and Bureaucratic Authoritarianism in Korea.*

Patrick Harries is Professor of African History at the University of Basel, Switzerland. He has taught at the universities of Cape Town, Lausanne and Madison-Wisconsin. He is presently engaged in a study of the community of 'Mozbieker' slaves liberated by the Royal Navy at the Cape in the mid-nineteenth century. He is author of *Work, Culture and Identity: Migrant Labour in Mozambique and South Africa, c. 1860–1910* (1994) and *Butterflies and Barbarians: Swiss Missionaries and Systems of Knowledge in Southeast Africa* (2007).

Bogumil Jewsiewicki is Professor of History at the History Department, Université Laval, Quebec, Canada, where he holds the Canada Research Chair in comparative history of memory. He is also a member of the Centre d'études africaines, École des hautes études en sciences sociales, Paris, France; director (with Philippe Joutard and Marie-Claire Lavabre) of the annual seminar Historical Memories from Here and from Elsewhere: Comparative Perspectives

(Paris, EHESS and IEP); and recipient of the African Studies Association 2006 Distinguished Africanist Award. Recent publications on related issues: *A Congo Chronicle: Patrice Lumumba in Urban Art* (B. Jewsiewicki et al. 1999); *An/Sichten, Malerei aus des Kongo, 1990–2000* (with Barbara Plankensteiner, 2001); *Mami Wata: La peinture urbaine au Congo* (2003); *Mourning and the Imagination of Political Time in Contemporary Central Africa* (edited with B. White, 2005); 'De la vérité de mémoire à la reconciliation: Comment travaille le souvenir?' *Le Débat* 122 (2002).

Annekie Joubert is Lecturer for Northern Sotho at the Institute for Asian and African Studies at the Humboldt University in Berlin and Research Fellow at the Department of Historical and Heritage Studies, University of Pretoria, South Africa. Her areas of specialization are African Languages (Northern Sotho), verbal art as literature, performance studies and folkloric filmmaking. She taught at the University of South Africa in the Department of African Languages from 1984 to 2001, and was Visiting Professor at the Instytut Filologii Angielskeij, Adam Mickiewicza University, Poznan, Poland, from 2002 to 2003. She is the author of *The Power of Performance: Linking Past and Present in Hananwa and Lobedu Oral Literature* (2004).

Eva Mozes Kor is Founder and Director of CANDLES, a museum dedicated to telling the stories of twins who were used as human guinea pigs in Dr Mengele's experiments in Auschwitz. She is one of the surviving twins. She has given over 2,500 lectures throughout the world, chiefly in the United States, Germany, Israel, England, South Africa and Poland. Her lectures describe her struggle to survive as a ten-year-old, liberation from Auschwitz in 1945 and the emotional liberation she achieved in 1995 by forgiving everybody, including Dr Josef Mengele. She is the author of two books and numerous chapters in other books.

Bernard C. Lategan is Founding Director of the Stellenbosch Institute for Advanced Study. He studied classical languages, linguistics, literary theory and theology at the Universities of the Free State, Stellenbosch and Kampen. His area of specialization is hermeneutics, with special interests in cultural diversity, value studies, historiography and processes of democratization. He taught at the Universities of the Western Cape, Stellenbosch, Göttingen and Hamburg and was the leader of an international research group of the Studiorum Novi Testamenti Societas for more than ten years. His publications include 'Current Issues in the Hermeneutical Debate', *Neotestamentica* 18 (1984); *The Option for Inclusive Democracy* (1987); *The Reader and Beyond* (1992); *The Relevance of Theology in the 1990's* (1994); and 'Questing or Sense-Making? Some Thoughts on the Nature of Historiography', *Biblical Interpretation* 11 (2003).

Elísio Macamo is Assistant Professor of African Studies at the University of Basel in Switzerland. He specializes in the sociology of development, risk, religion and knowledge and has a keen interest in the relevance of general social theory to African reality. He is currently a member of the scientific committee of CODESRIA, Dakar, and a member of the executive board of the German African Studies Association (VAD e.V.). He is the author of *Planície sem fim* (2008), *Trepar o País pelos ramos* (2006), *Negotiating Modernity: Africa's Ambivalent Experience* (2005), *Entsetzliche soziale Prozesse: Theoretische und empirische Annährungen* (co-edited with Lars Clausen and Elke Geenen, 2003); *Unraveling Ties: From Social Cohesion to New Practices of Connectedness* (co-edited with Yehuda Elkana, Ivan Krastev and Shalini Randeria, 2002), and *Was ist Afrika? Zur Soziologie und Kulturgeschichte eines modernen Konstrukts* (1999).

Jörn Rüsen is Senior Fellow of the Insitute for Advanced Study of Humanities and Professor for General History and Historical Culture at the University of Witten/Herdecke. He specializes in the theory and methodology of historical sciences, the history of historiography, intercultural aspects of historical thinking, theory of historical learning, the history of human rights and intercultural humanism. He has lectured at the Universities of Braunschweig, Berlin, Bochum and Bielefeld, and was Executive Director of the Centre for Interdisciplinary Research (ZIF) at Bielefeld and Visiting Professor at the Centre for Interdisciplinary Study at Stellenbosch University (South Africa). He is the author of *Zerbrechende Zeit* (2001), *Geschichte im Kulturprozeß* (2002), *Kann Gestern besser werden?* (2003), *History: Narration − Interpretation − Orientation* (2005), and *Kultur macht Sinn* (2006).

Index